HOME-KITCHEN FOOD STORAGE

Pantry-shelf Storage, Room Temperature

food item	storage time	keep in mind
baking powder, baking soda	18 months	keep dry, tightly covered
bouillon cubes & powders	1 year	
breads & rolls	3 days	in original wrapping
cake mixes	1 year	keep dry
cakes, baked	2-3 days	refrigerate if with cream or custard filling
canned foods, all kinds	1 year or more	use oldest first
coffee, vacuum can	1 year, unopened	store in refrigerator or freezer 1 week after opening
coffee, instant	6 months, unopened	store in refrigerator or freezer 1 week after opening
coffee lightener, nondairy	6 months	keep dry
cookies, packaged	4 months, unopened	1 week after opening
crackers	3 months	keep dry, tightly closed
crumbs, cracker/bread	6 months	keep dry, tightly closed
flour, all-purpose/cake	6 months	keep dry, tightly closed
frostings, mixes & canned	6 months	
fruit, dried	6-8 months	
gelatin, unflavored/fruit	6 months	keep dry
herbs & spices, whole	1 year	keep tightly closed
herbs & spices, ground	6 months	keep tightly closed
honey	1 year	do not refrigerate
hot-roll/quick-bread mixes	1 year	keep dry
jam, jelly	1 year	refrigerate after opening
molasses	1 year	
nonfat dry milk	6 months	keep dry; refrigerate after reconstituting
oil, salad & cooking	3 months	keep tightly closed
pancake, waffle mixes	6 months	keep dry, tightly closed
pasta	6 months, unopened	keep dry
peanut butter	6 months	2 months after opening
piecrust mixes	6 months	
pies & pastries	3 days	refrigerate cream, custard
pudding mixes	1 year	
rice, brown & wild	1 year	
rice, white	2 years	
rice, flavored mixes	6 months	
salad dressings	6 months	refrigerate after opening
sauce/soup/gravy mixes	3 months	
sauces/ketchup, barbecue	2 months	keep tightly closed
shortening, hydrogenated	8 months	keep tightly closed
soft drinks	3 months	
sugar, granulated	2 years	keep dry
sugar, brown & confectioners	4 years	
syrups	1 year	close tightly after use
tea, loose or bags	6 months	
tea, instant	1 year	
vegetables: onions, potatoes, rutabagas, sweet potatoes, winter squash	1 week	keep dry; provide for air circulation, will keep 2-3 months at 55°

Refrigerator Storage, Fruits & Vegetables
(in crisper or closed plastic bags)

food item	storage time	keep in mind
apples	1 month	or store at room temperature
apricots, avocados, pears, melons, bananas, grapes, nectarines, peaches, plums	5 days	ripen before refrigerating
berries & cherries	3 days	
citrus fruits	2 weeks	or store at room temperature
pineapples	2 days	
asparagus	3 days	
beets, carrots, parsnips, radishes, turnips	5 days	remove tops before storing
cabbage, cauliflower, celery, cucumbers, green beans, eggplant, peppers	1 week	
tomatoes	1 week	ripen tomatoes before refrigerating
corn on the cob	1 day	refrigerate in husks
lettuce, spinach, all green leafy vegetables	5 days	remove damaged leaves before refrigerating
lima beans, peas	5 days	leave in pods

Refrigerator Storage, Dairy Products
(tightly covered or wrapped)

food item	storage time	keep in mind
butter	2 weeks	
buttermilk	2 weeks	
cheese, spreads	2 weeks	if mold forms on hard cheese, remove before serving — it will do no harm
cheese, cottage & ricotta	5 days	
cheese, cream & neufchatel	2 weeks	
cheese, sliced	2 weeks	
cheese, in whole cuts	2 months	
cream, sweet/sour	1 week	ultrapasteurized, 1 month in original carton
eggs, whole in shell	1 month	
whites, separated	4 days	tightly covered
yolks, separated	4 days	cover with water
margarine	1 month	
milk, whole & skim	1 week	
milk, reconstituted nonfat, opened condensed & evaporated	1 week	

Refrigerator Storage, Meat, Fish & Poultry (uncooked)

food item	storage time	keep in mind
beef, pork, lamb & veal: steaks, chops, roasts	5 days	leave in store plastic wrap or rewrap loosely
ground & stew meats	2 days	
fresh sausage	2 days	
variety meats	2 days	
bacon, frankfurters	1 week	after opening
ham, canned	6 months	unopened
ham, slices	3 days	
ham, whole	1 week	
luncheon meats, cold cuts	5 days	after opening
sausage, dry & semidry	3 weeks	
fish, shellfish (all kinds)	1 day	keep closely wrapped
poultry, fresh or thawed	2 days	

Refrigerator Storage, Leftovers & Packaged Foods (after opening)

food item	storage time	keep in mind
broth, gravy, soup	2 days	tightly covered
cakes, pies: cream or custard fillings	2-3 days	
casserole dishes, stews	3 days	
coffee	1 week	after opening
coffee lighteners, frozen	3 weeks	after thawing
flour: rye, whole wheat, wheat germ	1 year	tightly covered container — not original package
fruits	3 days	
juices, beverages	6 days	
meat, fish, poultry	2 days	remove stuffing from poultry
nutmeats	6 months	tightly covered
pickles, olives	1 month	original container
refrigerated doughs: rolls, biscuits, cookies, breads	check final-use date on package; do not open until ready to use	
salad dressings	3 months	original container
salads: potato, chicken, fish, coleslaw	2 days	tightly covered
wine, white table	3 days	after opening

Continued on back Endsheet

Freezer Storage, Commercial Frozen Foods

food item	storage time	keep in mind
breads, rolls (baked)	3 months	overwrap commercial wrappings
breads, unbaked loaves	3 months	overwrap commercial wrappings
cakes: butter, pound-type	6 months	unfrosted, overwrap
cake, angel food	2 months	overwrap
cake, frosted layer	4 months	
coffee lighteners	1 year	
doughnuts, danish pastry	3 months	overwrap
fish (fat types): trout, mackerel, salmon	3 months	overwrap if package damaged
fish, (lean types): cod, flounder, sole	6 months	if thawed, do not refreeze
shellfish, breaded, cooked	3 months	
lobster, scallops	3 months	
king/queen crab	10 months	
shrimp, uncooked, unbreaded	1 year	
fruit	1 year	
ice cream, sherbet	1 month	overwrap leftovers
main-dish pies, fish or meat	3 months	
main-dish pies, poultry	6 months	
meats, beef roasts, steaks	1 year	overwrap
ground beef	4 months	overwrap
lamb, veal roasts, & steaks	9 months	overwrap
pork chops	4 months	overwrap
pork roasts	8 months	overwrap
pancake/waffle batter	3 months	
pies, unbaked	8 months	
pies, ready to thaw & eat	4 months	
poultry: chicken, turkey parts	6 months	
whole chicken, turkey	1 year	
duck, goose	6 months	
turkey rolls, roasts	6 months	
vegetables, all	8 months	

USEFUL SUBSTITUTIONS

if the recipe calls for	use instead
2 tablespoons all-purpose or whole wheat flour (for thickening)	1 tablespoon cornstarch or arrow-root or potato starch or quick-cooking tapioca
1 cup beef or chicken broth	1 bouillon cube or 1 envelope or 1 rounded teaspoon bouillon powder + 1 cup boiling water
2 egg yolks	1 whole egg
1 cup grated coconut	1⅓ cups flaked coconut
1 pound fresh mushrooms	12 ounces canned mushrooms, drained, or 3 ounces dried mush-rooms, rehydrated
1 teaspoon lemon juice	½ teaspoon distilled white vinegar
1 teaspoon grated lemon peel	½ teaspoon lemon extract
1 cup homogenized milk	1 cup skim milk + 2 tablespoons butter or margarine; or ½ cup evaporated milk + ½ cup water, or ¼ cup powdered whole milk + 1 cup water
1 square (1 ounce) unsweetened chocolate	3 tablespoons cocoa + 1 table-spoon butter or margarine
½ cup butter or margarine	7 tablespoons vegetable shortening
1 cup sifted cake flour	⅞ cup sifted all-purpose flour
1 teaspoon baking powder	½ teaspoon cream of tartar + ¼ teaspoon baking soda
1 cup sour cream (for use in cooking)	1 tablespoon lemon juice + evapo-rated milk (undiluted) to make 1 cup, or ⅓ cup butter + ¾ cup yogurt or buttermilk

1 cup buttermilk or sour milk	1 tablespoon lemon juice or white vinegar + milk to make 1 cup (let stand 5 minutes)
1 cup honey or corn syrup	1¼ cups sugar + ¼ cup liquid
1 tablespoon snipped fresh herb	1 teaspoon dried herb, same kind
1 medium onion, chopped	1 tablespoon instant minced onion, rehydrated
1 cup light cream or half-and-half	3 tablespoons butter + ⅞ cup milk
1 cup heavy (whipping) cream	⅓ cup butter + ¾ cup milk
2 cups tomato sauce	¾ cup tomato paste + 1 cup water
1 cup tomato juice	½ cup tomato sauce + ½ cup water
1 small clove garlic	⅛ teaspoon garlic powder or ¼ tea-spoon commercial garlic juice
1 tablespoon gelatin	1 envelope
1 cake compressed yeast	1 envelope active dry yeast
1 cup yogurt (in cooking)	1 cup buttermilk

FOOD-MEASURE EQUIVALENTS

start out with	to end up with
apples, 3 medium (1 pound)	3 cups sliced
bananas, 3 medium (1 pound)	1½ cups mashed
bread, 1-pound loaf	14 to 20 slices
bread, 1 slice (including crust)	½ cup crumbs
butter or margarine, ¼ pound	½ cup (1 stick or cube)
cheese, ¼ pound	1 cup shredded
cheese, cottage, 8-ounce container	1 cup
cheese, cream, 3-ounce package	6 tablespoons
chocolate, unsweetened, 1 square	1 ounce
chocolate, semisweet pieces, 6 ounces	1 cup
coconut, flaked, 3½-ounce can	1⅓ cups
coconut, shredded, 4-ounce can	1⅓ cups
cream, heavy or whipping, 1 cup	2 cups whipped
cream, sour, 8-ounce container	1 cup
egg whites, large, 8 to 10	1 cup
egg yolks, large, 12 to 14	1 cup
flour, all-purpose, 1 pound	about 3½ cups
flour, cake, 1 pound	about 4 cups
lemon, 1 medium	3 tablespoons juice, 1 tablespoon grated peel
lime, 1 medium	2 tablespoons juice, 1 teaspoon grated peel
milk, evaporated, 5⅓ or 6-ounce can	⅔ cup
12- or 14½-ounce can	1⅔ cups
sweetened condensed, 14-ounce can	1¼ cups
nuts, 1 pound almonds in shell	1 to 1¼ cups nutmeats
almonds, 1 pound shelled	3 cups
brazil nuts, in shell, 1 pound	1½ cups nutmeats
brazil nuts, shelled, 1 pound	3¼ cups
filberts, in shell, 1 pound	1½ cups nutmeats
filberts, shelled, 1 pound	3½ cups
peanuts, in shell, 1 pound	2 to 2½ cups nutmeats
peanuts, shelled, 1 pound	3 cups
pecans, in shell, 1 pound	2¼ cups nutmeats
pecans, shelled, 1 pound	4 cups
walnuts, in shell, 1 pound	2 cups nutmeats
walnuts, shelled, 1 pound	4 cups
onion, 1 large	¾ to 1 cup chopped
orange, 1 medium	¼ to ⅓ cup juice, 2 tablespoons grated peel
potatoes, 1 pound sweet, white	2¼ cups diced
raisins, 1 pound	3 cups
rice, long grain regular, 1 cup	3 cups cooked
salad oil, 16 ounces	2 cups
sugar, 1 pound granulated	2¼ to 2½ cups
brown, 1 pound	2¼ cups (packed)
confectioners, 1 pound	4 to 4½ cups
syrup, corn, 16 ounces	2 cups
maple, 12 ounces	1½ cups

Famous Brands

BREADS, QUICK BREADS & COFFEE CAKES

Brand Name Publishing Corp.

Gordon E. Smith compliments of Arnold Foods Company

Acknowledgments

The editors wish to thank the following companies for permission to use their recipes, photographs, and product names in this volume:

Almond Board of California

American Egg Board

Amstar Corp. Domino® Sugar is a registered trademark of the Amstar Corp.

Berio Importing Corp.

The Birkett Mills

ReaLemon® Lemon Juice from Concentrate Division of Borden Inc.

C & H Sugar Company

Calavo Growers of California

California Prune Advisory Board

California Raisin Advisory Board

Caloric Corporation

Campbell Soup Company

Carnation Company

The Cling Peach Advisory Board

CPC International Inc.

Cumberland Packing Corporation. Sweet 'N Low® is a registered trademark of the Cumberland Packing Corporation.

The Dow Chemical Company makers of SARAN WRAP™ brand plastic film

Durkee Famous Foods

Elam's

Simon Fischer Lekvar Prune Butter

Florida Department of Citrus

General Foods Corporation

General Mills, Inc. Bisquick® and Gold Medal® are registered trademarks of General Mills, Inc.

Georgia Egg Commission

Hamilton Beach Scovill Inc.

Hecker's Unbleached, All-Purpose, Naturally White Flour

HERSHEY Food Corporation. All recipes developed and tested in the HERSHEY Test Kitchen.

Heublein Inc.

Hiram Walker

Idaho Potato Commission

Kellogg Company

Lewis & Neale, Inc., on behalf of Hollywood Safflower Oil

Libby, McNeill & Libby, Inc., The Great Pumpkin Cookbook, A Harvest of Libby's Favorite Recipes. Libby's® is a registered trademark of Libby, McNeill & Libby, Inc.

Thomas J. Lipton, Inc., Englewood-Cliffs, NJ 07632

Martha White Foods, Inc.

Nabisco Brands, Inc.

Nestlé Foods Corporation. NESTLÉ TOLL HOUSE Semi-Sweet Chocolate Morsels, NESTLÉ Little Bits Semi-Sweet Chocolate, NESTLÉ Butterscotch Flavored Morsels, NESTLÉ Milk Chocolate Morsels, NESTLÉ Peanut Butter Morsels, NESTLÉ CHOCO-BAKE Unsweetened Baking Chocolate Flavor, TOLL HOUSE Cookies, and NESTLÉ QUIK Chocolate Flavor are registered trademarks of Nestlé Foods Corporation.

Nebraska Wheat Board

Norseland Foods, Inc.

North Carolina Yam Commission

Ocean Spray Cranberries, Inc.

Oklahoma Peanut Commission

H.G. Parks

The Quaker Oats Company

Consumer Products Division, Reynolds Metal Company

Riceland Foods

Roquefort Association

Sargento Cheese Company

Sioux Honey Association

Solo Food Products, Division of Sokol & Company

Sunbeam Appliance Co., a member company of Allegheny International, Inc. Sunbeam® is a registered trademark of the Sunbeam Corporation

Sun-Maid Growers of California

The Sweet Potato Council of the United States

Virginia State Apple Commission

Invitation

The Famous Brands Cookbook Library invites you, the modern cook, to a new experience in your own kitchen. Have you ever wished you had a larger repertoire of company's-coming menus? Ever searched for a different and exciting way to prepare favorite products? Ever felt that if you could just have a certain technique explained simply, you could master an entire new world of cooking?

The solutions to these dilemmas and others are the cornerstone of the twelve volumes that comprise *The Famous Brands Cookbook Library*. Whether you are just getting to know your kitchen—or have a long-standing relationship with it—the recipes and hints provided here offer the very best and latest information available from the test kitchens of many of America's finest food companies. Once you have had a chance to discover the treasures inside this volume, you'll want to collect each of the other volumes in this series—and an invaluable home cooking library will be yours.

Famous Brands Desserts

Famous Brands Every Oven Microwave Cookbook

Famous Brands Great Vegetable Dishes

Famous Brands Meat Cookbook

Famous Brands Chicken & Poultry

Famous Brands Breads, Quick Breads, & Coffee Cakes

Famous Brands Soups & Salads

Famous Brands Pasta Dishes

Famous Brands Fish & Seafood Cookbook

Famous Brands Cooking with Eggs & Cheese

Famous Brands Main Dishes

Famous Brands Chocolate Classics

Front cover: *Sour Cream-Date Muffins (page 72); Brown Sugar-Nut Bread (page 49); Sesame Quick Bread with Cream Cheese Spread (page 31).* C & H Sugar Co. Back cover: *Country Fair Bread (page 22).* Martha White Foods

Published by Brand Name Publishing Corp., 1950 Craig Road, St. Louis, Missouri 63146 and Brand Name Books, Inc., 122 East 25th Street, New York, New York 10010.

Bread Making: Challenge and Triumph

There is great satisfaction in being a good cook, in learning the basic kitchen skills and putting them to use, in regularly producing nourishing and flavorful food for the family and occasional big-production meals when guests are invited.

Perhaps the most enjoyable of the home cook's ventures is baking, and of baking's many facets, making bread, dinner and sweet rolls, tea loaves and coffee cakes, and all the other related good things that everyone so much enjoys is the high point. "You made it yourself?" is never quite as heartfelt—and never quite as flattering—as when it refers to a baking triumph.

Admittedly, baking can be a challenge. The difference between success and failure lies in know-how—in understanding what to do and how to do it, how the dough should look and feel and behave at every step of the way. If you have not been baking so long and so well that the know-how has become second nature, you need good recipes and you need to follow them faithfully. More, you need general knowledge: the meaning of baking terms, the kinds of leavening and how they work, what kinds of flour are available and which function best in bread making, how to tell when a loaf is done, and a host of other bits of information that can make all the difference.

In this book you'll find good, dependable, easy-to-understand recipes for a wide variety of breadstuffs that you will make with pleasure and serve with pride. And in this book, as well, you'll find the important hints of the ins and outs of baking that you need to go into the kitchen with confidence, knowing what you are going to do and how you will go about doing it.

The results? High-rise loaves, handsome and shapely buns and biscuits, nut- and fruit-studded quick breads, sweet rolls plump with filling or glistening with glaze, plus a wealth of the jams and preserves, spreads and butters, that make the serving of homemade bread such a pleasure at any meal, any time.

Contents

The Great Aroma of Baking Bread

Tall and shapely loaves—white and whole wheat, rye and pumpernickel—all yeast-raised.

Homemade French Bread

Makes 2 loaves

- 1⅓ **cups very warm (not hot) water**
- 1 **package (¼ ounce) active dry yeast**
- 2 **teaspoons salt**
- 3 to 3½ **cups unbleached all-purpose flour or regular all-purpose flour**

Step 1. Pour ⅓ cup of the warm water into a medium bowl. Stir in yeast and salt until dissolved. Stir in remaining cup of warm water.

Step 2. Gradually add 2½ cups of the flour, mixing with a large spoon. Dough will be soft and sticky.

Step 3. Sprinkle ½ cup of the remaining flour onto a smooth working surface; turn dough out onto the floured surface. Use a dough scraper, or a spatula if you don't have a dough scraper, to lift and turn the sticky dough until it can be shaped into a ball.

Step 4. Knead the dough for 15 minutes, adding only as much of the remaining flour as necessary to keep the dough from sticking. After 10 minutes of kneading, pick the dough up and slap it down on the work surface a few times during remaining kneading time. When dough is properly kneaded, it should feel smooth and springy.

Step 5. Place the dough in a clean, ungreased 2½-quart bowl. (If you are using a larger rising bowl, measure 10 cups of water into it and mark the level on the outside of the bowl so you'll know when the dough has tripled in volume. Pour out water and dry bowl well before adding dough.) Cover the bowl with plastic wrap. Let stand at room temperature, out of any drafts, until the dough reaches the top of, or the mark on, the rising bowl. This will take about 3 hours, or longer. Don't rush it.

Step 6. When the dough has tripled, punch it down, scoop it out of the bowl with your hands, and knead a few times on a lightly floured surface. (The dough can be covered and refrigerated at this point, or even wrapped in plastic wrap and frozen until you are ready to continue.) Return dough to bowl; cover and let rise until double in bulk, about 2 hours.

Step 7. At the end of the second rising time, punch the dough down, scoop it out of the bowl with your hands, and knead a few times on a lightly floured surface. Let rest about 5 minutes. (The dough can be refrigerated or frozen at this point, too.)

Step 8. Lightly grease a French bread pan. Set aside.

Step 9. Cut dough in half to make 2 loaves of traditional French bread. Flatten one piece of dough, then roll it into a sausage shape on a lightly floured surface. Place hands, palms down, on the center of the roll of dough. Push back and forth, working your way to the ends of the roll. Do this until the dough is just slightly shorter than the baking pan. Lift dough gently and place in pan. Repeat with remaining dough.

Step 10. Cover pan with plastic wrap or a towel and set aside until loaves have doubled in volume, about 1½ hours.

Step 11. About 20 minutes before baking, preheat oven to 425°F.

Step 12. Using a sharp knife or a single-edge razor blade, slash each loaf in three long diagonal lines about ½-inch deep.

Step 13. Immediately before placing slashed loaves in the oven, spray them with several pumps of water from an atomizer bottle, such as the kind used for misting plants.

Step 14. Place loaves in the oven and set a timer for 2 minutes. When timer rings, spray bread quickly to create steam in the oven. (To do this, open the oven door, but do not pull the bread out; spray liberally with several pumps and close the oven door as quickly as possible to retain steam and oven heat.) Repeat spraying 2 more times at 2-minute intervals. Bake bread about 25 minutes in all, or until a rich golden color, turning the pan around if loaves seem to be baking and browning unevenly.

Step 15. Slide out of pan onto a cooling rack.

Homemade French Bread. Courtesy *Parent's Magazine*

French Bread Ladder

Makes 2 ladders

Cutting slits in a flat loaf of French bread exposes more surface and produces more crust. This unusual-looking bread is smashing on a supper or buffet table.

1 recipe Homemade French Bread dough (see index)

Follow directions for Homemade French Bread through Step 6.

At the end of the second rising time, punch the dough down, scoop it out of the bowl with your hands, and knead a few times on a lightly floured surface. Let rest about 5 minutes.

Cut the dough in half. With a rolling pin, roll and push the dough to make 2 rectangles measuring roughly 8x12 inches each. If the dough is too springy, let it stand a bit, then continue rolling.

Lift the rectangles onto greased baking sheets. With a sharp knife or single-edge razor blade, make several diagonal cuts through each loaf of bread. Push the dough apart with fingers to open the cuts.

Cover with a towel and let rise about 1 hour.

Preheat oven to 400°F. about 20 minutes before baking time.

Spray loaves with water.

Follow Steps 14 and 15, baking about 25 minutes, or until crusty and golden.

French Bread Branches

Makes 2 branches

Sometimes called an "ear of wheat" or "a tree," this shape has baked points that are more like rolls than bread and are a crust-lover's delight.

1 recipe Homemade French Bread dough (see index)

Follow directions for Homemade French Bread through Step 7.

Lightly grease 2 large baking sheets. Set aside.

Follow Step 9 through shaping both halves of dough into an 18-inch roll.

Place each roll diagonally on a baking sheet. Cover with a towel and let rise until double in bulk, about 1½ hours.

Preheat oven to 425°F. about 20 minutes before baking time.

Using sharp scissors, make deep V-shape cuts about 2½ inches apart down the length of the loaf. As each cut is made, pull 1 side of the dough to the left with the point resting on the baking sheet. Pull the other side to the right with the point resting on the baking sheet. Continue alternating to the end of the loaf.

Spray loaves with water.

Follow Steps 14 and 15, baking for 20 to 25 minutes, or until loaves are golden.

Baguettes

Makes 4 baguettes

These smaller versions of the traditional loaf of French bread are popular with small families for whom a larger loaf would be too much.

1 recipe Homemade French Bread dough (see index)

Follow directions for Homemade French Bread through Step 7.

Lightly grease 2 French bread pans. If you have only 1 pan, see note at end of Baguette directions. Set pans aside.

Cut dough into quarters. Flatten one piece of dough, then roll it into a sausage shape on a lightly floured surface. Place hands, palms down, on the center of the roll of dough. Push back and forth, working your way to the ends of the roll. Do this until the dough is just slightly shorter than the baking pan. (Since you are working with only half as much dough as in the traditional loaf, this roll will be much thinner and will look more like a fat, slightly lumpy rope.) Lift dough gently and place in pan. Repeat with remaining dough.

Follow Steps 10 and 11.

Omit Step 12.

Follow Steps 13, 14, and 15.

Note: If you do not have 2 French bread pans, the loaves can be baked in 2 batches. In that case, roll out 4 baguettes, but leave 2 to rise on a floured surface covered with a towel. Bake the second pair of baguettes after the bread pan has cooled and has been greased again.

French Bread Wreath

Makes 2 wreaths

The wreath is similar to French Bread Branches. If you like, for variety, brush the loaf before baking with a beaten-egg wash, then sprinkle with poppy seeds. In that case, don't spray with water before baking or during baking.

1 recipe Homemade French Bread dough (see index)

Follow directions for Homemade French Bread dough through Step 7.

Lightly grease 2 large baking sheets. Set aside.

Follow Step 9 through shaping both halves of dough into 18-inch rolls. Place each roll on a baking sheet, forming a circle in the center of the sheet. Seal ends together by pinching firmly with fingers. Cover with a towel and let rise until double in bulk, about 1½ hours.

Preheat oven to 425°F. about 20 minutes before baking time.

Using a sharp scissors, make deep V-shape cuts about 2 inches apart around each wreath, starting at any point. As the cuts are made, pull each piece of dough to the outside so that the point is resting on the baking sheet.

Spray loaves with water.

Follow Steps 14 and 15, baking for 20 minutes, or until loaves are golden.

Focaccia

Makes 1 loaf

  2½ **to 3 cups all-purpose flour, divided**
    1 **package (¼ ounce) active dry yeast**
    1 **tablespoon sugar**
   ¾ **teaspoon salt**
    1 **cup milk**
    4 **tablespoons olive oil, divided**
   ½ **cup Sun-Maid® Zante Currants**
      Topping (recipe follows) (optional)

Combine 1 cup of the flour with the yeast, sugar, and salt in a large electric mixer bowl. Heat the milk and 3 tablespoons of the oil until very warm (120° to 130°F.). Beating at low speed, gradually add the warmed milk and oil to the flour mixture. Increase the speed to medium and beat for 2 minutes. Beat in ½ cup of the remaining flour, or enough to make a stiff dough. Increase the speed to high and beat for 5 minutes, or until the batter sheets off a spoon. Stir in the currants and about 1 cup of the remaining flour, or enough to make a firm dough. Turn out on a floured surface and knead until the dough is smooth and elastic, about 10 minutes. Place in a greased bowl and turn once to grease the surface. Cover and let rise in a warm place, free from draft, until double in bulk, about 45 minutes.

Prepare one of the toppings. Preheat the oven to 450°F. Grease a 15x10x1-inch jelly roll pan. Punch the dough down and press into the prepared pan. Brush the surface with the remaining 1 tablespoon oil and sprinkle with the topping. Bake for 12 to 15 minutes, or until golden brown. Cut into squares and serve hot.

Olive Topping

  ½ **cup sliced pitted black olives**
  ½ **cup chopped parsley**
  ½ **cup grated Parmesan cheese**

Combine black olives, chopped parsley, and Parmesan cheese until well blended.

Onion Topping

  3 **onions, sliced**
  ¼ **cup olive oil**
  ½ **cup grated Parmesan cheese**
    Salt

Cook onions in olive oil until the onions are soft but not browned. Spread over the dough and sprinkle with Parmesan cheese. The onions may be seasoned lightly with salt.

Bread-Making Terms

These commonly used bread-making terms are explained to help you short-cut your way through any recipe.

Kneading

This is the process that completes mixing through rhythmic pressure on the dough. Kneading should be done on a lightly floured board or pastry cloth. First, rub a little flour on your hands to keep the dough from sticking. Shape the dough into a ball. Fold the dough, bringing it toward you. Push down with the heel of your hand; give the dough a slight turn; fold and press again. Repeat until the dough becomes smooth, elastic, and satiny. This should take 8 to 10 minutes. If the dough is sticky, sprinkle the board or pastry cloth with a little flour. Use firm, steady, but gentle pressure. When kneading is completed, place the dough in a large greased bowl. Turn once to grease the top. Cover bowl with waxed paper, plastic wrap, or damp cloth.

Rising

Rising is the process of letting the dough double in bulk, at least once, and often twice. Rising of yeast breads, except refrigerator doughs, should be done in a warm place (80° to 85°F.), free from draft. An excellent place for dough to rise is in the oven. Place the bowl in a cold oven with a pan of hot water. Dough has risen sufficiently when it is double in bulk. To check for doubling, press 2 fingertips lightly about ½ inch into the dough. If a dent remains after you withdraw your fingers, the dough has risen sufficiently.

Punch Down

After the dough has risen, it must be punched down to expel air and redistribute the yeast. Push fist firmly into the center of the dough; bring edge toward center and turn dough over.

Let Rest

This step, after kneading but before shaping, makes dough easier to handle. Usually 10 minutes are allowed. If you are short of time, this step can be omitted.

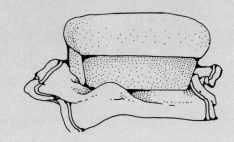

The ingredients: flour, yeast, water, salt.

Mix yeast with warm water until no lumps remain.

Add salt.

Gradually stir in all the flour, stirring constantly with wooden spoon.

When mixture forms a large ball, remove to pastry board and knead 5 to 10 minutes.

When dough begins to feel smooth and light and no longer sticky, it is ready.

Return dough to mixing bowl.

Allow to rise 30 to 40 minutes until double in bulk.

Divide dough into 4 sections; knead each for a minute and form into desired shape.

Allow to rise a second time, for about 10 to 15 minutes.

Slash tops about 1½-inch deep with sharp knife.

Bake for 45 to 50 minutes, until they are a light golden brown.

Bread Making—Step by Step
(see Lisa's Quick-Easy Italian Bread for more details)

Calabro Studios

Lisa's Quick-Easy Italian Bread

Makes 4 loaves
>   3 to 4 ounces fresh yeast
>   2 to 2½ cups lukewarm water (80° to 90°F.)
>   1 tablespoon salt
>   6 cups unbleached all-purpose flour

Mix yeast thoroughly with the warm water in a large bowl until completely dissolved and no lumps remain. Add salt. Gradually stir all the flour into the liquid yeast, stirring constantly with a wooden spoon. When mixture forms a large ball, remove to pastry board or marble surface and knead dough for 5 to 10 minutes, sprinkling lightly with flour to keep from sticking and/or if dough is too moist. When dough begins to feel smooth and light and no longer sticky, it is ready.

Return dough to mixing bowl and cover with 2 dish-cloths; place in a warm draft-free place, approximately 80°F., and allow to rise 30 to 40 minutes, until dough is double in bulk. After the first rising, divide dough into about 4 sections. Knead each for a minute and form into any selected shape: long, oval, round, or braided. Place loaves onto floured baking pans or baking stones, recover with cloth, and allow to rest and rise for second time, for approximately 10 to 15 minutes.

Preheat oven to 400°F. while loaves are rising. Just before placing the loaves into the oven, slash the tops about ½-inch deep with a sharp knife. Bake for 45 to 50 minutes, depending on thickness of dough. Do not open oven for at least 30 minutes before examining loaves for doneness. They should be a light golden brown. Remove bread from oven and place on a wooden rack or angled against a wall to permit bread to cool equally overall and to avoid any moisture from condensation. Bread should rest for a couple of hours before slicing and eating.

Country Rye Bread

Makes 1 loaf
>   1 cup mashed potatoes, at room temperature,
>   reserve 1½ cups potato water
>   2½ to 3 cups all-purpose flour, divided
>   1½ cups rye flour
>   1 package (¼ ounce) active dry yeast
>   1 tablespoon sugar
>   1 tablespoon butter or margarine
>   2 teaspoons caraway seed
>   1 teaspoon salt
>   1 egg, lightly beaten
>   2 tablespoons coarse salt

Heat reserved potato water in small saucepan to 120° to 130°F. Combine 1 cup all-purpose flour, rye flour, potatoes, warm potato water, yeast, sugar, butter, car-away seed, and salt in large bowl. Beat with electric mixer on high 2 minutes. Stir in remaining flour. Turn dough out onto lightly floured surface. Knead 10 minutes, or until dough is smooth and elastic. Place in lightly greased bowl; turn to coat entire surface. Cover and let rise in warm place, free from draft, until almost double in bulk, about 1 hour. Grease an 8-inch round cake pan; set aside. Punch dough down. Shape into a smooth, round ball. Place in prepared pan. Cover. Let rise in warm place, free from draft, until almost double in bulk, about 1 hour. Preheat oven to 375°F. Brush surface with beaten egg. Sprinkle with coarse salt. Bake 40 to 50 minutes, or until loaf sounds hollow when lightly tapped. Remove from pan. Cool on wire rack.

Q. *How do I know when the bread is done?*
A. Depend on your recipe for baking time and on your eye for well-risen, golden-brown baked goods. Or slip loaves of bread quickly from their pans—they will come out easily—and tap them on the bottom. A hollow sound tells you the loaf is done.

Homemade White Bread

Makes 2 loaves
>   1 package (¼ ounce) active dry yeast
>   ¼ cup warm water (105° to 115°F.)
>   2 cups warm milk
>   3 tablespoons sugar
>   1 tablespoon salt
>   3 tablespoons vegetable shortening, melted
>   5 to 5½ cups Martha White All-Purpose Flour,
>   divided
>   Vegetable oil

Dissolve yeast in water in measuring cup. Grease large bowl; set aside. Combine milk, sugar, salt, short-ening, and yeast mixture in separate bowl. Add 2 cups flour; blend well. Stir in enough remaining flour to make a stiff dough. Turn out onto floured board or pastry cloth. Cover with bowl. Let rest 10 minutes. Knead dough 8 to 10 minutes, or until smooth and elastic. Shape into ball. Place in prepared bowl. Turn once to grease top. Cover and let rise in warm place, free from draft, 1½ hours, or until double in bulk. Punch down. Let rest 10 minutes. Grease two 9x5x3-inch loaf pans. Divide dough in half. Shape each half into a loaf. Place in prepared pans. Brush tops with oil. Cover and let rise in warm place, free from draft, 1 hour, or until double in bulk. Preheat oven to 400°F. Bake 15 minutes. Reduce oven temperature to 300°F. Bake 20 to 25 minutes, or until loaves sound hollow when lightly tapped. Transfer to wire rack to cool.

Wholesome Wheat Bread

Makes 2 loaves

    6 cups (about) unsifted whole wheat flour,
        divided
    2 packages (¼ ounce each) active dry yeast
    1 teaspoon ground cinnamon
    1 teaspoon salt
    1 cup Karo Dark Corn Syrup
    1 cup water
    ½ cup Hellmann's or Best Foods Real Mayonnaise
    2 eggs

Grease and flour 1 large baking sheet. In small bowl, stir together 2 cups of the flour, yeast, cinnamon, and salt; set aside. In 2-quart saucepan, stir together corn syrup, water, and mayonnaise. Stirring occasionally, heat to 120° to 130°F. over medium heat. Pour into large mixer bowl. With mixer at medium speed, beat flour mixture 2 minutes. Reduce speed to low; beat in 2 more cups flour and eggs. Beat at medium speed 2 minutes. With wooden spoon, stir in enough additional flour (about 1½ cups) to make an easily handled dough. On floured surface, knead 10 minutes, or until smooth and elastic, adding ½ cup flour if necessary. Place in greased bowl; turn dough over so that top is greased. Cover with damp towel; let rise in warm place, free from draft, until doubled, about 1 hour. Punch dough down. Divide dough in half. Let rest 10 minutes. Shape each half into an 8x4-inch oval. Place on prepared baking sheet. Cut 3 slashes, ¼ inch deep, in top of each loaf. Cover with towel. Let rise in warm place, free from draft, until doubled, about 1½ hours. Bake in 350°F. oven 30 to 40 minutes, or until browned and loaves sound hollow when bottoms are tapped. Immediately remove from baking sheet. Cool on wire rack.

Variation

To prepare in loaf pans, grease and flour 2 8½x4½x2½-inch loaf pans. Prepare dough as in first paragraph in Wholesome Wheat Bread. Roll each dough half into 12x8-inch rectangle. Roll up from a short side. Press ends to seal; fold ends under. Place in prepared pans. Cover with towel. Let rise in warm place, free from draft, until doubled, about 1½ hours. Bake in 350°F. oven 30 to 40 minutes, or until browned and loaves sound hollow when bottoms are tapped. Immediately remove from pans. Cool on wire rack. *Makes 2 loaves*

Rye and Whole Wheat Bread

Makes 2 loaves

    2 cakes (6 ounce each) compressed yeast
    1 cup lukewarm water
    2 tablespoons shortening
    1 cup milk, scalded
    ¼ cup molasses
    2½ teaspoons salt
    2½ cups Elam's 100% Whole Rye Flour
    2½ cups Elam's 100% Whole Wheat Flour

Dissolve yeast in water. Add shortening to scalded milk; stir until melted. Cool to lukewarm. Stir in molasses, salt, and dissolved yeast. Add rye flour gradually; beat until smooth after each addition. Reserve ¼ cup of whole wheat flour. Stir in remaining whole wheat flour a small amount at a time. Turn dough out onto board sprinkled lightly with reserved whole wheat flour. Knead 8 to 10 minutes, adding more whole wheat flour to board as needed. Place in greased bowl. Cover; let rise in warm draftless area until double in size, about 1 hour. Punch dough down; cover and let rest 10 minutes. Shape dough into 2 loaves. Place each in a well-greased 8½x4½x2-inch loaf pan. Cover with towel. Let rise in warm, draftless area until nearly double in size, about 1 hour. Bake in moderate oven (375°F.) 45 minutes, or until done. Cool in pans 5 minutes. Turn onto wire rack to finish cooling.

Pumpernickel Bread

Makes two 9-inch loaves

    3 packages (¼ ounce each) active dry yeast
    1½ cups warm buttermilk (105° to 115°F.)
    2¾ cups rye graham flour
    2¾ cups enriched all-purpose flour, divided
    1 egg, lightly beaten
    ½ cup warm honey
    3 tablespoons soft shortening
    1 tablespoon caraway seed
    1 tablespoon sesame seed
    1 tablespoon salt
    Cornmeal

Soften yeast in the buttermilk. Combine rye flour, 1 cup all-purpose flour, egg, honey, shortening, seeds, salt, and softened yeast. Beat well. Stir in enough remaining all-purpose flour to make a stiff dough. Knead on floured board until smooth, 8 to 10 minutes. Place in a greased bowl. Cover, let rise until double. Punch down, divide in half. Cover, let rest 10 minutes. Form into balls and put into greased 9-inch round pans sprinkled with cornmeal. Bake at 375°F. until well browned, about 30 to 35 minutes.

What Kind of Flour?

Shopping at supermarkets, health food stores, and food specialty shops, you can find a wide variety of flours. Although when we mention flour, we are subconsciously thinking of "wheat," and although the largest number of those we find on supermarket shelves are wheat flours, there are actually a number of other kinds. Here is an overview of the flours readily available to today's home baker.

Wheat Flours

White flour is the soft, white lightweight flour that comes first to mind when we think of flour. This is the most widely used variety. **Unbleached** is wheat flour left the normal pale yellow-tan color of flour after the milling process. White flour is bleached, either by time or by chemicals, or both. **All-purpose** flour is simply another term for white flour—it may be used for all purposes to which flour is put. **Bread** flour has a higher gluten content than all-purpose flour, and is therefore useful in bread making where gluten is an important factor. However, note that most recipes in cookbooks and magazine cooking articles are tailored for all-purpose flour. **Whole wheat** flour, which may also be labeled "graham," is made from cleaned, unrefined, unbleached wheat. Light brown in color, it retains the natural constituents (bran, embryo, endosperm) that are removed during the milling process of white flour. **Bran** flour is white flour with the milled-out bran returned to it at the end of the milling process. **Cracked wheat** flour is all-purpose flour into which the entire wheat kernel, somewhat crushed, has been mixed. **Wheat germ** flour has the "germ"—the embryo—of the grains mixed into it. **Cake** flour is highly refined and bleached and feels very light and silky to the touch. It is used in cake mixes, and is available for home baking—but, because proportions vary, should be used only in recipes that call for it. **Self-rising** flour is bleached flour into which leavening—baking powder, soda—and salt have been mixed. Available as self-rising all-purpose and self-rising cake flours, it should not be used in any recipes that call for yeast unless the recipe so specifies. In other baking, if the recipe calls for all-purpose flour and you wish to use self-rising, omit leavening and salt. **Enriched** flour returns to the flour certain nutrients that are lost in the milling process. Enriching restores the all-purpose flour to the approximate nutrient value of whole wheat flour. Government regulations specify minimum and maximums of each nutrient that may be added per pound of flour. Iron, niacin, riboflavin, and thiamin must be added for flour to qualify as "enriched," and calcium and vitamin D may also be added. **Instant-type** flour has a granular texture which makes it easy to measure. It need not be sifted, and blends readily with cold liquid without lumping. It should be used only in recipes especially developed for its use and never substituted for all-purpose flour when that is called for.

Non-Wheat Flours

Arrowroot flour, from the roots of a tropical plant, is used as a thickening agent, largely by commercial bakers; it is very easily digestible and so particularly suitable for plain biscuits for babies and invalids. **Barley** flour, lower in protein than wheat but rich in minerals, is more used in Europe than in this country; it is difficult to use in bread making. **Buckwheat** flour is finely ground and has the sweet/sour flavor peculiar to buckwheat. **Carob** flour is made from the pods of the carob tree, also known as St. John's bread or locust; it is high in protein and has a sweetish, faintly chocolatelike flavor. **Corn** flour is finer than cornmeal, of which it is a by-product; find it labeled "masa harina" in stores in the Southwest. **Cottonseed** flour is made from the residue remaining after the extraction of oil from specially treated cotton seeds. **Lima bean** flour is produced by milling ripe, dried lima beans; the skins are removed in the milling. **Peanut** flour is the residue remaining after the oil has been extracted from peanuts. **Potato** flour is made of potatoes that are cooked, dried and ground; it is used extensively in Europe. **Rice** flour, made from white rice, is starchy; it is used as a thickener, and in foods for those allergic to wheat. A second type, **waxy rice flour,** made from a variety of rice with waxy, adhesive qualities, is used as a stabilizer in sauces and gravies to prevent separation of these foods when frozen. **Rye** flour is used extensively in Europe, notably in northern countries where the climate is not suitable for wheat, and in this country particularly where migrants from northern Europe have settled. **Soy** flour comes in two varieties, full-fat and low-fat; the former is made from soybeans with only the hull removed, the latter from the residue remaining after the oil is expressed from the beans. **Tapioca** flour is made from the root of the tropical manioc (cassava) plant; it is high in carbohydrate nutrients. Although you may seldom, or never, use them at home, these flours are employed extensively in the manufacture of commercial foods (read labels and see); many are a godsend to those allergic to wheat flours.

Rye-Caraway Cheese Bread (page 16). Caloric Corporation

Earth Grains Bread

Makes 2 loaves

- 1½ **cups undiluted Carnation® Evaporated Milk**
- ¾ **cup water**
- 2 **packages (¼ ounce each) active dry yeast**
- ⅔ **cup firmly packed brown sugar**
- ½ **cup quick-cooking oats**
- 2 **teaspoons salt**
- 1 **cup whole wheat flour**
- 1 **cup rye flour**
- 3 to 3¾ **cups all-purpose flour**
  Undiluted Carnation® Evaporated Milk

Combine 1½ cups evaporated milk and water; heat to lukewarm (105° to 115°F.). Place in large bowl. Dissolve yeast in warm mixture. Add brown sugar, oats, salt, whole wheat flour, and 1 cup all-purpose flour. Stir vigorously 1 minute. Stir in 1½ cups additional flour to make a stiff dough. Knead on floured surface, working in additional flour until smooth and elastic, about 8 minutes. Place in buttered bowl turning to butter top. Cover; let rise in warm place until double in bulk. Punch dough down. Roll into rectangle; cut into 6 strips. Carefully roll and pull each strip into 12-inch rope. Place 3 ropes on buttered baking sheet and braid; tuck ends under. Repeat with other 3 ropes. Brush with evaporated milk. Cover, let rise in warm place until double in bulk. Bake in slow oven (325°F.) 25 to 30 minutes, or until bread sounds hollow when tapped.

Lisa's Quick-Easy Italian Bread (page 11). Lisa Trozza/Calabro Studios

Old-Fashioned Wheatena Bread

Makes 2 loaves

- **2 packages (¼ ounce each) active dry yeast**
- **½ cup warm water**
- **1¾ cups milk**
- **6 to 6½ cups Hecker's Unbleached, All-Purpose, Naturally White Flour, sifted**
- **1 cup Wheatena, uncooked**
- **2 tablespoons sugar**
- **1 tablespoon honey**
- **1 tablespoon salt**
- **2 tablespoons shortening, softened**

Dissolve yeast in water. Scald milk and cool to lukewarm. To the yeast mixture, add the milk, half the flour, and all other ingredients. Beat until smooth and add the remaining flour. Turn out onto floured board and knead until smooth and elastic. Place in a greased bowl, cover, and leave in a warm (80° to 85°F.) place for 1 hour, or until doubled in size. Punch down, cover, and let rise again for 30 minutes. Divide into 2 pieces and roll each piece into a ball. Let rest 10 minutes.

Shape into loaves and place each in a well-greased 9x5x3-inch loaf pan. Return to warm place and let rise for 50 to 55 minutes. Bake in a preheated 425°F. oven about 30 to 35 minutes.

Rye-Caraway Cheese Bread

Makes 10 servings
  2½ cups all-purpose flour
  1½ cups rye flour
   ¼ cup firmly packed brown sugar
   2 teaspoons salt
   1 teaspoon caraway seed
   2 packages (¼ ounce each) active dry yeast
   1 cup milk
   ¼ cup butter or margarine
   ½ cup shredded cheddar cheese

Combine flours and measure 2 cups of flour mixture into mixing bowl. Add brown sugar, salt, caraway seed, and yeast. In small saucepan, cook milk, butter, and ⅔ cup water over medium heat until very warm (120° to 130°F.). Pour into flour mixture and beat 5 minutes. Stir in cheese and remaining flour. Place in greased 2½-quart casserole and turn to coat entire surface. Cover and let rise in warm place, free from draft, until almost double in bulk, about 45 minutes.

Preheat oven to 400°F. Bake 35 to 40 minutes until loaf sounds hollow when tapped on bottom. Remove from casserole immediately and cool on wire rack.

Shaping

For recipes yielding 2 loaves, divide the dough in half. Roll out each half with a rolling pin or pat into a 14x9-inch rectangle (for an 8½x4½x2½-inch pan) or 15x10 inches (for a 9x5x3-inch pan). Roll up the rectangles tightly from the narrow side, pressing with your thumbs to seal the dough at each turn. Pinch the edges and ends to seal. Fold the ends under. Place the loaf in the pan with both ends touching the pan. Brush the top of the loaf with melted butter or vegetable oil. Cover and place in a warm place, free from draft, until double in bulk.

Refrigerator Whole Wheat Bread

Makes 2 loaves
   2 cups milk
   ¾ cup water
   ¼ cup butter or margarine
   4 cups Martha White All-Purpose Flour, divided
   3 tablespoons brown sugar
   4 teaspoons salt
   2 packages (¼ ounce each) active dry yeast
  3½ to 4 cups Martha White Whole Wheat Flour
      Vegetable oil

Heat milk, water, and butter in saucepan until very warm (120° to 130°F.). Combine 3 cups all-purpose flour, sugar, salt, and yeast in mixing bowl. Gradually stir in heated mixture; beat at high speed of electric mixer 2 minutes, scraping bowl occasionally. Add remaining cup all-purpose flour; beat at high speed 2 minutes. Stir in enough whole wheat flour to make a stiff dough. Sprinkle board or pastry cloth with whole wheat flour. Turn dough out onto floured surface. Knead 8 to 10 minutes, or until smooth and elastic. Cover with plastic wrap, then a towel. Let rest 20 minutes. Grease two 9x5x3-inch loaf pans; set aside. Divide dough in half. Roll each half into 14x9-inch rectangle. Roll up, jelly roll fashion, from long side; press ends under. Place loaves in prepared pans. Brush tops with oil. Cover with plastic wrap. Refrigerate at least 6 hours. When ready to bake, remove from refrigerator. Carefully remove plastic wrap. Let stand at room temperature 10 minutes. Preheat oven to 400°F. Bake 40 minutes, or until loaves sound hollow when lightly tapped. Transfer to wire rack to cool.

Houska

Makes 1 large loaf
   1 package (¼ ounce) dry yeast
   1 teaspoon sugar
   ½ cup warm water (105° to 115°F.)
  7½ cups (about) enriched all-purpose flour
   ½ cup butter
   ½ cup sugar
   1 tablespoon salt
   2 cups warm milk
      Rind of ½ lemon, grated
   1 egg, beaten
   2 egg yolks, beaten
   ¾ cup white raisins
   ½ cup shredded almonds
      Egg white, beaten
      Whole blanched almonds

Dissolve yeast and sugar in warm water. Add enough of the flour to make a thin batter, about 2 heaping tablespoons. Let rise until light. Add butter, sugar, and salt to warm milk. When cool, add grated lemon rind and beaten egg and egg yolks. Combine sponge and milk mixture. Add aproximately 7 cups flour, beating and kneading with a wooden spoon until mixture is smooth and elastic. Cover and let rise until double in bulk. When light, turn on to a floured board and knead in raisins and almonds. Divide into 5 portions. Work each portion into a long strand. Braid 3 strands together. Place on greased pan. Twist 2 remaining strands and place on top of braid, tucking ends under length of braid. Set aside to rise. Cover. When light, brush with beaten egg white and decorate with whole blanched almonds. Bake about 1 hour in a 350°F. oven. **Note:** Instead of 1 large Houska, you might prefer to divide dough and make 2 smaller loaves. Bake smaller Houska for 45 minutes.

Anadama Bread

Makes 2 loaves
  1 cup water
  1 cup milk
  ¼ cup butter or margarine
  6 to 6½ cups Martha White All-Purpose Flour, divided
  1 cup Martha White Self-Rising Corn Meal
  2 teaspoons salt
  2 packages (¼ ounce each) active dry yeast
  ½ cup molasses

Grease large bowl; set aside. Heat water, milk, and butter in saucepan until very warm (120° to 130°F.). Combine 3 cups flour, cornmeal, salt, and yeast in separate bowl. Add heated mixture and molasses; stir until blended. Add 3 cups flour; blend well. If dough is sticky, add remaining flour. Turn out onto floured board or pastry cloth. Cover with bowl. Let rest 10 minutes. Knead 8 to 10 minutes, or until smooth and elastic. Shape into ball. Place in prepared bowl. Turn once to grease top. Cover and let rise in warm place, free from draft, 1 to 1½ hours, or until double in bulk. Grease two 9x5x3-inch loaf pans; set aside. Punch dough down; divide in half. Shape each half into a loaf. Place in prepared pans. Cover and let rise in warm place, free from draft, 1 hour, or until double in bulk. Preheat oven to 375°F. Bake 35 minutes, or until loaves sound hollow when lightly tapped. Transfer to wire racks to cool.

No-Knead Bran Bread

Makes 1 loaf
  3 cups all-purpose flour
  ½ cup instant nonfat dry milk (in dry form)
  1½ teaspoons salt
  2 packages (¼ ounce each) active dry yeast
  ¼ cup sugar
  1½ cups warm water (110° to 115°F.)
  2 cups Kellogg's® All Bran® Cereal or Kellogg's® Bran Buds® Cereal
  1 egg
  ⅓ cup margarine or butter, softened

Stir together flour, dry milk, and salt. Combine yeast, sugar, warm water, and cereal in large bowl of electric mixer. Let stand 2 minutes. Add egg, margarine, and 1 cup of the flour mixture. Beat at medium speed for 2 minutes. Gradually mix in remaining flour mixture by hand to form a stiff, sticky dough. Cover. Let rise in warm place until double in volume, about 1 hour. Stir down dough to original volume. Spoon into greased 9x5x3-inch loaf pan. Bake at 375°F. about 40 minutes, or until browned. Remove from pan. Brush with melted margarine.

Kulich

Makes 2 loaves
  ½ cup milk
  ¼ cup sugar
  1 teaspoon salt
  2 tablespoons butter
  1 package (¼ ounce) or cake yeast, active dry or compressed
  3 cups (about) all-purpose flour
  1 egg
  ¼ cup white raisins
  ¼ cup chopped blanched almonds
  1 teaspoon grated lemon peel
  ¾ cup confectioners sugar
    Few drops vanilla extract
  1 tablespoon (about) milk

Scald ½ cup milk. Stir in sugar, salt, and butter. Cool to lukewarm. Measure ¼ cup warm (105° to 115°F.) water in a bowl. Sprinkle or crumble in yeast. Stir until dissolved. Add lukewarm milk mixture. Stir in 1 cup of the flour and beat thoroughly. Beat in egg. Stir in raisins, almonds, and lemon peel. Stir in about 1½ cups of the remaining flour. Sprinkle remaining flour on breadboard. Turn dough out onto flour and knead until smooth and elastic. Place in well-oiled bowl; turn dough to oil on all sides. Cover and let rise in a warm place, free from draft, until double in bulk, about 2 hours. Punch dough down and divide in half. Shape into 2 balls. Press each ball into an oiled 1-pound coffee can. Cover and let rise until double in bulk, about 1¼ hours. Bake in a preheated 350°F. oven for 30 to 35 minutes. Turn out of cans at once and cool. Mix confectioners sugar, vanilla, and 1 tablespoon milk. Add more milk as necessary to bring icing to pouring consistency. Frost breads, letting some glaze drip down the sides.

To Caraway or Not

When you buy rye flour, be sure to read the label. Some rye flours are flavored with crushed caraway seed. This is fine if you propose to make bread flavored with caraway, provided you know in advance so that you can omit additional caraway seed when you make up the dough—too much caraway is anathema to even the most dedicated lover of the little seeds. But if you wish to make a bread without the caraway flavor, or if your family doesn't like the little seeds—lots of people don't— be sure to buy flour without the seed flavoring in it. Actually, you're better off with the plain flour in any case, adding caraway if you wish it in amounts that you like.

Overnight Oatmeal Bread

Makes 1 loaf

½ cup uncooked quick oats
1 cup boiling water
1 package (¼ ounce) active dry yeast
⅓ cup warm water (105° to 115°F.)
¼ cup molasses or honey
1 tablespoon butter or margarine
1¼ teaspoons salt
3 cups Martha White All-Purpose Flour, divided

Combine oats and boiling water in bowl; let stand until just warm. Dissolve yeast in warm water. Keep in warm place until oat mixture cools. Stir yeast mixture into oat mixture. Add molasses, butter, and salt; blend thoroughly. Stir in 2 cups flour; blend well. Knead in remaining cup flour; blend well. Add additional flour, if necessary, to make a fairly stiff dough. Let rest 3 to 5 minutes. Grease a 9x5x3-inch loaf pan; set aside. Turn dough out onto lightly floured board or pastry cloth. Knead 8 to 10 minutes, or until smooth. Shape into a loaf. Place in prepared pan. Lightly oil top of loaf. Cover and refrigerate at least 8 hours or up to 24 hours. Remove from refrigerator at least 10 minutes or up to 1 hour before baking. Preheat oven to 350°F. Bake 50 minutes, or until loaf sounds hollow when lightly tapped. Transfer to wire rack to cool.

Spiced Oatmeal Raisin Bread

Makes 1 loaf

1 package (¼ ounce) active dry yeast
2½ cups rolled oats
¾ cup Sun-Maid® Puffed Seeded Muscat Raisins
¼ cup vegetable oil
¼ cup firmly packed light or dark brown sugar
2 teaspoons salt
1 teaspoon ground cinnamon
½ teaspoon ground ginger
½ teaspoon ground nutmeg
¼ teaspoon ground cloves
⅓ cup sesame seed
1¾ to 2¼ cups all-purpose flour
Oil

Combine the yeast and 1½ cups lukewarm water and stir until dissolved. Add the oats, raisins, oil, sugar, salt, and spices and let stand for 15 minutes. Stir in the sesame seed and about 1¾ cups of the flour, or enough to form a firm dough. Work into a ball and knead for 1 minute on a lightly floured board. Place in a greased bowl and turn once to grease the surface. Cover and let

Overnight Oatmeal Bread; Riz Biscuits (page 111). Martha White Foods

rise in a warm place, free from draft, for about 2 hours. (This is a compact bread and will not double in rising.) Punch down the dough and shape into a ball. Grease a 1½-quart soufflé or round baking dish. Punch down the dough and shape into a ball. Place in the prepared dish, cover, and let rise. Preheat the oven to 375°F. Bake for 20 minutes; reduce the oven temperature to 325°F. and bake 30 minutes longer. Turn out onto a wire rack to cool. While still warm, brush the top of the bread with oil.

Raisin Pumpernickel Bread

Makes 1 loaf

2 cups all-purpose flour
2 cups whole wheat flour
½ cup wheat bran morsel cereal
1 package (¼ ounce) active dry yeast
2 teaspoons salt
1 tablespoon freeze-dried coffee granules
¼ cup dark molasses
1 square (1 ounce) unsweetened chocolate
2 tablespoons butter or margarine
1 teaspoon caraway seed
1¼ cups Sun-Maid® Puffed Seeded Muscat Raisins
1 egg yolk beaten with 1 teaspoon water

Combine the flours with the bran and stir to mix well; measure 1½ cups of the mixture into a large electric mixer bowl. Add the yeast and salt. Combine 1½ cups water with the coffee, molasses, chocolate, butter, and caraway seed in a saucepan and heat until very warm (120°F. to 130°F.). Beating at low speed, gradually add the warmed liquid to the flour mixture. Increase the speed to medium and beat for 2 minutes. Beat in ½ cup of the remaining flour mixture, or enough to make a thick batter. Increase the speed to high and beat for 5 minutes. Stir in the remaining 2½ cups flour mixture, or enough to make a stiff dough. Turn out onto a floured surface and knead until smooth and elastic, about 10 minutes. Place in a greased bowl and turn once to grease the surface. Cover and let rise in a warm place, free from draft, until double in bulk, about 1½ hours. Grease a large baking sheet. Punch the dough down and roll it out into a 15-inch square. Sprinkle with the raisins and roll up, jelly roll fashion. Place seam side down on the prepared sheet. Cover and let rise until almost double in bulk, about 45 minutes. Preheat the oven to 400°F. Brush the loaf with the egg yolk mixture and bake for 30 minutes, or until the bread sounds hollow when tapped. Cool on a wire rack.

Raisin Bread

Makes 2 loaves

    1 cup milk
    ¼ cup butter or margarine
    ¼ cup sugar
    1½ teaspoons salt
    2 packages (¼ ounce each) active dry yeast
    ¾ cup warm water (110° to 115°F.)
    2 eggs, beaten
    5½ to 6 cups all-purpose flour
    2 cups raisins
      Melted buter

Heat milk to scalding; add butter, sugar, and salt. Cool to lukewarm. In large mixer bowl, dissolve yeast in warm water. Add the lukewarm mixture. Stir in eggs. By hand, or using an electric mixer, gradually beat in 4 cups flour. Add raisins. By hand, work in remaining flour to make a medium-firm dough. Continue to knead until dough is smooth and satiny. Place in deep greased bowl, turning to grease top. Cover; let rise in warm place until double in size, about 1½ hours. Punch down dough. Turn out onto floured board and knead lightly. Form into 2 loaves and place in greased 9x5x3-inch loaf pans. Cover; let rise in warm place until double in size, about 1 hour. Bake at 375°F. for 30 to 35 minutes, or until nicely browned. Remove from pans; brush tops with butter and cover with cloth. Cool on wire rack.

Making a Crusty Crust

To many, the crust is the best part of the bread, particularly of a homemade loaf. How you treat the crust, during and after baking, determines the end result. **Very crisp crust**—Brush the tips of the loaves with plain water before baking. For a very crisp, thick crust, the kind found on good French or Italian bread, brush with plain water before baking and also several times during the baking period. **Soft, tender crust**—When the bread is done, immediately after removing it from the oven, brush the crust with soft butter or shortening; cover the loaves with a towel until they are cool. **Highly glazed crust**—Brush the crust before baking with **dorure,** made by beating the yolk of an egg with a tablespoon of water. This is the "baker's varnish" that gives a glistening, golden shine to many kinds of baked goods prepared by professionals. **Naturally crisp crust**—Don't brush with anything, either before or after baking; simply let the bread cool uncovered at room temperature when it is done.

Stovepipe Bread

Makes 2 small loaves

    3½ cups all-purpose flour, divided
    1 package (¼ ounce) active dry yeast
    ½ cup milk
    ½ cup salad oil
    ¼ cup sugar
    1 teaspoon salt
    2 eggs

Measure 1½ cups of the sifted flour into large bowl of Sunbeam Mixmaster Mixer. Add yeast and blend at low speed ½ minute. Combine milk, ½ cup water, oil, sugar, and salt in a small saucepan. Heat on low heat until mixture is just warm. Add to dry ingredients in the mixer bowl and beat at low speed until smooth. Add eggs and beat at medium-low speed until mixture is blended. Turn to lowest speed and gradually add 1 cup flour. Beat until smooth and well blended. Scrape beaters. Remove bowl and stir in remaining 1 cup flour with a spoon to make a soft dough. Spoon batter into 2 well-greased 1-pound coffee cans. Cover with the plastic lids and let stand in a warm place, free from draft. When dough has risen almost to top of cans, remove lids. Bake in preheated 375°F. oven 30 to 35 minutes, or until browned. Let cool about 10 minutes in cans before removing to cooling racks.

Honey-Oatmeal Bread

Makes 2 loaves

    1 cup boiling water
    1 cup rolled oats
    ⅓ cup soft shortening
    ½ cup Sue Bee Honey
    1 tablespoon salt
    2 packages (¼ ounce each) active dry yeast
    1 cup warm (not hot) water
    1 egg
    4 to 5 cups sifted all-purpose flour
      Butter

Stir the boiling water, oats, shortening, honey, and salt together in a large mixing bowl. Cool to lukewarm. Dissolve yeast in warm water. Measure out all-purpose flour. Add dissolved yeast and water, egg, and 2 cups of flour to the first mixture. Beat 2 minutes at medium speed with mixer or by hand until batter is smooth. By hand, gradually stir in remaining flour to make a stiff batter. Spread batter evenly in 2 greased 9x5x3-inch loaf pans. Smooth tops of loaves by patting into shape. Cover and let rise in warm place about 1½ hours. Heat oven to 375°F. and bake 50 to 55 minutes. Remove from pan and brush with melted butter.

Swedish Rye Bread

Makes 2 loaves
- 1 cup milk
- 1 cup water
- ¼ cup vegetable shortening
- 4 cups Martha White All-Purpose Flour, divided
- 2 packages (¼ ounce each) active dry yeast
- ¼ cup firmly packed brown sugar
- 2 teaspoons caraway seed
- 1½ cups rye flour
- 1 tablespoon butter or margarine, melted and slightly cooled

Grease large bowl; set aside. Heat milk, water, and shortening in saucepan until very warm (120° to 130°F.). Combine 3 cups all-purpose flour, yeast, brown sugar, and caraway seed in separate bowl. Add heated mixture; stir until moistened, then beat well. Add remaining cup all-purpose flour; beat 2 minutes. Stir in enough rye flour to make a soft dough. Turn out onto lightly floured board or pastry cloth. Cover with bowl. Let rest 10 minutes. Knead 8 to 10 minutes, or until smooth and elastic. If dough is sticky, knead in additional rye flour. Shape into ball. Place in prepared bowl. Turn once to grease top. Cover and let rise in warm place, free from draft, 1½ hours, or until double in bulk. Grease two 8-inch round cake pans. Punch dough down; divide in half. Shape each half into smooth ball. Place in prepared pans. Make 3 slashes ½ inch deep in top of each. Brush with butter. Cover and let rise in warm place, free from draft, 45 minutes, or until double in bulk. Preheat oven to 375°F. Bake 35 minutes, or until loaves sound hollow when lightly tapped. Transfer to wire racks to cool.

Sifting Flour

Many brands of white all-purpose flour are now presifted and need not be sifted again before using; however, they should be stirred before measuring. Let the recipe you are using be your guide as to whether or not to sift. If it calls for sifted flour, sift—in a flour sifter or through a fairly fine-mesh sieve—before measuring, then spoon the sifted flour lightly into the measuring cup. Cake flour should always be sifted. Whole wheat flour and wheat germ flour should not be sifted—it removes the bran and wheat embryo, the reasons you bought that kind of flour in the first place. These, too, should be stirred before measuring.

Sifting flour onto a piece of waxed paper or foil makes it easy to return unused flour to the container; just pick up the paper or foil and pour. Use the same trick when sifting flour with other dry ingredients; foil or paper makes it simple to add the dry ingredients to the dough or batter.

Braided Sesame Ring

Makes 1 loaf
- 7½ cups (about) all-purpose flour, divided
- 2 packages (¼ ounce each) active dry yeast
- ¼ cup sugar
- 1 teaspoon salt
- 1½ cups warm water (120° to 130°F.)
- ½ cup Hellmann's or Best Foods Real Mayonnaise
- 4 eggs, divided
- 2 tablespoons sesame seed

Grease 1 large baking sheet. In large mixer bowl, stir together 2 cups of the flour, yeast, sugar, and salt. With mixer at medium speed, gradually beat in warm water; beat 2 minutes. Reduce speed to low; beat in 2 more cups flour, mayonnaise, and 3 of the eggs. Beat at medium speed 2 minutes. Stir in enough additional flour (about 3 cups) to make an easily handled dough. On floured surface, knead 10 minutes or until smooth and elastic, adding ½ cup flour if necessary. Place in greased bowl; turn dough over so that top is greased. Cover with damp towel; let rise in warm place, free from draft, until doubled, about 1 hour. Punch dough down; divide into thirds. Let rest 10 minutes.

Roll each third into a 24-inch rope. Place side by side on prepared baking sheet and loosely braid. Shape into a circle, pinching ends together to seal well. Cover with towel. Let rise in warm place, free from draft, until doubled, about 1½ hours. Beat remaining egg lightly; brush onto surface of dough. Sprinkle with sesame seed. Bake in 375°F. oven about 40 minutes, or until bread sounds hollow when bottom is tapped. Immediately remove from baking sheet. Cool on wire rack.

Challah

Grease 2 large baking sheets. Follow recipe for Braided Sesame Ring through first paragraph. Omit sesame seed. Use 2 tablespoons poppy seed. Divide one-third of dough into balls; roll each into a 14-inch rope. Place side by side on baking sheet and loosely braid; pinch ends. Repeat with another one-third of dough; place on separate baking sheet. Cut remaining third of dough into sixths. Roll each piece into a 16-inch rope; make 2 braids. Place on top of large braids, tucking ends of top braid under bottom braid. Cover with towel; let rise in warm place, free from draft, until doubled, about 1 hour. In small bowl, beat remaining egg lightly. Brush top and sides of each loaf with egg. Sprinkle with poppy seed. Bake in 375°F. oven about 35 minutes, or until loaves sound hollow when bottoms are tapped. Remove from baking sheets. Cool on wire rack. *Makes 2 loaves.*

County Fair Bread

Makes 1 loaf

   6 **to 6½ cups sifted Martha White All-Purpose**
     Flour, divided
 ¼ **cup sugar**
  2 **teaspoons salt**
  1 **package (¼ ounce) active dry yeast**
1½ **cups milk**
 ¼ **cup butter or margarine**
  2 **eggs, at room temperature**
  1 **egg white**
  1 **tablespoon water**
    Sesame seed

Grease large bowl; set aside. Combine 1 cup flour, sugar, salt, and yeast in mixing bowl; set aside. Heat milk and butter in saucepan until very warm (120° to 130°F.); butter need not melt completely. Add heated mixture and eggs to flour mixture; blend well. Add 2 cups flour; beat with electric mixer 2 minutes. Stir in enough remaining flour to make a stiff dough. Turn out onto floured board or pastry cloth. Knead 8 to 10 minutes, or until smooth and elastic. Place in prepared bowl. Turn once to grease top. Cover and let rise in warm place, free from draft, 1½ hours, or until double in bulk. Grease large baking sheet; set aside. Punch dough down. Turn out onto floured surface. Pinch off about one-third of dough; set aside. Divide remaining dough into thirds. Roll out each third into an 18-inch rope. Braid ropes; pinch ends to seal. Place on prepared baking sheet. Divide remaining dough into thirds. Roll out each third into a 12-inch rope. Braid ropes; pinch ends to seal. Place on top of large braid. Cover and let rise in warm place, free from draft, 1 hour, or until double in bulk. Preheat oven to 375°F. Beat egg white and water with fork in small dish. Brush braids with egg wash. Sprinkle with sesame seed. Bake 40 to 45 minutes, or until golden brown and loaf sounds hollow when lightly tapped. If bread begins to brown too rapidly, cover with tent of aluminum foil or brown paper. **Note:** Two single braids can be made by dividing dough in half. Bake 35 to 40 minutes.

Walnut-Date Loaf (page 40); Wholesome Wheat Bread (page 12); Braided Sesame Ring (page 21).
Hellmann's/Best Foods Real Mayonnaise

Casserole Honey-Rye Bread

Makes 1 loaf

3½ to 4 cups all-purpose flour
1½ cups rye flour
2 packages (¼ ounce each) active dry yeast
2 teaspoons caraway seed
1 tablespoon salt
1 cup milk
1 cup water
½ cup Sue Bee Honey
3 tablespoons shortening
1 egg

In large mixer bowl, combine 1 cup all-purpose flour, all of rye flour, yeast, half of the caraway seed, and salt. Mix well. In a saucepan, heat milk, water, honey, and shortening until warm. Add to flour mixture. Add egg. Blend at low speed until moistened; beat 3 minutes at medium speed. By hand, gradually stir in enough remaining all-purpose flour to make a stiff dough. Cover and let rise 50 minutes, or until double in bulk. Stir dough and turn into a very well greased 1½-quart casserole. Brush lightly with oil and sprinkle with remaining caraway seed. Let rise about 30 minutes. Then bake in a 375°F. oven 40 to 45 minutes.

Kugelhopf

Makes 1 loaf

1 can (10¾ ounces) condensed chicken broth
1 package (¼ ounce) active dry yeast
¾ cup butter or margarine, softened
¾ cup sugar
4 eggs
4 cups all-purpose flour
½ teaspoon salt
1¼ cups golden raisins
¾ cup chopped almonds
¼ cup ground almonds

Heat chicken broth to lukewarm (110°F.). Sprinkle yeast over broth; stir until dissolved. In large bowl of electric mixer, beat butter and sugar until light and fluffy. Add eggs, one at a time, beating after each addition, scraping sides and bottom of bowl constantly. Add yeast mixture; blend. Add flour and salt; beat on low speed until smooth. Stir in raisins and chopped almonds. Butter large Kugelhopf mold (or 10-cup Turk's Head mold); sprinkle with ground almonds, tilting pan to coat bottom and sides. Pour batter into pan. Cover; let rise in warm place until ¼ inch from top of pan (about 2 hours). Bake at 375°F. for 1 hour 15 minutes, or until done. Remove from pan; cool.

Orange-Oatmeal Bread

Makes 3 loaves

1 package (¼ ounce) active dry yeast
¼ cup warm water
2 cups milk
2 cups uncooked oats, regular or quick-cooking
¼ cup butter or margarine
2 cups Florida orange juice
½ cup molasses
1 tablespoon salt
⅔ cup sugar
2 cups raisins
10 cups sifted all-purpose flour

In small cup, sprinkle yeast over warm water, stir until dissolved, and set aside. Scald milk, pour over oats and butter in large mixing bowl. Let stand ½ hour. Add orange juice, molasses, salt, sugar, raisins, and dissolved yeast mixture to oats. Stir in enough flour to make a soft dough. Place in greased clean bowl, cover, and let stand until double in bulk, about 1½ hours. Turn out onto floured surface and knead 10 minutes. Shape into 3 loaves and place in 3 greased 9x5x3-inch loaf pans. Cover and let rise until double, 1½ to 2 hours. Bake in 350°F. oven 1 hour, or until loaves sound hollow when tapped on top. Cool.

Orange Sally Lunn

Makes 1 loaf

1 package (¼ ounce) active dry yeast
¼ cup warm water
¾ cup milk
¼ cup sugar
¼ cup butter or margarine
1 teaspoon grated orange rind
1 teaspoon salt
1 cup Florida orange juice
2 eggs, beaten
6 cups all-purpose flour

Sprinkle yeast over warm water, stir until dissolved, and set aside. Scald milk in medium saucepan. Add sugar, butter, orange rind, and salt; stir until sugar is dissolved and butter melts. Cool. In large bowl, combine milk mixture, yeast, orange juice, eggs, and flour. Beat until smooth (dough will be very soft). Turn into greased Bundt pan or 10-inch tube pan. Let rise in warm place, covered, until double in bulk, about 1 hour. Bake in 400°F. oven 15 minutes, reduce oven to 350°F., and bake 15 to 20 minutes longer, or until bread is browned and sounds hollow when tapped. Cool 5 minutes, turn out on wire rack, and cool completely.

Spiced Bubble Bread

Makes 12 servings

   2 teaspoons ground cinnamon
   ½ teaspoon ground cloves
   ½ teaspoon ground ginger
   ½ teaspoon ground nutmeg
   1 package (¼ ounce) active dry yeast
   1 cup warm water (105° to 115°F.)
1½ cups sugar, divided
 14 tablespoons butter, divided, melted
   1 teaspoon salt
   ½ cup nonfat dry milk solids
   1 can (16 ounces) Libby's Solid Pack Pumpkin
   5 cups flour
   ½ cup finely chopped nuts

Combine spices, mixing well; set aside. In large mixer bowl, dissolve yeast in water. Stir in ½ cup sugar, 6 tablespoons butter, salt, dry milk, and pumpkin. Add 2 teaspoons of spice mixture and 2½ cups flour. Beat on low speed 3 minutes, scraping bowl often. Gradually beat in enough remaining flour, about 2½ cups, to form a stiff dough. On lightly floured surface, knead until smooth, adding flour as needed. Place in greased bowl. Cover; let rise in warm place until double in volume, about 1½ hours. Lightly grease a 10-inch tube pan; if pan has removable bottom, line the bottom and sides with foil. Combine remaining spice mixture and 1 cup sugar; mix well. Punch down dough; divide into thirds. Shape each third into a smooth 18-inch rope; cut each into eighteen equal pieces. Shape pieces into smooth balls. Dip each ball in remaining melted butter and roll in sugar mixture. Arrange eighteen balls in a single layer in bottom of pan so they just touch; sprinkle with one-third of the nuts. Top with two remaining layers of eighteen balls each, staggering balls; sprinkle each layer with remaining nuts. Cover pan lightly; let rise in warm place, about 45 minutes. Preheat oven to 325°F. Bake 70 minutes, or until golden brown. Cool on wire rack 20 minutes; invert onto serving plate. To serve, break apart with forks.

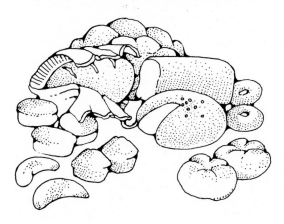

About Rye Grain

This is a cereal grass, one that is closely related to wheat—so closely that an amateur cannot distinguish between the two when they are growing in fields.

The grain is used to make rye flour—which in turn is used, combined with wheat flour, to make rye bread, all rye-pumpernickel, and certain kinds of flat breads, as well as whisky, gin, and malt liquors. Because it can withstand colder temperatures than wheat, rye is a staple in northern Europe and in Russia, and early settlers in New England found that they could grow rye more successfully than wheat.

Rye flour can be had in some supermarkets, as well as in specialty and health food shops. All-rye and rye-combination flours must be refrigerated. Rye cereals, both dry and to be cooked, are widely available, as is rye bread—light and dark, with caraway seeds or without—and pumpernickel.

Nutritionally, rye flour—which is not enriched, as is usually true of wheat flour—is a source of carbohydrate, with small amounts of protein, potassium, and the B vitamins.

Honey Whole Wheat Batter Bread

Makes 2 round loaves

   1 cup undiluted Carnation® Evaporated Milk
   ½ cup water
   2 packages (¼ ounce each) active dry yeast
   ⅓ cup honey
1½ teaspoon salt
1¼ cups whole wheat flour
1¾ to 2¼ cups all-purpose flour
     Melted butter
   1 tablespoon sesame or 1 teaspoon poppy seed

Combine evaporated milk and water; heat to lukewarm (105° to 115°F.). Place in large mixer bowl. Dissolve yeast in warm mixture. Add honey, salt, whole wheat flour, and 1 cup all-purpose flour. Beat with dough hooks until smooth and elastic, 2 to 3 minutes on medium speed. Gradually add additional all-purpose flour to make a soft, sticky dough, beating 6 to 8 minutes on slow speed. Turn into well-buttered bowl. Cover; let rise in warm place until doubled. Punch dough down. Divide dough in half and place in 2 well-buttered 1-quart round casserole dishes. Let rise in warm place until doubled. Carefully brush with melted butter; sprinkle with seeds. Bake in slow oven (325°F.) about 25 to 30 minutes, or until bread sounds hollow when tapped. Remove from dishes and cool on wire racks.

Babka (Polish Easter Bread). Wisconsin Potato Growers Auxiliary

Babka (Polish Easter Bread)

Makes 1 large loaf

- 1¼ **cups milk**
- ½ **cup butter or margarine**
- 2 **packages (¼ ounce each) active dry yeast**
- 7 **to 7½ cups all-purpose flour, divided**
- ½ **cup sugar**
- 1 **teaspoon salt**
- 1 **cup Riced Potatoes (recipe follows)**
- 4 **eggs**
- 1 **egg, separated**
- 1 **tablespoon grated lemon peel**
- ¾ **cup golden raisins**
- 2 **tablespoons all-purpose flour**
- 2 **tablespoons sugar**
- ¼ **teaspoon ground cinnamon**
- 2 **teaspoons butter or margarine, softened**

Heat milk and butter in small saucepan to 120° to 130°F. Combine yeast, 3 cups flour, ½ cup sugar, salt, potatoes, 4 eggs, egg yolk, lemon peel, and warm milk-butter mixture in large bowl. Beat with electric mixer on high until smooth. Beat in 3 cups flour. Stir in raisins. Knead in enough remaining flour to form a soft dough. Place dough in lightly greased bowl; turn to coat entire surface. Cover and let rise in warm place, free from draft, until almost double in bulk, about 1 hour. Grease and flour 9-inch springform pan. Fold a 3-inch strip of aluminum foil lengthwise in half; grease one side of strip. Circle top of springform pan with foil, greased side in, extending 2 inches above rim of pan. Fasten ends with paper clips. Punch down dough. Shape into a ball. Place in prepared pan. Cover with oiled waxed paper. Let rise in warm place, free from draft, until dough is ¾ inch from top of aluminum foil, about 40 minutes. Preheat oven to 350°F. Combine egg white and 1 tablespoon water in small bowl; mix with fork. Brush over top of bread. Combine 2 tablespoons flour, 2 tablespoons sugar, cinnamon, and butter in small bowl. Sprinkle over dough. Bake 50 to 60 minutes, or until golden brown. Cut into wedges and serve slightly warm.

Riced Potatoes

Makes 6 servings

- 6 **medium potatoes, washed and peeled**
- ½ **teaspoon salt**
- 2 **tablespoons butter or margarine, melted**

Cut potatoes in quarters. Bring 1 quart water and salt to a boil in large saucepan. Add potatoes. Cover and boil 20 to 30 minutes, or until tender. Drain thoroughly. (Reserve potato water for other uses, such as soup.) Let stand uncovered until dry. Process through food mill or ricer. Spoon into warm serving dish. Pour melted butter over top.

Cranberry Bread Wreath (page 28). Ocean Spray Cranberries

Mexican Pull-Apart Bread

Makes 2 loaves

   1 **cup undiluted Carnation® Evaporated Milk**
   ½ **cup water**
   1 **package (¼ ounce) active dry yeast**
   2 **tablespoons sugar**
  1½ **teaspoons salt**
   3 **to 3½ cups all-purpose flour**
  1½ **cups (6 ounces) shredded Monterey Jack cheese**
   ¼ **cup diced green chilies**
   1 **tablespoon chili powder**
     Melted butter

Combine evaporated milk and water; heat to luke-warm (105° to 115°F.). Place in large bowl. Dissolve yeast in warm mixture. Add sugar, salt, and 2½ cups flour. Stir vigorously about 1 minute. Stir in enough addtional flour to make a stiff dough. Knead on floured surface, working in additional flour, until smooth and elastic, about 8 minutes. Place in buttered bowl, turning to butter top. Cover; let rise in warm place until double in bulk. Punch dough down. Roll out to 14x12-inch rectangle on lightly floured surface. Combine cheese, chilies, and chili powder; sprinkle over dough. Roll up starting at long end. Cut into 1-inch sections; cut each section into quarters. Divide pieces of dough between 2 well-buttered 8½x4½x2½-inch loaf dishes, being careful that cut surfaces of dough do not touch sides or bottoms of dishes. Cover; let rise in warm place until double in bulk. Bake in moderate oven (350°F.) 20 to 25 minutes. Cool in dishes 10 minutes.

Flour Facts

Wheat flour, either white or whole wheat, is the flour most commonly used to make bread because it contains gluten, a substance that causes the dough to expand into an elastic framework that holds the gas formed by the yeast. Because whole wheat flour contains less gluten, it is usually used in combination with white. Other flours can be used to make bread, but only in combination with white flour. When using all-purpose and whole wheat flours to make bread, it is not necessary to sift the flour before measuring. Simply spoon flour lightly into a measuring cup, and level with a knife. Self-rising flour may be substituted in any yeast bread recipe by omitting the salt from the recipe ingredients. Because heat and humidity can effect the amount of flour needed for a given recipe, you might have to add up to 1 cup more flour on a hot, humid day.

Cranberry Bread Wreath

Makes 1 large wreath

   1 **package (¼ ounce) active dry yeast**
   ½ **cup warm water (105° to 110°F.)**
   3 **tablespoons sugar**
   ½ **cup milk**
   ¼ **cup soft butter or margarine**
   1 **teaspoon salt**
   ½ **teaspoon ground nutmeg**
   2 **large eggs**
   1 **teaspoon grated lemon rind**
   4 **cups (about) all-purpose flour**
     Cranberry Filling (recipe follows)
   1 **egg white**

In large bowl, dissolve yeast in water and sprinkle in sugar. Let stand a few minutes. Meanwhile, in a small saucepan, heat milk and butter just until lukewarm. Stir milk mixture, salt, nutmeg, eggs, and lemon rind into dissolved yeast. With mixer, beat in 1 cup of flour. With spoon, stir in enough of the remaining flour to form stiff dough. Turn out and knead 5 to 10 minutes, or until smooth and elastic, adding flour as needed. Place dough in greased bowl; cover; let rise 1½ hours, or until doubled. Meanwhile, prepare and chill Cranberry Filling. Cut dough in half. Roll half to 18x9-inch rectangle. Brush with some egg white. Sprinkle with half of Cranberry Filling to within 1 inch of edges. Roll up from long edge. Seal ends and seam securely. Repeat with other half of dough and filling. Grease a large baking sheet; dust with flour. Place rolls, seam side down, on sheet and cut ½ inch off ends of each to use for making leaves. Shape bread into a wreath, crossing the ends together over one another and tucking the ends under. Brush top with egg white. Reroll end pieces and cut into leaves, and shape some dough into holly berries. Let wreath rise in warm place uncovered until puffy-looking, about 30 minutes. Bake in a preheated 375°F. oven 50 minutes, or until nicely browned, covering leaves midway through baking with pieces of foil to prevent overbrowning. Cool wreath on wire rack. Tie with ribbon and decorate with ornaments, if you wish.

Cranberry Filling

   ¼ **cup soft butter**
   ¼ **cup all-purpose flour**
   ½ **cup sugar**
   ½ **cup chopped walnuts**
   ¾ **cup chopped Ocean Spray Fresh Cranberries**
   ½ **teaspoon grated lemon peel**

Combine all ingredients. Chill until butter is firm.

Classic Cinnamon-Raisin Bread

Makes two 9-inch loaves

5½ to 6 cups all-purpose flour, divided
2 packages (¼ ounce each) active dry yeast
¼ cup firmly packed dark brown sugar
2 teaspoons salt
1 teaspoon ground cinnamon
1¾ cups milk
¼ cup butter or margarine
2 eggs
2 cups Sun-Maid® Seedless Raisins

Combine 2 cups of the flour with the yeast, sugar, salt, and cinnamon in a large electric mixer bowl. Heat the milk and butter with ⅓ cup water until very warm (120° to 130°F.). Beating at low speed, gradually add the warmed milk, butter, and water to the flour mixture. Increase the speed to medium and beat for 2 minutes. Beat in the eggs and 1 cup of the remaining flour, or enough to make a thick batter. Increase the speed to high and beat for 5 minutes. Stir in the raisins and about 2½ cups of the remaining flour, or enough to make a firm dough. Turn out onto a floured surface and knead until the dough is smooth and elastic, about 10 minutes. Place in a greased bowl and turn once to grease the surface. Cover and let rise in a warm place, free from draft, until almost double in bulk, about 2 hours. Grease two 9x5x3-inch loaf pans. Punch down the dough and divide in half. Shape into loaves and place in the prepared pans. Cover and let rise until almost double in bulk, about 1 hour. Preheat the oven to 375°F. Bake the bread for 40 to 45 minutes, or until loaves sound hollow when tapped. Remove from pans and cool on wire racks.

Wheat Germ Batter Bread

Makes 1 loaf

2¾ cups Martha White All-Purpose Flour, divided
½ cup plus 1 teaspoon wheat germ, divided
2 packages (¼ ounce each) active dry yeast
1½ teaspoons salt
1 cup very warm water (120° to 130°F.)
¼ cup honey
2 tablespoons butter or margarine
1 egg, at room temperature

Combine 2 cups flour, ½ cup wheat germ, yeast, and salt in bowl. Add water, honey, butter, and egg; beat well. Add enough remaining flour to make a stiff batter. Cover and let rise in warm place, free from draft, 1 hour, or until double in bulk. Grease 9x5x3-inch loaf pan. Stir down batter. Spoon into prepared pan. Sprinkle with remaining teaspoon wheat germ. Cover with plastic wrap. Let rise in warm place, free from draft, 45 minutes, or until double in bulk. Preheat oven to 350°F. Bake 35 to 40 minutes, or until loaf sounds hollow when lightly tapped. Transfer to wire rack to cool.

Poppy Seed Batter Bread

Makes 1 loaf

1¼ cups warm water (105° to 115°F.)
1 package (¼ ounce) active dry yeast
2 tablespoons butter or margarine, softened
4 tablespoons (about) whole poppy seed
2 tablespoons sugar
2 teaspoons salt
3 to 3½ cups all-purpose flour
1 egg white
1 tablespoon cold water

Measure warm water into a large warm bowl. Sprinkle in yeast. Stir until dissolved. Add butter, 2 tablespoons poppy seed, sugar, and salt. Stir in 2 cups flour. Beat until well blended, about 1 minute. Stir in enough additional flour to make a soft dough. Cover; let rise in a warm place, free from draft, until double in bulk, about 35 minutes. Stir down. Spread dough evenly in a greased 9x5x3-inch loaf pan. Cover; let rise in a warm place, free from draft, until double in bulk, about 40 minutes. Preheat oven to 375°F. Combine egg white and cold water. Carefully brush on top of loaf. Sprinkle with additional poppy seed. Bake about 45 minutes, or until done. Remove from pan and cool on wire rack before slicing.

Satisfaction Guaranteed

There's an ego trip in baking bread, and something a little awe-inspiring about your first try. You assemble the ingredients carefully, controlling temperature so that the yeast is neither under- nor over-stimulated. You knead the dough, feeling the elastic life under your hands, feeling the change in texture, feeling the strength in it. You set it to rise, and you must wait until it is ready for you, not you ready for it. Then you punch it down, shape it, put it in its pan, and set it to rise again, enjoying the miracle of the yeast's aliveness once more. You bake it, turn it out, thump its backside to be sure it's done (it is if it sounds hollow), and butter its top for a tender crust. And then—well, if you have any pride about you, you call the family to taste this miracle you've wrought while it's still a fresh, new miracle. But probably you won't have to call. They'll be assembled and waiting, looking wistfully hopeful, drawn to the kitchen by the irresistible aroma. (You may even have drawn a few neighbors, possibly a stranger or two off the street.) Bring out the butter, open a jar of preserves. Be smug. You deserve it. You have mastered a living force.

Fresh From the Oven

*All the best quick breads, and tea loaves studded with nuts
and fruit, are easy to make and wonderful to eat at any
meal or in between.*

Spiced Zucchini Bread

Makes 1 loaf

    1 cup C & H Granulated Sugar
    ½ cup butter or margarine, softened
    2 eggs
    1¾ cups all-purpose flour
    ½ teaspoon *each* salt, baking soda, and ground
        nutmeg
    1 cup finely grated unpeeled zucchini
    ½ cup chopped walnuts
    1 teaspoon vanilla extract

Preheat oven to 350°F. Grease 9x5x3-inch loaf pan.
Cream sugar and butter. Beat in eggs. Combine flour,
salt, baking soda, and nutmeg. Stir half the dry ingredients into the creamed mixture. Stir in zucchini (batter
may look curdled). Stir in remaining dry ingredients,
then walnuts and vanilla. Bake 50 to 60 minutes. Turn
out onto rack to cool.

Bishop's Date Bread

Makes 1 loaf

    ¾ cup firmly packed C & H Golden Brown Sugar
    ¼ teaspoon salt
    6 eggs, separated
    1 cup chopped walnuts
    1 cup snipped dates
    ½ cup diced candied citron
    1 teaspoon grated lemon rind
    2 ounces unsweetened chocolate, grated
    1 cup all-purpose flour
        Pinch *each* salt and cream of tartar

Preheat oven to 300°F. Grease 9x5x3-inch loaf pan
and line bottom with greased paper. Gradually beat
sugar and salt into egg yolks; continue beating until
thick, smooth, and lemon colored. Stir in walnuts,
dates, citron, lemon rind, and chocolate. Blend in flour.

Beat egg whites with salt and cream of tartar until stiff,
then fold into flour mixture (yes it will—just keep folding). Pour into loaf pan. Bake 1½ hours. Remove from
pan, peel off paper, and cool on rack.

Sesame Quick Bread

Makes 1 loaf

    ¾ cup firmly packed C & H Golden Brown Sugar ·
    2 cups whole wheat flour
    ½ cup unprocessed bran
    1 tablespoon baking powder
    1 teaspoon ground cinnamon
    ½ teaspoon salt
    1½ cups buttermilk or whole milk
    ¼ cup vegetable oil
    1 egg, lightly beaten
    3 tablespoons sesame seed, toasted★
        Cream Cheese Spread (recipe follows)

Preheat oven to 350°F. Grease and flour 9x5x3-inch
loaf pan. In large bowl, combine all ingredients except
1 tablespoon sesame seed and the spread. Stir just until
blended. Turn into loaf pan. Sprinkle remaining sesame
seed over top. Bake 1 hour, or until cake tester inserted
in center comes out clean. Cool 10 minutes in pan.
Turn out onto rack to finish cooling. Serve with
Cream Cheese Spread.
★ To toast sesame seeds, spread in shallow pan and bake,
stirring frequently, 8 to 10 minutes in 350°F. oven until
brown.

Cream Cheese Spread

    2 tablespoons C & H Golden Brown Sugar
    1 package (3 ounces) cream cheese, softened
    1 tablespoon grated orange rind
    1 tablespoon orange juice

Mix all ingredients until well blended. Refrigerate
until ready to serve.

*Crunchy Mixed-Grain Banana Bread (page 32); Apricot-
Banana Tea Bread (page 32); Banana Muffin Surprise (page 72).*
Florida Department of Citrus

Basic Banana Bread

Makes 1 loaf

½ cup butter or margarine, softened
1 teaspoon vanilla extract
1 cup sugar
2 eggs
1⅓ cups mashed ripe bananas (3 or 4 medium)
1 tablespoon milk
2 cups all-purpose flour
1 teaspoon baking soda
¼ teaspoon salt
1 cup chopped nuts

In large bowl, cream butter, vanilla, and sugar until light and fluffy. Beat in eggs. Combine bananas and milk. Mix flour, soda, and salt. Blend dry ingredients into creamed mixture alternately with bananas. Stir in nuts. Turn into greased 9x5x3-inch loaf pan. Bake in 350°F. oven 1 hour and 10 minutes, or until cake tester inserted in center comes out clean. Cool 10 minutes, turn out of pan, and cool completely.

Crunchy Mixed-Grain Banana Bread

Makes 1 loaf

½ cup butter or margarine, softened
½ cup firmly packed light brown sugar
2 eggs
1 cup unsifted whole wheat flour
1 cup regular or quick oats, uncooked
1 teaspoon baking soda
½ teaspoon salt
1½ cups mashed ripe bananas (4 or 5 medium)
¼ cup milk
½ cup chopped peanuts

In a large bowl, cream butter and sugar. Beat in eggs 1 at a time, blending well after each addition. Mix flour, oats, baking soda, and salt; add to creamed mixture with bananas and milk. Blend only until ingredients are well mixed. Stir in chopped peanuts. Turn into a greased 9x5x3-inch loaf pan. Bake in 350°F. oven 1 hour, until cake tester inserted in center comes out clean. Cool 10 minutes, then turn out of pan. Serve warm or cooled.

Banana-Oat Wheat Muffins

Divide batter among 18 greased muffin cups. Bake in 350°F. oven 25 minutes, until cake tester inserted in center comes out clean. Remove from pan. Serve warm. *Makes 18 muffins*

Banana-Spice Bread

Makes 1 large loaf or 2 small loaves

1¾ cups sifted all-purpose flour
2 teaspoons baking powder
¼ teaspoon soda
½ teaspoon salt
1 teaspoon ground cinnamon
¼ teaspoon ground cloves
½ cup Sue Bee Honey
2 eggs, well beaten
⅓ cup salad oil
1 cup mashed bananas (2 to 3)
½ cup chopped nuts
Confectioners Sugar Glaze (see index) (optional)

Sift dry ingredients together. Combine honey, eggs, salad oil, and mashed bananas. Add to dry ingredients and beat until smooth. Add nuts. Pour into greased 9x5x3-inch loaf pan or 2 small greased 8½x4½x2½-inch loaf pans. Bake in 350°F. oven for 50 to 65 minutes in a large loaf or 45 to 50 minutes in small loaf pans, or until toothpick inserted in center comes out clean. Remove from pan and cool before slicing. If desired, glaze loaf with thin Confectioners Sugar Glaze, if you like, or serve plain.

Apricot-Banana Tea Bread

Makes 1 loaf

⅔ cup butter or margarine
1 cup sugar
2 eggs
1½ cups mashed ripe bananas (4 to 5 medium)
1 tablespoon lemon juice
1¾ cups all-purpose flour
1 teaspoon baking soda
1 teaspoon salt
½ cup chopped dried apricots mixed with 1 tablespoon all-purpose flour
Confectioners sugar (optional)

In a large bowl, cream butter and sugar. Beat in eggs one at a time, beating well after each addition. Blend in bananas and lemon juice. Mix together flour, baking soda, and salt. Blend into banana mixture; stir in apricots. Turn into greased and floured 9x5x3-inch loaf pan. Bake in 325°F. oven for 1 hour and 10 to 1 hour and 20 minutes, or until cake tester inserted in center comes out clean. Remove from pan and cool. Sift confectioners sugar over top, if desired, before serving.

Primer on Leavening Agents

Those things that make baked goods rise high are called leavening agents. Without them, the dough or batter would lie, gray and sulky, in the bottom of the pan. Today, leavening agents are available everywhere, but early-day cooks were not so lucky. The early Egyptians, who thoughtfully discovered beer before they discovered leavened bread, learned somewhere along the line that if they added beer to their bread dough, the dough would magically rise and produce a far superior product. Colonial housewives used hartshorn, which had to be dissolved in liquid before being used, or saleratus, a form of baking soda; both were iffy performers, both were scarce, and both required a trip to the chemist's, as the earlyday drugstore was called. Otherwise, air—free, and readily available— was the leavening agent in the colonies, as in the air incorporated into egg whites for angel food cakes and other such baked delights. However, air works only in light-bodied foods; it had no efficacy in sturdier foods, such as breads. Alaskan prospectors saved a bit of to-day's dough (which needed to turn sour in order to do its work) to leaven tomorrow's biscuits or flapjacks and, all unthinking, launched the present-day sour-dough fad.

Today's more fortunate cooks have a number of leavening agents at their disposal: **Double-action baking powder,** available virtually everywhere, is what is meant in modern recipes when "baking powder" is called for. Unless you do a great deal of baking, buy it in reasonably small amounts; it is very effective, but does lose its potency after a time. **Single-action baking powder** was the first baking powder on the market, introduced many years ago. Although it is still available—but not widely—it is not reliable as a substitute, measure for measure, for the double-acting kind in today's recipes. If you wish to try a recipe from an old cookbook, sift together 2 tablespoons cream of tartar, 1 tablespoon baking soda, and 1 tablespoon cornstarch; use 1 teaspoon of this mixture for each teaspoon of single-action baking powder called for in the recipe. **Compressed yeast (in cake form)** is available in limited supply; find it in the dairy case if your market carries it. Yeast cakes, .6- and 1-ounce sizes, are moist and easily crumbled, and may be used in recipes calling for active dry yeast as well as those specifying compressed yeast. Use the .6-ounce size to substitute for 1 envelope of dry yeast. Store compressed yeast in the refrigerator and use within 2 weeks of purchase. **Active dry yeast** is granular in form; it comes in ¼-ounce sealed envelopes. It's also available in jars, for those who do a lot of baking; use 2¾ teaspoons of this bulk yeast for each envelope the recipe calls for. Both envelopes and jars carry expiration dates—abide by them for good results. **Rapid-rise yeast,** relatively new on the market, is active dry yeast that rises in just about half the time as the regular active dry yeast, for which it can be substituted measure for measure. **Baking soda** is a leavening agent—indeed, it is one of the ingredients of baking powder—and has a large number of other household uses as well. When used alone as a leavener, the dough or batter in which it is used must have an acid ingredient. Some of the common ones are sour cream, sour milk, buttermilk, and molasses.

Time is the enemy of all leavening agents. Yeast is end-dated, but baking powder and soda are not. Date the can of baking powder and the box of soda when you buy them and use within 6 months.

Bread of Barbados

Makes 1 loaf
- ⅓ **cup chopped blanched almonds**
- 1 **cup all-purpose flour**
- ¾ **cup fine graham cracker crumbs**
- 2 **tablespoons ground baking chocolate**
- 2 **teaspoons baking powder**
- 1 **teaspoon baking soda**
- ½ **teaspoon salt**
- ⅓ **cup butter or margarine**
- ⅔ **cup sugar**
- 2 **eggs**
- 1 **cup mashed ripe bananas (2 or 3)**
  Butter or cream cheese, softened (optional)

Combine almonds with flour, graham cracker crumbs, chocolate, baking powder, soda, and salt; mix well. Cream butter with sugar until fluffy. Beat in the eggs, one at a time, then the mashed bananas; beat until smooth. Stir in the almond mixture. Spoon into well-greased 9x5x3-inch loaf pan. Bake at 350°F. for 1 hour, or until done. (Light touch with fingertip should not leave depression.) Turn out onto wire rack to cool, then chill before slicing. To serve, cut thin slices; spread, if you wish, with soft butter or cream cheese.

Granola-Carrot Bread

Makes 1 loaf

½ cup firmly packed C & H Golden Brown Sugar
1½ cups granola
1½ cups whole wheat flour
1½ cups grated carrots
½ cup vegetable oil
1 tablespoon baking powder
1 teaspoon vanilla extract
½ teaspoon salt
2 eggs
½ cup milk, buttermilk, or sour milk

Preheat oven to 350°F. Grease and flour 8½x4½x2½-inch loaf pan. Combine all ingredients in bowl; stir until just mixed. Turn into loaf pan. Bake 55 to 60 minutes, or until cake tester inserted in center comes out clean. Cool 10 minutes in pan. Turn out onto rack to finish cooling.

Sweet Potato-Walnut Bread

Makes 1 loaf

1 cup vegetable oil
¾ cup brown sugar
2 eggs
1 teaspoon vanilla extract
1½ cups all-purpose flour
1½ teaspoons baking soda
½ teaspoon salt
1 teaspoon ground cinnamon
1 teaspoon grated orange peel
1½ cups grated peeled sweet potatoes
1 cup chopped walnuts
Orange Glaze (recipe follows) (optional)

In large bowl, mix oil, brown sugar, eggs, and vanilla. Sift together flour, soda, salt, and cinnamon; stir in orange peel. Add to sugar mixture; mix well. Fold in grated sweet potatoes and walnuts. Pour into greased and floured 9x5x3-inch loaf pan. Bake in 350°F. oven 55 to 60 minutes, or until center springs back when gently pressed. Cool in pan 10 minutes; turn out on wire rack; cool completely. Top with Orange Glaze, if desired.

Orange Glaze

½ cup confectioners sugar
1 teaspoon orange peel
1 tablespoon grated orange juice

Combine sugar, orange peel, and orange juice; stir until smooth. Drizzle over top of loaf.

North Carolina Sweet Potato Tea Bread

Makes 1 loaf

2 large sweet potatoes
2 cups sifted all-purpose flour
1 cup firmly packed brown sugar
2 teaspoons baking powder
1 teaspoon salt
1 teaspoon baking soda
1 teaspoon ground ginger
1 teaspoon ground cinnamon
½ teaspoon ground nutmeg
2 eggs, beaten
¾ cup orange juice
2 tablespoons vegetable oil or melted shortening
1 cup chopped nuts

Prepare sweet potatoes by baking at 350°F. for 40 minutes, or boiling in water 20 minutes, until tender. Cool. Remove peel, mash well, and measure 1 cup. Sift flour, brown sugar, baking powder, salt, baking soda, ginger, cinnamon, and nutmeg into large mixing bowl. Combine eggs, orange juice, and oil in small bowl; beat until well mixed. Add to dry ingredients with cold mashed sweet potato and nuts. Mix until well blended. Turn into greased 9x5x3-inch loaf pan; bake at 300°F. for 1½ hours, or until tester inserted in center comes out clean. Cool in pan 10 minutes, turn out, and cool completely. Bread is best if kept overnight and then sliced. Frost, if desired.

New Orleans Praline Bread

Makes 2 loaves

1 cup chopped pecans
½ cup Praline® Liqueur
1 cup butter
2 cups sugar
1 tablespoon vanilla extract
5 large eggs
¼ cup milk
2¼ cups all-purpose flour
1 teaspoon ground cinnamon
½ teaspoon baking powder
¼ cup Praline Liqueur

Heat oven to 300°F. Marinate pecans in ½ cup Praline Liqueur. Beat butter, sugar, and vanilla in large bowl until smooth and creamy. Add remaining ingredients except ¼ cup Praline Liqueur, beating until well blended, 1 to 2 minutes. Pour into 2 greased 8½x4½x2½-inch loaf pans. Bake 1¼ hours, or until wooden toothpick inserted in center comes out clean. Cool. Wrap in cheesecloth, pour remaining Praline Liqueur over breads, and wrap in foil. Let stand 1 to 2 weeks.

Sour Cream-Date Muffins (page 72); Brown Sugar-Nut Bread (page 49); Sesame Quick Bread with Cream Cheese Spread (page 31). C & H Sugar Co.

Mini Hearth Loaves

Makes three 6-inch loaves or one 9-inch loaf
- ⅓ cup butter or margarine, softened
- ⅔ cup sugar
- 2 teaspoons grated lemon peel
- ¼ teaspoon ground cinnamon
- 2 eggs
- 3 tablespoons milk
- 1 teaspoon lemon juice
- 2 cups all-purpose flour
- 1 teaspoon baking powder
- 1 teaspoon salt
- ½ teaspoon baking soda
- 1½ cups peeled shredded apple
- 1 cup chopped Sun-Maid® Seedless Raisins
- ½ cup chopped walnuts
- Lemon Glaze (recipe follows)

Grease three 6x3x2-inch loaf pans. Cream the butter with the sugar, lemon peel, and cinnamon until fluffy. Beat in the eggs until light and fluffy. Beat in the milk and lemon juice. Preheat the oven to 350°F. Combine the flour with the baking powder, salt, and baking soda and add to the batter, stirring just until the flour is moistened. Fold in the apple, raisins, and nuts and spoon the batter into the prepared pans. Bake for 40 to 50 minutes, or until a toothpick inserted in the center comes out clean. Let stand on a wire rack for 5 minutes before removing from the pans to cool completely on the rack. Drizzle Lemon Glaze over the loaves and garnish as desired.

Lemon Glaze
- ¾ cup sifted confectioners sugar
- 1 tablespoon lemon juice

Combine sugar and lemon juice and mix well.

Apricot Bread

Makes 1 loaf
- 3 cups all-purpose flour
- 5 teaspoons baking powder
- ½ teaspoon salt
- 1 cup finely chopped pecans
- 1 egg, well beaten
- 1 cup milk
- ¾ cup grated orange rind
- 1 tablespoon Simon Fisher Apricot Butter (or Simon Fisher Prune Butter)

Mix and sift flour, baking powder, and salt; stir in nutmeats. Combine egg, milk, grated orange rind, and apricot butter, then stir in dry ingredients. Pour into greased 9x5x3-inch loaf pan. Bake at 350°F. for 1¼ hours. Let bread cool before slicing.

Quick Fig Bread

Makes 1 loaf
- 1 cup California dried figs
- 2 cups sifted all-purpose flour
- 2 teaspoons baking powder
- 1½ teaspoons salt
- ¾ cup sugar
- 2 cups whole wheat flour
- 4 tablespoons butter or margarine
- 1½ cups sour milk
- 1 teaspoon soda
- 2 eggs
- ¾ cup coarsely chopped walnuts

Cover figs with boiling water, let stand 10 minutes, drain, and dry on towel. Clip stems and cut figs into thin strips. Sift all-purpose flour with baking powder, salt, and sugar. Add whole wheat flour and stir to blend. Work butter into flour mixture. Add sour milk, in which soda has been dissolved and mix. Add beaten eggs, nuts, and figs, and beat. Pour into a paper-lined loaf pan (about 9x5x3 inches). Bake in moderate oven (350°F.) about 1 hour and 25 minutes. Serve hot with butter, or cool and slice very thin for tea sandwiches. Makes excellent toast when 1 or 2 days old.

Cranberry-Raisin Loaf

Makes 2 loaves
- 4½ cups sifted all-purpose flour
- 2 cups sugar
- 4½ teaspoons baking powder
- 2 teaspoons salt
- 1 teaspoon ground cinnamon
- ½ teaspoon ground nutmeg
- 2 cups Wheat Chex® Cereal, crushed
- ⅔ cup raisins
- 2 eggs, lightly beaten
- 4 tablespoons salad oil
- ⅔ cup orange juice
- 2 cups cranberry sauce, drained and cubed

Grease two 8½x4½x2½-inch loaf pans. Sift together flour, sugar, baking powder, salt, and spices. Stir in cereal and raisins. In large mixing bowl, combine eggs, oil, orange juice, and cranberry sauce. Add dry ingredients, stirring just until moistened. Pour into pans. Bake in preheated 350°F. oven for 60 to 65 minutes, or until knife inserted in center comes out clean. Cool 15 minutes before removing from pan.

Almond Bread

Makes 2 loaves

    3 eggs, well beaten
    ⅔ cup sugar
       Juice and rind of medium-size lemon
    ¾ tablespoon vanilla extract or grated vanilla
       beans
    3 cups all-purpose flour
    3 teaspoons baking powder
    ½ cup blanched almonds
       Scant ½ cup Filippo Berio Olive Oil

Beat eggs, add sugar, beat together. Add lemon, vanilla, and 1 cup of flour, which has been sifted with baking powder. Add almonds cut in half lengthwise. Add Filippo Berio Olive Oil and the rest of the flour; knead into 2 long loaves about 2 inches wide, place in oiled floured pan, and bake in a moderately slow oven (325°F.) 20 to 30 minutes. Remove from pan, and while warm cut into ½-inch slices. Lay out on pan and place in oven at 250°F. to be slightly browned.

Golden Thread Loaf

Makes 2 loaves

    2 cups all-purpose flour
    1 cup sugar
    1½ teaspoons baking powder
    1¼ teaspoons salt
    ½ teaspoon soda
    ¼ teaspoon ground mace
    ¼ cup shortening
    1 egg
    ¼ cup frozen orange juice
    ½ cup water
    1½ cups shredded raw sweet potatoes
    ¼ cup (or more) raisins
    1 tablespoon lemon juice
       Ground cinnamon
       Sugar

Mix dry ingredients; cut in shortening. Beat egg; add orange juice and water, mixed together. Blend into dry ingredients just until moistened. Fold in shredded sweet potatoes and raisins that have been sprinkled with lemon juice. Fill greased and floured loaf pans one-half to two-thirds full and sprinkle cinnamon and sugar on top. Bake at 350°F. for 30 to 40 minutes. Use two 9x5x3-inch loaf pans or 4 smaller size. Freezes well.

Note: Can also be baked in square or oblong pans and cut in squares to serve.

Baking and Storing Know-how
Preheat
The proper preheated temperature provides the "oven spring," which is the final expansion of the dough. If using glass pans, reduce oven temperature by 25°F.

Pan Placement
Place pans 2 inches apart on the middle shelf of the oven. Four pans should be staggered on 2 shelves. Avoid placing pans directly above and below each other.

Testing Doneness
When baking time is completed, remove the pan from the oven. Turn the loaf out of the pan. Tap the bottom and sides of the loaf. If the loaf sounds hollow, it is fully baked.

Cooling
Immediately turn bread out onto a wire rack to keep it from becoming soggy as it cools.

Storing
Bread should be cooled completely before wrapping, storing, or freezing. Homemade breads stay fresh and moist when tightly wrapped in aluminum foil, plastic wrap, or an airtight plastic bag, and stored in a cool, dry place.

Soy-Corn Bread

Makes about 16 pieces

    1½ cups Elam's Stone Ground 100% Whole Yellow
        Corn Meal
    ½ cup sifted Elam's Soy Flour
    2½ teaspoons baking powder
    ¾ teaspoon salt
    3 tablespoons sugar
    3 eggs, separated
    1 cup milk
    2 tablespoons soybean or cooking oil or melted
       butter

Combine first 4 ingredients and sift into mixing bowl. Stir in sugar. Combine egg yolks, milk, and oil or butter; beat slightly. Add liquids to dry ingredients; stir just until dry ingredients are moistened. Beat egg whites until they form soft peaks. Fold egg whites into batter; pour into well-greased 8x8x2-inch pan. Bake in moderate oven (375°F.) until done, about 20 minutes. Cool 5 minutes before cutting into 2-inch squares.

Orange Oatmeal Bread (page 25); Orange Sally Lunn (page 24); Orange Crackling Bread. Florida Department of Citrus

Sugarplum Bread (page 54). The Reynolds Wrap Kitchen

Orange Crackling Bread

Makes 8 servings

½ **pound salt pork, cut in cubes**
2 **tablespoons finely chopped onion**
1½ **cups yellow cornmeal**
½ **cup all-purpose flour**
3 **teaspoons baking powder**
1½ **teaspoons salt**
1 **teaspoon sugar**
2 **eggs**
½ **cup buttermilk**
1 **cup Florida orange juice**
   Butter

In 9-inch ovenproof skillet, cook salt pork over low heat until very crisp; remove and chop finely. Drain off all but 1 tablespoon fat, add onion, and cook until tender. In large bowl, mix together cornmeal, flour, baking powder, salt, and sugar. In small bowl, beat eggs with buttermilk and orange juice. Add egg mixture all at once to dry ingredients and stir just until mixed; stir in salt pork and onion. Heat the skillet, turn in batter, and bake in 350°F. oven 30 to 35 minutes. Serve hot with butter.

Banana-Orange Bread (page 57); Walnut-Apple Ring (page 80). Hollywood Safflower Oil

Banana-Peanut Bread

Makes 1 loaf

- ⅔ **cup shortening**
- 1 **cup sugar**
- 2 **eggs**
- 1½ **cups mashed ripe bananas (5 medium)**
- 1 **tablespoon lemon juice**
- 2 **cups sifted all-purpose flour**
- 1 **teaspoon baking soda**
- ½ **teaspoon salt**
- ¼ **teaspoon ground nutmeg**
- ½ **cup chopped cocktail peanuts**

In a large bowl, cream shortening with sugar. Beat in eggs, one at a time. Blend in bananas and lemon juice. Sift together flour, baking soda, salt, and nutmeg. Blend into banana mixture; stir in peanuts. Turn into greased and floured 9x5x3-inch loaf pan. Bake in 325°F. oven for 1 hour to 1 hour 10 minutes, or until cake tester inserted in center comes out clean. Remove from pan. Cool completely on wire rack. Wrap; store at room temperature overnight to mellow flavor.

To Grease or Not

Do as the recipe directs. Breads of all kinds are temperamental. Some require well-greased pans, some lightly greased, some grease only on the pan's bottom, some no greasing at all. Use butter, margarine, or hydrogenated shortening, but never oil.

Walnut-Date Loaf

Makes 1 loaf

- 2½ **cups all-purpose flour**
- ¾ **cup sugar**
- 1 **tablespoon baking powder**
- ¼ **teaspoon salt**
- 1 **package (8 ounces) pitted dates, chopped (about 1¼ cups)**
- 1 **cup coarsely chopped walnuts**
- 2 **eggs**
- ¾ **cup water**
- ½ **cup Hellmann's or Best Foods Real Mayonnaise**
- 1½ **teaspoons vanilla extract**

Grease and flour 9x5x3-inch loaf pan. In large bowl, stir together flour, sugar, baking powder, and salt. Stir in dates and walnuts; set aside. In small bowl, beat eggs lightly with fork; beat in water, mayonnaise, and vanilla until smooth. Add to flour mixture; stir just until moistened. Spoon into prepared pan. Bake in 350°F. oven 50 to 60 minutes, or until cake tester inserted in center comes out clean. Cool in pan 10 minutes. Remove and cool completely on wire rack.

Peanut Butter Bread

Makes 1 loaf

- 1 **cup all-purpose flour**
- ½ **cup whole wheat flour**
- 2 **teaspoons baking powder**
- ¼ **teaspoon salt**
- ½ **teaspoon ground cinnamon**
- ¼ **teaspoon ground nutmeg**
- ¼ **teaspoon ground allspice**
- ½ **cup peanut butter**
- 3 **tablespoons butter**
- ¾ **cup brown sugar**
- 2 **eggs**
- ⅔ **cup milk**
- ½ **teaspoon vanilla extract**
- 1 **cup chopped peanuts**

Combine flours, baking powder, salt, cinnamon, nutmeg, and allspice. Cream peanut butter, butter, and brown sugar. Add eggs, one at a time, beating after each addition. Combine milk and vanilla; add alternately with dry ingredients to creamed mixture, ending with dry ingredients. Stir in chopped peanuts. Pour into a greased 8½x4½x2½-inch loaf pan. Bake in a preheated 325°F. oven for 1 hour, or until done. Cool 10 minutes and remove from pan. Cool before slicing.

Spicy Honey Bread

Makes 2 loaves

- ⅔ **cup honey**
- 1 **cup sugar**
- 4 **cups finely milled rye flour**
- 1 **teaspoon baking soda**
- 4 **teaspoons baking powder**
- 1½ **tablespoons ground cinnamon**
- 1 **teaspoon ground cloves**
- 1 **teaspoon ground allspice**
- ¼ **teaspoon ground cardamom**
- ¾ **cup shredded blanched almonds**
- 2 **tablespoons grated orange peel**
- ¾ **cup finely**
- ¾ **cup chopped citron**

In the top of a double boiler, heat honey, 1½ cups water, and sugar until small bubbles appear. Mix flour, baking soda, baking powder, and spices. Beat in the honey mixture. Beat 10 minutes with electric mixer at medium speed. Beat in nuts, peel, and citron. Pour mixture into 2 oiled 8x4x2-inch loaf pans. Place a pan of water on lowest shelf of oven. Bake bread on top shelf in preheated 350°F. oven for about 1 hour.

Helpful to know: Like good wine, this ages gracefully. Will keep 2 weeks, and should be aged at least 3 days in plastic or tin before serving.

Raisin-Nut Bread

Makes 1 loaf

  3 cups all-purpose flour
3½ teaspoons baking powder
  1 teaspoon salt
1½ teaspoons ground cinnamon
  1 cup firmly packed Domino Light Brown Sugar
  1 egg, beaten
1⅓ cups milk
  ¼ cup shortening, melted
  1 cup raisins, plumped★
  ¾ cup chopped walnuts or pecans

Sift together flour, baking powder, salt, and cinnamon. Mix in sugar. Combine egg and milk. Add milk mixture and shortening to flour; mix just until blended. Fold in raisins and nuts. Bake in 9x5x3-inch loaf pan lined on bottom with greased waxed paper. Bake in moderate oven (350°F.) 1 hour to 1 hour and 10 minutes. Cool 5 minutes; remove from pan and cool on rack. Wrap in foil and store overnight before slicing.
★To plump raisins, pour boiling water over raisins; let stand 5 minutes. Drain well.

Coconut Bread

Makes 3 loaves

  1 tablespoon butter, softened
  5 cups plus 1 tablespoon all-purpose flour
  2 cups sugar
  1 tablespoon baking powder
  ½ teaspoon ground cinnamon
  ¼ teaspoon ground cloves
  1 teaspoon salt
   Meat from 1 coconut, finely grated
  2 cups milk
  4 tablespoons butter, melted

Brush 1 tablespoon butter evenly on bottom and sides of three 3½x7-inch loaf pans. Sprinkle 1 tablespoon flour in each pan. Tip pan side to side to spread evenly. Tap pan (upside down) to remove excess. Into deep bowl, sift flour, sugar, baking powder, cinnamon, cloves, and salt. Add coconut. Mix well. Add milk, ½ cup at a time, blending thoroughly. Stir in 4 tablespoons melted butter. Ladle batter into pans, none more than two-thirds full. Bake 1 hour in 350°F. oven, or until bread pulls away from pan and top is crusty, golden brown. Cool 5 minutes. Turn bread out onto wire cake racks. Serve warm or cool.

Boston Brown Bread. Caloric Corporation

Q. *Is there a better way to make stale bread and rolls seem fresh than warming them in the oven?*
A. The oven is the right way, but perhaps you're going about it the wrong way. Breads warmed in the oven on a baking sheet or in foil will get warm, but you need dampness to refresh the bread. For biscuits and rolls, dampen a brown paper bag well and put them inside it. For bread, sprinkle the loaf (or part of a loaf) lightly with water, then put it into a brown paper bag. Either way, twist the end of the bag closed and place in a 300°F. oven, 5 to 7 minutes for biscuits or rolls, 15 minutes for bread.

Boston Brown Bread

Makes 10 servings
  1 cup yellow cornmeal
  1 cup whole wheat flour
  ½ cup rye flour
  2 teaspoons baking soda
  1½ teaspoons salt
  2 cups buttermilk
  ⅔ cup molasses
  1 cup raisins

Combine cornmeal, flours, baking soda, and salt. Stir in buttermilk, molasses, and raisins until well mixed. Pour into well greased 2-quart casserole. Cover casserole. Place casserole in large casserole and add boiling water to come about halfway up side of covered casserole. Bake at 300°F. 2 hours, or until toothpick inserted in center comes out clean. Invert onto serving plate and cut into wedges.

Steamed Boston Brown Bread

Makes 2 loaves
  1¼ cups Sun-Maid® Puffed Seeded Muscat Raisins, chopped
  1 cup whole wheat flour
  1 cup yellow cornmeal
  1 cup rye flour
  1¼ teaspoons baking soda
  1 teaspoon salt
  2 cups buttermilk
  ¾ cup molasses

Combine raisins, whole wheat flour, cornmeal, rye flour, baking soda, and salt in large bowl. Toss until raisins are well coated. Add buttermilk and molasses and stir until batter is smooth. Grease two 1-pound coffee cans (or one 2-pound coffee can). Divide batter into cans. Cover cans with a square of greased foil. Mold the foil tightly to the cans and tie snugly with a piece of string. Place cans on a rack in a large kettle of simmering water deep enough to come halfway up the sides of the cans. Cover and simmer 2 hours and 15 minutes, or until toothpick inserted in bread comes out nearly clean. Invert cans to cool slightly, then finish cooling on a rack.

Irish Soda Bread

Makes 1 loaf
  3½ cups all-purpose flour
  ¼ cup sugar
  1 teaspoon baking powder
  1 teaspoon baking soda
  1 teaspoon salt
  2 tablespoons caraway seed
  ¼ cup butter or margarine
  1 cup Sun-Maid® Seedless Raisins
  1 egg, beaten
  1⅓ cups buttermilk
    Melted butter or margarine

Grease an 8-inch layer cake pan. Combine the flour with the sugar, baking powder, baking soda, salt, and caraway seed. Cut in the butter until the mixture resembles fine crumbs. Stir in the raisins. Preheat the oven to 375°F. Combine the egg and buttermilk and stir into the dry ingredients. Turn out onto a board with 2 tablespoons flour and knead lightly. Form the dough into a ball and place in the prepared pan. Brush with melted butter and bake for 30 minutes. Reduce oven temperature to 350°F. and bake 20 minutes longer, or until a toothpick inserted in the center comes out clean. Remove from pan and cool on a wire rack.

Chocolate-Coconut Doughnuts (page 109); Butterscotch-Banana Bread (page 56). Nestlé Foods Corporation

Raisin-Apple Bran Bread

Makes one 9-inch loaf
   2 eggs, beaten
   ⅓ cup butter or margarine, melted
   ⅔ cup milk
   1 cup wheat bran morsel cereal
   1⅓ cups all-purpose flour
   ⅔ cup firmly packed light brown sugar
   1½ teaspoons baking powder
   ¾ teaspoon salt
   ½ teaspoon baking soda
   1 teaspoon ground cinnamon
   1 cup chopped cooking apple
   1 cup Sun-Maid® Seedless Raisins

Grease a 9x5x3-inch loaf pan. Combine the eggs, butter, milk, and bran in a bowl; let stand for 5 minutes. Preheat the oven to 350°F. Mix the flour with the brown sugar, baking powder, salt, baking soda, and cinnamon in a separate bowl before adding to the bran mixture; stir just until flour is moistened. Fold in the apple and raisins and turn the batter into the prepared pan. Bake for 50 minutes, or until a toothpick inserted in the center comes out clean. Let stand for 10 minutes on a wire rack before removing from the pan to cool completely on the rack.

Flour in Your Pantry

Unless you do a good deal of baking, the larger sizes of flour, even though they may cost less per pound, are not necessarily a good buy. This is particularly true in warm weather. You're better off buying the smaller sizes, and bringing home a fresh batch more often. Even if you use enough all-purpose flour to warrant buying the large size, the other household-use flours, such as whole wheat and rye, should be purchased only in quantities that will be used up within a month or so.

How to Store

Remove the flour from the bag (or box) in which you buy it to a container—metal, glass, plastic—with an airtight cover as soon as you bring it home. This helps to keep the flour fresh, and it also discourages weevils, those pantry pests to whom flour is especially appealing. White all-purpose and cake flour can be stored at room temperature, in a cool, dry place. Those that incorporate the embryo—whole wheat and wheat germ flours—should be refrigerated, also in a container with an airtight cover, as the germ deteriorates rapidly at room temperature and the oil it contains becomes rancid. Flours from grains other than wheat should also be refrigerated, and if your kitchen shelves do not offer a sufficiently cool storage place, refrigerate flours of all kinds. Tightly covered containers prevent flour from losing its own moisture content and from absorbing moisture from outside sources.

Crunchy Prune Loaf

Makes 1 loaf
   1½ cups coarsely chopped pitted prunes
   ⅓ cup apple or orange juice
   2 eggs
   ½ cup honey
   ½ cup vegetable oil
   2¼ cups all-purpose flour
   ⅓ cup wheat germ
   1 teaspoon salt
   2 teaspoons baking powder
   2 teaspoons baking soda
   3 tablespoons yogurt or sour cream
   ⅔ cup coarsely chopped nuts
   ⅓ cup sunflower seed

In small bowl, combine prunes and juice; set aside. In large bowl, combine eggs, honey, and oil; mix thoroughly. Beat in flour, wheat germ, salt, baking powder, and baking soda. Mix in yogurt and prune mixture. Stir in nuts and sunflower seed. Spread evenly in buttered 9x5x3-inch loaf pan. Bake in 325°F. oven about 1 hour and 30 minutes, until toothpick inserted in center comes out clean. Cool on wire rack. Wrap in aluminum foil while still slightly warm.

Zucchini-Cranberry Bread

Makes 18 servings
   3¼ cups all-purpose flour, divided
   ¼ cup sugar
   ⅔ teaspoon (2 packets) Sweet 'N Low granulated
      sugar substitute
   1 tablespoon baking powder
   ½ teaspoon ground cinnamon
   ½ teaspoon salt
   ¾ cup skim milk
   ¼ cup vegetable oil
   1 egg, lightly beaten
   1 teaspoon vanilla extract
   2 cups loosely packed shredded zucchini
   ¾ cup fresh or frozen chopped cranberries
   ⅓ cup raisins

Preheat oven to 350°F. Spray 9x5x3-inch loaf pan with nonstick cooking spray. In large bowl, combine 3 cups flour, sugar, Sweet 'N Low, baking powder, cinnamon, and salt; set aside. In small bowl, beat together skim milk, oil, egg, and vanilla; set aside. In medium bowl, toss together zucchini, cranberries, raisins, and remaining ¼ cup flour. Add to dry ingredients with liquid ingredients until just moistened; do not overstir. Spoon into prepared pan. Bake for about 1¼ hours, or until wooden toothpick inserted in center comes out clean. Cool in pan 10 minutes. Remove from pan and completely cool on rack.

Holiday Mincemeat Quick Bread

Makes 1 loaf
  2 cups all-purpose flour
  ⅔ cup sugar
  1 tablespoon baking powder
  1 teaspon salt
  1 cup Holiday Mincemeat (recipe follows)
  ¼ cup chopped nuts
  1 egg, beaten
  1 cup milk
  3 tablespoons vegetable oil
  1 teaspoon vanilla extract

Sift together flour, sugar, baking powder, and salt into large mixing bowl. Add mincemeat and nuts in flour mixture, tossing until well coated. Blend together egg, milk, oil, and vanilla. Add liquid mixture all at once to flour mixture, stirring only until flour is moistened. Turn into greased 8x4x2-inch loaf pan. Bake in preheated 350°F. oven 65 minutes, or until wooden toothpick or cake tester inserted in center comes out clean. Cool in pan on wire rack 10 minutes before removing from pan. Cool completely before slicing. (For best results, wrap and store overnight before slicing.)

Holiday Mincemeat

Makes about 6 cups
  ½ pound ground pork
  6 cups (about 2 pounds) cooking apples, chopped, peeled, and cored
  1 package (12 ounces) pitted prunes, finely chopped (about 2 cups)
  1 cup firmly packed brown sugar
  1 cup raisins
  ¼ cup Kikkoman Soy Sauce
  ¼ cup cider vinegar
  1 tablespoon ground cloves
  1 tablespoon grated orange rind
  ¼ cup orange juice
  2 tablespoons brandy

Brown pork in Dutch oven or large saucepan until meat is thoroughly cooked and crumbly. Stir in apples, prunes, brown sugar, raisins, soy sauce, vinegar, cloves, orange rind, and juice. Bring mixture to boil, reduce heat, and simmer uncovered 35 minutes. Remove from heat and cool slightly. Stir in brandy. Pack into sterilized jars and refrigerate a few days for flavors to blend. Use to make mincemeat pies, cookies, or quick breads.

Zucchini Bread

Makes 1 loaf
  2 cups all-purpose flour
  ¾ teaspoon baking powder
  ¾ teaspoon baking soda
  ¾ teaspoon salt
  ¾ teaspoon ground cinnamon
  3 eggs
  1 cup Domino Granulated Sugar
  ⅔ cup salad oil
  1⅓ cups grated unpeeled zucchini
  ¾ teaspoon lemon extract
  ⅔ cup chopped pecans
  ⅔ cup raisins

Sift together flour, baking powder, baking soda, salt, and cinnamon. Set aside. Beat eggs with sugar for 2 minutes. Gradually add oil and beat 2 minutes. Add extract. Alternately fold in flour mixture and zucchini until evenly moistened. Stir in pecans and raisins. Do not overmix. Pour batter into well-greased 9x5x3-inch loaf pan. Bake at 350°F. 1 hour and 10 minutes to 1 hour and 15 minutes, until bread tests done. Cool 10 minutes; remove from pan and cool completely on wire rack. Wrap in plastic wrap or foil.

Golden Corn Bread

Makes one 8-inch square bread
  1 cup sifted all-purpose flour
  1 cup yellow cornmeal
  ½ teaspoon salt
  ⅓ cup sugar
  1 teaspoons baking powder
  2 eggs
  ⅓ cup butter or margarine, melted
  1 cup milk

Heat oven to 425°F. Grease 8x8x2-inch baking pan. Combine flour, cornmeal, salt, sugar, and baking powder in medium-size bowl. Put remaining ingredients into blender container in order listed. Cover; blend at low speed until well mixed. Add dry ingredients to blender container in 3 additions. Cover; blend at low speed after each addition just until mixed. Pour into baking pan. Bake 25 to 30 minutes, or until top is golden brown.

Golden Corn Muffins

Fill 12 greased 2½-inch muffin-pan cups two-thirds full with batter. Bake 15 to 20 minutes, or until golden brown.

Corn Bread. Caloric Corporation

Corn Bread

Makes 8 servings

  1 **cup yellow cornmeal**
  ¾ **cup all-purpose flour**
  1 **tablespoon sugar**
  1 **tablespoon baking powder**
  1 **teaspoon salt**
  ½ **teaspoon baking soda**
  6 **slices bacon, cooked and crumbled**
  1 **cup buttermilk**
  1 **egg**
  ⅓ **cup vegetable oil**

Combine cornmeal, flour, sugar, baking powder, salt, and baking soda in mixing bowl. Add bacon and toss until evenly mixed. Blend buttermilk, egg, and oil until smooth. Stir into cornmeal mixture until well mixed. Pour into greased 8-inch square baking dish. Preheat oven to 425°F. Bake 20 to 25 minutes until toothpick inserted in center comes out clean.

Country-Style Corn Bread

Makes 12 muffins, 16 sticks or 1 skilletful

  2 **cups Martha White Self-Rising Corn Meal**
  ½ **teaspoon baking soda**
 1½ **cups buttermilk**
  ¼ **cup bacon drippings or vegetable shortening, melted**

Preheat oven to 450°F. Grease muffin cups, corn-stick mold, or 8-inch skillet; preheat in oven. Combine corn meal and baking soda in bowl. Add buttermilk and bacon drippings; blend thoroughly. Pour into hot pans. (Fill muffin cups and corn-stick pans two-thirds full.) Bake 20 to 25 minutes, or until golden brown.
Note: Whole milk can be substituted for buttermilk by reducing amount to 1⅓ cups and omitting baking soda.

Traditional southern corn bread is brown and crusty. To make it this way, use black iron pans which have been greased and heated in the oven until they begin to smoke; batter should sizzle when poured into the pan.

Indian Corn Bread

Makes 6 servings
  1 cup all-purpose flour
  1 cup cornmeal
  ⅓ cup sugar
  2 teaspoons baking powder
  ½ teaspoon salt
  1 cup Libby's Solid Pack Pumpkin
  ¼ cup butter or margarine, melted
  2 eggs
    Butter or honey (optional)

Preheat oven to 425°F. In medium bowl, combine flour, cornmeal, sugar, baking powder, and salt; mix well. Add combined remaining ingredients; beat vigorously 1 minute. Spread batter evenly into greased 8x8-inch baking pan. Bake 20 to 25 minutes, or until golden brown. Cut into squares. Serve with butter and/or honey, if desired.

Double-Good Corn Bread

Makes 16 squares
  1 package (7½ ounces) Martha White Corn
    Muffin Mix
  1 can (17 ounces) cream-style corn
  ½ cup butter or margarine, melted
  2 eggs, lightly beaten

Preheat oven to 350°F. Butter 8-inch square baking pan; set aside. Combine all ingredients in bowl; blend thoroughly. Spread in prepared pan. Bake 35 to 40 minutes, or until golden brown. Cut into 2-inch squares. Serve as a vegetable or bread.

Bread-Making Substitutions and Equivalents

Flour: 1 cup self-rising flour = 1 cup all-purpose flour plus 1½ teaspoons baking powder and scant ½ teaspon salt. ("All-purpose" flour is the same as "plain" flour.)
Milk: 1 cup whole milk = ½ cup evaporated milk plus ½ cup water, or 1 cup reconstituted nonfat dry milk plus 2½ teaspoons melted butter or margarine.
Buttermilk: 1 cup buttermilk = 1 cup sweet milk plus 1 tablespoon lemon juice or vinegar. Let stand 5 minutes.
Yeast: 1 cake compressed yeast (.6 ounces) = 1 package (¼ ounce) active dry yeast = 2⅔ teaspoons active dry yeast.
Chocolate: 1 square (1 ounce) unsweetened baking chocolate = 3 tablespoons cocoa plus 1 tablespoon butter or margarine.

Egg Corn Bread

Makes 14 muffins, 18 sticks, or 1 skilletful
  2 cups Martha White Self-Rising Corn Meal
  1 teaspoon sugar
  2 eggs, lightly beaten
  1¼ cups milk
  ¼ cup bacon drippings or vegetable shortening,
    melted

Preheat oven to 450°F. Grease muffin cups, corn-stick mold, or 8-inch skillet; preheat in oven. Combine cornmeal and sugar in bowl; set aside. Combine eggs, milk, and bacon drippings in separate bowl. Add cornmeal mixture; blend thoroughly. Pour into hot pans. (Fill muffin cups and corn-stick pans two-thirds full.) Bake 15 to 20 minutes, or until golden brown.

Buttermilk-Egg Corn Bread
Substitute 1½ cups buttermilk for whole milk and add ¼ teaspoon baking soda.

Mango Bread

Makes 1 loaf
  1 cup C & H Granulated Sugar
  ½ cup butter or margarine, softened
  2 eggs
  2¼ cups all-purpose flour
  1 tablespoon baking powder
  ½ teaspoon salt
  1 cup puréed mangoes (2 to 3 medium)
  1 tablespoon lemon juice

Preheat oven to 350°F. Grease and flour 9x5x3-inch loaf pan. Cream sugar and butter until fluffy. Add eggs, 1 at a time, beating well after each addition. Combine flour, baking powder, and salt. Blend half the dry ingredients into creamed mixture. Combine mangoes and lemon juice, then stir into batter. Add remaining flour and mix well. Pour into loaf pan. Bake 55 to 60 minutes. Remove from pan and cool on rack.

Golden Coconut Loaf

Makes 1 loaf
  2 cups sifted all-purpose flour
  1 cup sugar
  2 teaspoons baking powder
  1 teaspoon salt
  ½ cup shortening
  1 teaspoon Durkee Lemon Extract
  4 egg yolks
  ¾ cup milk
  1 package (3½ ounces) Durkee Flaked Coconut

Sift together dry ingredients. Add shortening, extract, egg yolks, and ½ cup milk. Beat 2 minutes. Add remaining milk. Beat 2 minutes more. Fold in coconut. Pour batter into greased and floured 11x7-inch pan. Bake at 350°F. about 35 to 40 minutes.

Apple Bread

Makes 1 loaf

   1 cup sugar
   ½ cup vegetable shortening
   1 teaspoon vanilla extract
   2 eggs
   1 tablespoon buttermilk
   2 cups sifted Martha White Self-Rising Flour
   1 teaspoon grated lemon peel
1½ cups chopped peeled tart apples
   1 tablespoon sugar
   ½ teaspoon ground cinnamon

Preheat oven to 350°F. Grease bottom of 9x5x3-inch loaf pan; set aside. Cream 1 cup sugar, shortening, and vanilla with electric mixer in mixing bowl until light and fluffy. Add eggs and buttermilk. Blend well. Add flour; blend well. Stir in lemon peel and apples. Pour into prepared pan. Combine 1 tablespoon sugar and cinnamon; sprinkle over batter. Bake 1 hour, or until toothpick inserted in center comes out clean. Cool in pan 10 minutes. Gently loosen sides of loaf. Turn out onto wire rack to cool completely.

Brown Sugar-Nut Bread

Makes 1 loaf

1 cup firmly packed C & H Brown Sugar
2 cups all-purpose flour
1 teaspoon salt
½ teaspoon baking soda
1 cup coarsely chopped walnuts
1 egg, lightly beaten
1 cup buttermilk or sour milk

Preheat oven to 350°F. Grease 9x5x3-inch loaf pan. Mix sugar, flour, salt, baking soda, and walnuts in bowl. Combine egg and milk. Stir into dry ingredients, mixing just until moistened. Pour into loaf pan. Rest 20 minutes in warm place, then bake 60 to 70 minutes, or until cake tester inserted in center comes out clean. Turn out onto rack to cool. Slices easily even while warm.

Keeping Bread

No matter what you've heard, the refrigerator is not the best place to store bread, whether bought or home-made. True, it won't mold in the refrigerator, but it does get stale just about as rapidly as it does at room temperature. Instead, store bread in the freezer, from which it will emerge (once it's thawed, which takes very little time) fresh and moist and delicious. If little bread is used in your house, slice the loaf before you freeze it, so you can take it out a slice or two at a time. Whole or sliced, be sure to wrap the bread airtight, in freezer paper or heavy-duty foil, before freezing.

Specially Flavored Breads

Try some of the following variations to basic breads—then invent a few ideas of your own.

Sliced Herb Bread: Take a loaf of thinly sliced sour-rye bread and spread each slice with garlic-flavored butter and sprinkle each slice with finely chopped parsley and a hint of dried thyme or rosemary. Place the slices together, loaf fashion, wrap in foil, and bake at 375°F. for 15 to 20 minutes, or until the butter is thoroughly melted and the herb flavor is blended.

Italian Cheese Bread: Start by spreading halves of long French or round Italian loaves lavishly with butter. Add a layer of sliced mozzarella cheese, a layer of anchovy fillets, a layer of thinly sliced onions, and a layer of chopped parsley. Press them together and heat in a 375°F. oven for 15 to 20 minutes. Another very satisfactory way to prepare this exceptionally tasty—and different—bread is to wrap the layers in aluminum foil and heat them on the back of the grill.

Garlic Bread: Rub 2 to 3 cloves garlic well into the crust of French or Italian loaves. Heat in a 350°F. oven in the house or wrap in foil and heat on the back of your grill, turning often.

Mustard Bread: Combine ½ pound butter with 1 cup finely chopped green onions, ½ cup chopped parsley, and a few drops lemon juice. Cream it well and spoon onto split halves of French or Italian bread. Top with mustard and sprinkle with toasted sesame seed. Heat on grill or—much better—in the oven, and serve hot from the kitchen.

Cheese Loaf: Combine ½ pound well-softened butter, ½ pound grated sharp cheddar cheese, 2 teaspoons dry mustard, a few specks cayenne pepper, and blend well. Spread or split loaves of French or Italian bread, press halves together, and heat in a 375°F. oven until the cheese is melted, or wrap in foil and heat on the back of the grill, turning quite often while they heat.

Herbed Loaf: Chop a bunch of green onions or scallions, enough parsley to make ½ cup, enough fresh basil to make 2 tablespoons. Combine with ½ pound softened butter and 1 teaspoon dry mustard. Split 1 long French loaf or 2 round Italian loaves and, through the middle, spread with this mixture. Heat in a 375°F. oven for 15 minutes, or wrap in foil and heat on the back part of the grill.

Rolls: Any of these mixtures may be used with French or Italian hard rolls split and prepared the same way. This may be more advantageous for a large party.

Cranberry-Banana-Nut Bread

Makes 1 cake

- 1½ cups sugar
- ⅔ cup vegetable shortening
- 3 eggs
- 3½ cups sifted Martha White Self-Rising Flour
- 1 cup chopped walnuts
- ¼ teaspoon baking soda
- 2 cups mashed bananas (4 medium)
- 1 can (16 ounces) whole berry cranberry sauce

Preheat oven to 325°F. Grease and flour 12-cup Bundt-type pan; set aside. Cream sugar and shortening with electric mixer in mixing bowl until light and fluffy. Add eggs; blend well. Add flour, walnuts, baking soda, and bananas; blend well. Stir in cranberry sauce. Pour into prepared pan. Bake 1 hour and 10 minutes to 1 hour and 15 minutes, or until toothpick inserted in center comes out clean. Cool in pan 10 minutes. Turn out onto wire rack to cool.

Apricot Bread

Makes 1 loaf

- 2¾ cups sifted Martha White Self-Rising Flour
- ¾ cup sugar
- ¼ teaspoon baking soda
- 1 cup buttermilk
- 1 egg, lightly beaten
- 3 tablespoons butter or margarine, melted
- 1½ cups uncooked dried apricots, cut into strips
- ½ cup chopped pecans

Preheat oven to 350°F. Grease bottom of 9x5x3-inch loaf pan; set aside. Sift flour, sugar, and baking soda into bowl. Combine buttermilk, egg, and butter in separate bowl. Combine buttermilk mixture and flour mixture; mix just until blended. Stir in apricots and pecans. Pour into prepared pan. Bake 55 to 60 minutes, or until toothpick inserted in center comes out clean. Cool in pan 10 minutes. Gently loosen sides of loaf. Turn out onto wire rack to cool completely.

Q *Is there a way to incorporate nuts and fruits into a recipe?*

A. When the sweet-dough bread or roll recipe calls for nuts and/or raisins and/or other fruits, such as snipped dried apricots, place them in a small bowl—combining them if more than one kind is used—and toss with a tablespoon or two of the flour the recipe requires. This will coat the nuts or fruit, keeping the pieces from sinking to the bottom during the baking process. But be sure only to use some of the flour called for—extra flour will make the finished product dry.

Cranberry-Banana-Nut Bread. Martha White Foods

All Seasons Tea Bread with Creamy Cheese Spread (page 52); Pumpkin-Raisin Muffins (page 76). Libby, McNeill & Libby, Inc., The Great Pumpkin Cookbook, A Harvest of Libby's Favorite Recipes.

All Seasons Tea Bread with Creamy Cheese Spread

Makes 1 loaf
- 1 cup Libby's Solid Pack Pumpkin
- 1 cup grated zucchini
- ¾ cup sugar
- 2 eggs, lightly beaten
- ¼ cup oil
- ¼ cup butter or margarine, melted
- 2 cups all-purpose flour
- 1 teaspoon baking soda
- ½ teaspoon baking powder
- ½ teaspoon ground cinnamon
- ¼ teaspoon salt
- ½ cup chopped pecans or walnuts
- Creamy Cheese Spread (recipe follows)

Preheat oven to 350°F. In large bowl, combine pumpkin, zucchini, sugar, eggs, oil, and butter; mix well. In separate bowl, combine flour, baking soda, baking powder, cinnamon, and salt. Add dry ingredients to pumpkin mixture, mixing until just moistened. Stir in nuts. Spoon into well-greased 9x5x3-inch pan. Bake 60 minutes, or until wooden toothpick inserted in center comes out clean. Cool 10 minutes; remove from pan.

Variation
Substitute grated carrot for zucchini.

Creamy Cheese Spread
- 1 package (3 ounces) cream cheese, softened
- 3 tablespoons butter or margarine, softened

Combine ingredients; mix until well blended. Spread between slices of All Seasons Tea Bread.

Homemade Whipped Butter
When you make homemade bread, take an extra few minutes to prepare whipped butter—so delicious, so far superior to the store-bought kind, that your family and guests will be won over for life. Bring 1 pound butter to room temperature; place in small bowl of electric mixer. Add 1 whole egg. Beat at low speed until blended, then at high speed 5 minutes. Add ¼ cup cold heavy (whipping) cream. Blend at low speed; beat at high speed 10 to 15 minutes, until very light and fluffy. Refrigerate; you'll need two 1-pound containers—besides being so good, the butter will have doubled in bulk. Let stand at room temperature 10 minutes before serving.

Whole Wheat Health Bread

Makes 1 loaf
- 1 cup Martha White Whole Wheat Flour
- 1 cup sifted Martha White Self-Rising Flour
- ¼ cup sugar
- ½ teaspoon salt
- ¼ teaspoon baking soda
- 1 egg, lightly beaten
- 1½ cups buttermilk
- ¼ cup honey
- ¼ cup butter or margarine, melted
- ½ cup chopped walnuts
- ½ cup raisins

Preheat oven to 375°F. Grease bottom of 9x5x3-inch loaf pan; set aside. Combine flours, sugar, salt, and baking soda in large bowl. Combine egg, buttermilk, honey, and butter in separate bowl. Add buttermilk mixture to flour mixture; stir just until moistened. Stir in walnuts and raisins. Pour into prepared pan. Bake 45 to 50 minutes, or until toothpick inserted in center comes out clean. Cool in pan 10 minutes. Gently loosen sides of loaf. Turn out onto wire rack to cool completely.

Note: This loaf does not rise as high as many of the quick breads and will be more compact.

Peanut Butter-Orange Bread

Makes 1 loaf
- ¾ cup peanut butter
- ½ cup butter or margarine
- 2 cups sifted all-purpose flour
- ½ cup sugar
- 1½ teaspoons baking powder
- 1 teaspoon salt
- ½ teaspoon baking soda
- 1 tablespoon grated orange rind
- 1 egg, beaten
- 1 cup milk

Preheat oven to 350°F. In large Sunbeam Mixmaster Mixer bowl, cream together peanut butter and butter at medium high until light and fluffy. Sift flour, sugar, baking powder, and salt together into creamed mixture and beat at lowest 1 minute, or until crumbs form. Add orange rind, egg, and milk; beat at low until all of mixture is moistened. Pour into greased 9x5x3-inch loaf pan. Bake 55 minutes, or until cake tester inserted in center comes out clean. Remove from pan. Cool before slicing.

Lemon Tea Bread

Makes 1 loaf
- ¾ cup sugar
- ⅓ cup butter or margarine
- 2 eggs, lightly beaten
- 3 teaspoons grated lemon peel
- 2 cups sifted Martha White Self-Rising Flour
- ¾ cup milk
- ½ cup chopped walnuts
- 2 tablespoons sugar
- 1 tablespoon lemon juice

Preheat oven to 350°F. Grease bottom of 9x5x3-inch loaf pan; set aside. Cream ¾ cup sugar and butter with electric mixer in mixing bowl until light and fluffy. Add eggs and lemon peel; blend thoroughly. Alternately add flour and milk to creamed mixture, beginning and ending with flour. Stir in walnuts. Pour into prepared pan. Bake 55 to 60 minutes, or until toothpick inserted in center comes out clean. Combine 2 tablespoons sugar and lemon juice in small dish. Remove bread from oven. Spoon lemon juice mixture evenly over hot bread. Cool in pan 10 minutes. Gently loosen sides of loaf. Turn out onto wire rack to cool completely.
Note: This recipe works well in an 8½x4½x2½-inch glass loaf pan.

Orange-Date Loaf

Makes 1 loaf
- 2 cups sifted all-purpose flour
- 2 teaspoons baking powder
- ½ teaspoon salt
- 1 egg
- 2 tablespoons shortening
- ¾ cup sugar
- ¾ cup orange juice
- 1 piece orange rind, ½x2 inches
- ½ teaspoon almond extract
- ½ cup nutmeats
- ½ cup pitted dates

Preheat oven to 350°F. Grease an 8x4x2-inch loaf pan. Sift flour, baking powder, and salt into a large bowl of Sunbeam Mixmaster Mixer. Put egg, shortening, sugar, orange juice, and rind into blender; cover and blend at Mix until smooth. Stop blender, add extract, nuts, and dates; cover and process at Chop only until nuts and dates are chopped. Pour mixture over dry ingredients. Turn dial to lowest; mix only until dry ingredients are moistened. Turn into greased pan. Bake for 55 to 60 minutes.

Oatmeal-Nut Bread

Makes 1 loaf
- 1½ cups sifted all-purpose flour
- ½ teaspoon salt
- ½ teaspoon baking powder
- 1 teaspoon baking soda
- ¾ cup quick-cooking oatmeal
- 1 egg
- ½ cup sugar
- 1 cup sour cream
- ⅓ cup dark molasses
- ½ cup pitted dates
- 1 cup nuts

Preheat oven to 350°F. Line a greased 8x4x2-inch loaf pan with wax paper; grease again. Sift flour, salt, baking powder, and soda into mixing bowl. Add oatmeal. Put egg, sugar, sour cream, and molasses into blender; cover and process at Mix until smooth and well blended. Add dates and nuts and process at Chop until dates are chopped. Empty into dry ingredients and stir well. Fill prepared pan and bake 45 to 55 minutes.

Onion Bread

Makes 2 loaves
- 1 package (¼ ounce) active dry yeast
- 1 cup warm water (105° to 115°F.)
- 3¼ to 3¾ cups sifted Martha White All-Purpose Flour, divided
- 2 teaspoons sugar
- 2 teaspoons salt
- 2 tablespoons butter or margarine, melted
- ⅔ cup chopped onions
- 2 teaspoons paprika

Grease large bowl; set aside. Dissolve yeast in water in separate bowl. Add 2 cups flour, sugar, and 1 teaspoon salt; stir until moistened, then beat well. Add enough remaining flour to make a soft dough. Turn out onto floured board or pastry cloth. Knead 8 to 10 minutes, or until smooth and elastic. Shape into ball. Place in prepared bowl. Turn once to grease top. Cover and let rise in warm place, free from draft, 1 hour, or until double in bulk. Grease two 9-inch round baking pans; set aside. Punch dough down; divide in half. Press each half into prepared pans. Brush tops with butter. Sprinkle onions evenly over tops. Use fingertips to press onions lightly into dough. Cover with plastic wrap. Let rise in warm place, free from draft, 40 minutes, or until double in bulk. Preheat oven to 450°F. Sprinkle each loaf with ½ teaspoon remaining salt and 1 teaspoon paprika. Bake 20 to 25 minutes, or until well browned and loaves sound hollow when lightly tapped. Transfer to wire racks to cool.

Sugarplum Bread

Makes 2 loaves or 3 mini-loaves

1⅓ cups sugar
2⅔ cups all-purpose flour
 1 tablespoon baking powder
 2 teaspoons pumpkin pie spice
 1 teaspoon salt
 3 eggs
 1 cup vegetable oil
 2 jars (4¾ ounces each) strained plum baby food
    (1 cup)
 1 cup chopped pecans

Preheat oven to 350°F. Combine sugar, flour, baking powder, pumpkin pie spice, and salt in large bowl; set aside. Combine eggs, oil, and baby food in a separate bowl. Stir liquid mixture into dry ingredients; mix just until moistened. Fold in pecans. Divide batter evenly between 2 ungreased Reynolds Redi-Pan loaf pans or 3 ungreased Reynolds Redi-Pan mini-loaf pans. Bake 45 to 55 minutes, or until toothpick inserted in loaf comes out clean. Cool in pan.

For gift giving: One recipe converts into 3 gifts by using the mini-loaf pans. Overwrap with Reynolds Plastic Wrap and tie with a bow.

Fruit and Nut Bread

Makes 1 loaf

 1 cup sugar
 ½ cup vegetable shortening
 1 teaspoon vanilla
 2 eggs
 1 tablespoon buttermilk
 2 cups sifted all-purpose flour
 2 teaspoons baking powder
 1 teaspoon grated lemon peel
 ½ cup chopped dried apricots
 ½ cup seedless white raisins
 ½ cup seedless dark raisins
 ½ cup chopped walnuts
 1 tablespoon sugar
 ½ teaspoon cinnamon

In large bowl of electric mixer, cream together 1 cup sugar, shortening, and vanilla. Add eggs and buttermilk and blend well. Add flour and blend well. Stir in lemon peel, apricots, raisins, and nuts. Pour into 9x5x3-inch loaf pan with a greased bottom. Combine 1 tablespoon sugar and cinnamon; sprinkle over batter. Bake in preheated 350°F. oven 1 hour, or until toothpick inserted in center comes out clean. Cool 10 minutes. Loosen sides of loaf and turn out onto wire rack to cool completely.

Fruit and Nut Bread. Gordon E. Smith compliments of Arnold Foods Company

Banana-Spice Bread (page 32)

Strawberry Bread

Makes 1 loaf

½ cup sugar
½ cup butter or margarine
1 teaspoon vanilla extract
2 eggs
2 cups sifted Martha White All-Purpose Flour
½ teaspoon salt
¼ teaspoon baking soda
1 cup strawberry preserves
½ cup buttermilk
½ cup chopped walnuts

Preheat oven to 325°F. Grease bottom of 9x5x3-inch loaf pan; set aside. Cream sugar, butter, and vanilla with electric mixer in mixing bowl until light and fluffy. Add eggs, 1 at a time, beating well after each addition. Sift flour, salt, and baking soda into separate bowl; set aside. Combine preserves and buttermilk in small bowl; blend thoroughly. Alternately add flour mixture and preserves mixture to creamed mixture; beat just until blended. Stir in walnuts. Pour into prepared pan. Bake 1 hour and 30 minutes, or until toothpick inserted in center comes out clean. Cool in pan 10 minutes. Gently loosen sides of loaf. Turn out onto wire rack to cool completely.
Note: For an especially attractive loaf, try an 8½x4½x2½-inch glass loaf pan.

Toasted Coconut Bread

Makes 1 loaf

1⅓ cups shredded coconut
3 cups sifted Martha White Self-Rising Flour
1 cup sugar
1 tablespoon grated orange peel
1 egg, lightly beaten
1⅓ cups milk
1 teaspoon vanilla extract
Almond Butter Spread (see index)

Preheat oven to 350°F. Spread coconut in shallow baking pan. Bake 7 to 12 minutes, or until lightly browned, stirring or shaking pan often to toast coconut evenly; set aside. Grease bottom of 9x5x3-inch loaf pan; set aside. Sift flour and sugar into bowl. Stir in toasted coconut and orange peel. Combine egg, milk, and vanilla in separate bowl; mix lightly. Combine milk mixture with flour mixture; mix just until blended; do not beat. Pour into prepared pan. Bake 55 to 60 minutes, or until toothpick inserted in center comes out clean. Cool in pan 10 minutes. Loosen sides of loaf. Turn out onto wire rack to cool completely. Cut into thin slices and serve with Almond Butter Spread.

Blueberry-Sour Cream Loaf

Makes 1 loaf

2 eggs
1 cup (8 ounces) sour cream
½ cup milk
2 tablespoons butter or margarine, melted
2 packages (7 ounces each) Martha White Blueberry Muffin Mix
½ cup chopped pecans

Preheat oven to 350°F. Grease bottom of 9x5x3-inch loaf pan; set aside. Break eggs into bowl and beat lightly. Add sour cream, milk, butter, and muffin mix; stir just until blended. Stir in pecans. Pour into prepared pan. Bake 45 to 50 minutes, or until toothpick inserted in center comes out clean. Cool in pan 10 minutes. Gently loosen sides of loaf. Turn out onto wire rack to cool completely.

Variation

For Apple-Cinnamon-Sour Cream Loaf, substitute Apple Cinnamon Muffin Mix for Blueberry Muffin Mix.

Currant-Cheese Bread

Makes 1 9-inch loaf

¼ cup bulgur
2 cups whole wheat flour
3 tablespoons firmly packed light or dark brown sugar
2½ teaspoons baking powder
½ teaspoon baking soda
½ teaspoon salt
½ cup Sun-Maid® Zante Currants
1 egg, lightly beaten
¾ cup milk
2 tablespoons vegetable oil
½ cup cream-style cottage cheese

Combine the bulgur with 1 cup water and let stand for 15 to 20 minutes; drain well. Grease a 9x5x3-inch loaf pan. Preheat the oven to 350°F. Mix the flour, sugar, baking powder, baking soda, salt, and currants in a large bowl. In a separate bowl, combine the egg, milk, oil, cottage cheese, and drained bulgur; stir until well mixed. Add to the flour mixture all at once, stirring just until the flour is moistened. Turn the batter into the prepared pan. Bake 1 hour and 10 minutes, or until a toothpick inserted in the center comes out clean. Let stand on a wire rack for 10 minutes before turning out of the pan to cool completely on the rack.

Butterscotch-Banana Bread

Makes 2 loaves

- 3½ cups all-purpose flour
- 4 teaspoons baking powder
- 1 teaspoon baking soda
- 1 teaspoon ground cinnamon
- 1 teaspoon ground nutmeg
- 1 teaspoon salt
- 2 cups ripe mashed bananas (4 to 6 medium bananas)
- 1½ cups sugar
- 2 eggs
- ½ cup butter, melted
- ½ cup milk
- 2⅔ cups chopped pecans, divided
- 2 cups (12-ounce package) Nestlé Butterscotch Flavored Morsels

Preheat oven to 350°F. In a small bowl, combine flour, baking powder, baking soda, cinnamon, nutmeg, and salt; set aside. In a large bowl, combine bananas, sugar, eggs, and butter; beat until creamy. Gradually add flour mixture alternately with milk; mix until well blended. Stir in 2 cups pecans and the Nestlé Butterscotch Flavored Morsels. Pour batter equally into 2 well-greased and floured 9x5x3-inch loaf pans. Sprinkle tops equally with remaining ⅔ cup pecans. Bake 60 to 70 minutes; remove from pans.

Note: To make 1 loaf, divide ingredients in half.

Breakfast Cheddar Bread

Makes 1 loaf

- ½ cup C & H Granulated Sugar
- ½ cup shortening
- 3 eggs
- 2 cups all-purpose flour
- 1 tablespoon baking powder
- ¾ teaspoon salt
- 1 cup milk
- 1 cup shredded sharp cheddar cheese
- ½ cup chopped nuts

Preheat oven to 375°F. Grease 9x5x3-inch loaf pan. Cream sugar and shortening until fluffy. Add eggs, 1 at a time, beating well after each addition. Combine flour, baking powder, and salt. Add alternately to creamed mixture with milk, beginning and ending with dry ingredients. Stir in cheese and nuts. Pour into loaf pan. Bake 1 hour, or until cake tester inserted in center comes out clean. Turn out onto rack to cool.

Biscuit Mixes

This is one of the earlier of the hundreds of convenience foods that have proliferated in this generation. A great many baked foods can be made with biscuit mix as a base—biscuits, of course, and dumplings, shortcake, simple snack-type cakes, pancakes and waffles, quick breads, coffee cakes, and so on. In fact, the maker of the mix in widest distribution offers a cookbook containing more than 200 biscuit-mix recipes.

The chief advantage of convenience foods is ease of preparation. Another point in their favor is that they may contain ingredients that the average home cook doesn't store in her kitchen and/or doesn't want to buy in quantity because she may not use them again before they deteriorate from age.

In spite of its wide popularity, neither of these 2 important points is true of biscuit mix. It is almost as easy—and as quick—to measure and combine the ingredients from scratch as it is to measure and use the biscuit mix. And the ingredients—flour, shortening, leavening, salt, and in the case of some mixes, dried milk—are available in most kitchens in which any amount of baking is done. (Liquid milk, from the container, can be substituted for the dried milk when baking from scratch, although many kitchens these day use dried milk regularly for both drinking and cooking.) The total cost of these ingredients, when baking from scratch, is less than that of a comparable amount of biscuit mix.

Nevertheless, many households swear by biscuit mix. Part of this is psychological—inexperienced or inept cooks feel that through some magic the foods they bake with a mix will turn out better than if they measured and combined the ingredients themselves—although there is nothing that can be made of biscuit mix alone, without adding, at the very least, water, in the case of even very simple foods—pancakes, for instance—milk, eggs, and often sugar must be added to the mix to make an acceptable product.

If you're addicted to biscuit mix, you might like to try assembling your own. In a large mixing bowl, combine 10 cups of all-purpose flour, 1 tablespoon of salt, ½ cup of baking powder, and, if you wish, ¼ cup of sugar. Measure 2 cups of shortening—the type that does not require refrigeration—and cut into the dry ingredients with a pastry blender or two knives until the mixture resembles coarse meal. Store covered at room temperature—it will keep about 6 weeks.

Even for the cook who is not intimidated by the thought of whipping up a batch of from-scratch biscuits, this mix or the commercial kind can be useful on occasions—camping trips, visits to summer cottages—when it's expedient to take along as few separate items as possible.

Banana-Orange Bread

Makes 1 loaf

- 1¼ cups unsifted whole wheat flour
- 1¼ cups all-purpose flour
- 2½ teaspoons baking powder
- ½ teaspoon baking soda
- ¼ teaspoon ground nutmeg
- 1 cup mashed ripe bananas
- ¾ cup honey
- 2 tablespoons Hollywood Safflower Oil
- 2 egg whites or 1 whole egg
- ¾ teaspoon grated orange peel
- Orange slices (optional)
- Orange marmalade or apricot jam, melted (optional)

Preheat oven to 325°F. Grease a 9x5x3-inch loaf pan; set aside. In a medium bowl, combine flour, baking powder, baking soda, and nutmeg; set aside. In another bowl, combine bananas, honey, safflower oil, egg whites, and orange peel. Add flour mixture to banana mixture; mix just until combined. Spoon into prepared pan. Bake until a cake tester inserted into center comes out clean, about 65 minutes. Let stand in pan for 10 minutes. Loosen edges with a spatula and turn onto a wire rack to cool. Serve warm garnished, if desired, with orange slices topped with melted orange marmalade or apricot jam. Wrap loaf and store in the refrigerator.

Cheddar Spoon Bread

Makes 6 to 8 servings

- 2 cups milk
- 1 cup water
- 1 cup yellow cornmeal
- 2 tablespoons butter or margarine
- 1½ teaspoons salt
- ⅛ teaspoon cayenne
- 3 eggs, beaten
- 1½ cups (6 ounces) Sargento Shredded Natural Cheddar Cheese
- Butter

In medium saucepan, bring to boil milk, water, cornmeal, 2 tablespoons butter, salt, and cayenne; cook and stir until smooth and thickened. Remove from heat and beat in eggs until well blended; stir in cheese. Bake in greased 1½-quart casserole in preheated 400°F. oven 35 minutes, or until knife inserted in center comes out clean. Serve hot with butter.

Pumpkin Bread

Makes 4 loaves

- 2⅓ cups sugar
- ⅔ cup cooking oil
- 4 eggs, lightly beaten
- 1 can (2 cups) pumpkin
- ⅔ cup water
- 3⅓ cups Hecker's Unbleached, All-Purpose, Naturally White Flour, sifted
- ½ teaspoon baking powder
- 2 teaspoons baking soda
- 1½ teaspoons salt
- ½ teaspoon ground cinnamon
- ½ teaspoon ground cloves
- ⅔ cup finely chopped nuts
- ⅔ cup raisins (soaked in boiling water 1 minute, drained and dried)

Mix together sugar, oil, eggs, pumpkin, and water in a large bowl. Sift dry ingredients together; add raisins and nuts. Add to pumpkin mixture and blend well. Grease and flour four 1-pound coffee cans. Fill halfway with batter. Bake in preheated 350°F. oven 1¼ hours.

Pineapple-Coconut Bread

Makes 1 loaf

- ¾ cup C & H Granulated Sugar
- ¼ cup butter or margarine, softened
- 2 eggs
- 1 cup (8¾-ounce can) crushed pineapple, undrained
- ½ cup grated coconut
- 2 cups all-purpose flour
- 1 tablespoon baking powder
- ½ teaspoon salt

Preheat oven to 350°F. Grease 9x5x3-inch loaf pan. In bowl, beat sugar, butter, and eggs until smooth and creamy. Stir in pineapple and coconut. Combine flour, baking powder, and salt; stir into creamed mixture. Pour into loaf pan. Bake 1 hour. Turn out onto rack to cool.

Small Wonders

Grandma called them "gems" and that's what they are—jewels of muffins and related individual quick and yeast breads to enrich breakfast, brunch, or lunch.

Sweet Potato Pan Rolls

Makes 2 dozen rolls

    1 package (¼ ounce) active dry yeast
    ¼ cup warm water
    ½ cup lowfat milk
    ¼ cup firmly packed brown sugar
    1 teaspoon salt
    1 teaspoon ground cinnamon
    ½ teaspoon ground nutmeg
    ¼ cup butter or margarine
    ¾ cup cooked mashed sweet potatoes (fresh or canned)
    1 egg, beaten
    4½ to 5 cups all-purpose flour
       Melted butter

Line a 13x9x2-inch baking pan with Heavy Duty Reynolds Wrap aluminum foil. Dissolve yeast in warm water; set aside. Scald milk; add sugar, salt, spices, and butter. Stir until butter is almost melted. Pour over sweet potatoes; beat well with electric mixer. Stir in dissolved yeast and egg. Add 2 cups flour; beat well. Stir in enough additional flour to make a soft dough. Turn out onto floured surface; knead until smooth and elastic, 8 to 10 minutes. Place in greased bowl; cover and let rise in warm place until double in size, about 1 hour. Divide dough into 24 equal pieces. Shape to form round balls. Place in prepared pan. Brush with melted butter; cover and let rise in warm place until double in bulk, about 30 minutes. Bake in preheated 375°F. oven 20 to 25 minutes, or until golden brown. If desired, serve only 1 dozen rolls. Cool remaining rolls completely. Wrap in aluminum foil liner by bringing longer sides of foil together over rolls. Fold down in locked folds, pressing air out until foil is tight against rolls. Fold up short ends; crimp to seal. Label, date, and freeze. To thaw and heat, bake fully wrapped frozen rolls in 375°F. oven 30 to 35 minutes, or until heated through.

Sweet Potato Pan Rolls. The Reynolds Wrap Kitchen

Hot Cheese Rolls

Makes 24 rolls

    1 cup water
    2 tablespoons vegetable shortening
    3½ to 4 cups Martha White All-Purpose Flour, divided
    1 tablespoon sugar
    ½ teaspoon salt
    1 package (¼ ounce) active dry yeast
    1 egg, lightly beaten
    2 cups (8 ounces) sharp cheddar cheese, shredded
    2 tablespoons butter, melted

Grease large bowl; set aside. Heat water and shortening in saucepan until very warm (120° to 130°F.). Combine 2 cups flour, sugar, salt, and yeast in separate bowl. Add heated mixture; mix well. Stir in egg and cheese. Stir in enough remaining flour to make a soft dough. Turn out onto lightly floured board or pastry cloth. Cover with bowl. Let rest 10 minutes. Knead dough 8 to 10 minutes, or until elastic. Shape into ball. Place in prepared bowl. Turn once to grease top. Cover and let rise in warm place, free from draft, 1 hour, or until double in bulk. Grease 24 muffin cups. Punch dough down. Shape into Cloverleaf Rolls (see index). Brush tops with melted butter. Cover and let rise in warm place, from from draft, 30 minutes, or until double in bulk. Preheat oven to 375°F. Bake 12 to 15 minutes, or until golden brown.

Light Dinner Rolls

Makes 54 rolls

- 1½ **cups milk**
- 1½ **cups water**
- ½ **cup butter or margarine**
- 9 **to 10 cups Martha White All-Purpose Flour, divided**
- ½ **cup sugar**
- 4 **teaspoons salt**
- 2 **packages (¼ ounce each) active dry yeast**
- 1 **egg**

Grease large bowl; set aside. Heat milk, water, and butter in saucepan until very warm (120° to 130°F.). Combine 3 cups flour, sugar, salt, and yeast in mixing bowl. Add heated mixture and egg; beat at high speed of electric mixer 2 minutes. Stir in enough remaining flour to make a soft dough. Turn out onto floured board or pastry cloth. Cover with bowl. Let rest 10 minutes. Knead 8 to 10 minutes, or until smooth and elastic. Shape into ball. Place in prepared bowl. Turn once to grease top. Cover and let rise in warm place, free from draft, 45 minutes, or until almost double in bulk. Grease 2 large baking sheets; set aside. Punch dough down; divide into 4 portions. Shape into rolls as desired. Place on prepared baking sheets. Cover and let rise in warm place, free from draft, 45 minutes, or until double in bulk. Preheat oven to 350°F. Bake 15 to 20 minutes, or until golden brown. Transfer to wire racks to cool.

Shaping Yeast Rolls

Pan Rolls

Gently shape pieces of dough into smooth, 1½-inch balls by pulling the dough down and under with your thumb. Place, smooth sides up, in greased muffin cups or an 8-inch round baking pan about ½ inch apart.

Cloverleaf Rolls

Shape pieces of dough into smooth, ¾-inch balls. Place 3 balls in each greased muffin cup.

Easy Cloverleaf Rolls

Shape dough as for pan rolls. Place 1 ball in each greased muffin cup. Use scissors dipped in flour to cut each ball crosswise in half, then into quarters, cutting almost through to the bottom.

Parker House Rolls

Roll out dough to ¼-inch thickness on lightly floured board or pastry cloth. Cut out with a floured 2½-inch round cutter. Use the floured handle of a knife to make a deep, off-center crease in the top of each round. Fold the larger section over the smaller section. Press edges together lightly. Place about 1½ inches apart on greased baking sheet.

Fan Tans

Roll out dough into 12x9-inch rectangle. Brush with melted butter. Cut lengthwise into 6 strips. Stack the strips. Cut into twelve 1-inch pieces. Place, cut sides up, in greased muffin cups.

Twists

Shape pieces of dough into 1½-inch balls. Roll each ball into a thin, 12-inch rope. Fold in half; twist in center. Pinch ends to seal. Place about 2 inches apart on a greased baking sheet.

Double Knots

Shape pieces of dough into 1½-inch balls. Roll each ball into a thin, 12-inch rope. Form into a loose knot at center, leaving 2 long ends. Bring the top end under the rope, tucking it into the center of the knot. Bring the bottom end over the rope, tucking it into the center of the knot. Place 2½ inches apart on greased baking sheet.

Cloverleaf Rolls

Easy Cloverleaf Rolls

Parker House Rolls

Double Knots

Easy Refrigerator Rolls

Makes 3 dozen rolls

1¾ **cups warm water (105° to 115°F.)**
2 **packages (¼ ounce each) active dry yeast**
½ **cup sugar**
1 **tablespoon salt**
1 **egg**
¼ **cup butter or margarine, softened**
6 **cups sifted all-purpose flour**
  Melted butter or margarine

Put water and yeast into blender container; let stand 3 to 5 minutes. Cover; blend at low speed until mixed. Add sugar, salt, egg, and butter. Cover; blend at low speed until smooth. Add 3 cups flour. Cover; blend at high speed until smooth. If necessary, stop blender during processing and push ingredients toward blades with rubber spatula. Put remaining 3 cups flour into large mixing bowl. Add mixture from blender container; stir with wooden spoon to mix. Work dough with hands until smooth. Brush top of dough with melted butter. Cover with double thickness of plastic wrap or clean towel. Let rise in refrigerator at least 2 hours, or until double in bulk. Punch dough down. Dough is now ready to shape into rolls. (It may be stored in refrigerator up to 3 days if it is punched down once each day.) When ready to bake, heat oven to 400°F. Shape rolls according to following directions and bake 12 to 15 minutes. Serve hot.

Parker House Rolls

Roll dough out on lightly floured surface to ½-inch thickness. Cut into rounds with lightly floured 2½-inch biscuit cutter. Press deep crease, just off center, across each round with dull edge of knife. Brush rounds lightly with melted butter. Fold smaller section over larger; press edge lightly to seal with tines of a fork. Place 1 inch apart on lightly greased cookie sheet. Let rise in warm place (85°F.) about 20 minutes, or until double in bulk. Brush with melted butter. *Makes 1 dozen rolls.*

Cloverleaf Rolls

Divide dough in half. Roll each half with palms of hands on lightly floured surface into an 18-inch-long rope. Cut each rope into 18 equal pieces. Shape each piece into ball, tucking edges under so that tip is smooth. Place 3 balls in each greased 2½-inch muffin-pan cup. Cover with clean towel. Let rise in warm place (85°F.) about 20 minutes, or until double in bulk. Brush with melted butter or margarine. *Makes 1 dozen rolls.*

Pan Rolls

Roll dough with palms of hands on lightly floured surface into a 12-inch-long strip. Cut into 12 equal pieces. Shape each piece into ball, tucking edges under so that top is smooth. Place ¼ inch apart in greased 8- or 9-inch round cake pan. Cover with clean towel. Let rise in warm place (85°F.) about 20 minutes, or until double in bulk. Brush with melted butter or margarine. *Makes 1 dozen rolls.*

Easy Sweet Rolls

Follow directions for Easy Refrigerator Rolls, using 2 eggs instead of 1 and increasing softened butter to ½ cup. Use dough to make Prune or Apricot Swirls.

Double-Quick Dinner Rolls

Makes 1 dozen rolls

2¼ **cups Gold Medal all-purpose flour★**
2 **tablespoons sugar**
1 **teaspoon salt**
1 **package (¼ ounce) active dry yeast**
1 **cup very warm water (120° to 130°F.)**
2 **tablespoons shortening**
1 **egg**

Mix 1¼ cups of the flour, sugar, salt, and yeast in large bowl. Add water, shortening, and egg; beat until smooth. Stir in remaining flour until smooth. Scrape batter from side of bowl. Cover and let rise in warm place until double, about 30 minutes.

Stir down batter by beating about 25 strokes. Spoon into 12 greased medium muffin cups. Let rise until batter rounds over tops of cups, 20 to 30 minutes.

Heat oven to 400°F. Bake until golden brown, 15 to 20 minutes.
Note: Unbleached flour can be used in this recipe.
★If using self-rising flour, omit salt.

Whole Wheat Dinner Rolls

Substitute 1¼ cups whole wheat flour for 1¼ cups of the all-purpose flour; mix in with the sugar.

About Baking with Yeast

Yeast is a leavening agent that acts with sugar in the dough to form carbon dioxide gas. It is this action which causes the dough to rise and gives the finished bread lightness. There are 2 forms of yeast: compressed cakes (in .6-ounce packages) and active dry yeast (in ¼ ounce packages and 4-ounce jars). They can be used interchangeably. One package dry yeast equals 2⅔ teaspoons or one .6-ounce cake.

Brioche. American Egg Board

Brioche

Makes 1 large loaf or 2 dozen individual rolls
- **1 package (¼ ounce) active dry yeast★**
- **¼ cup warm water (105° to 110°F.)**
- **1 cup butter, softened**
- **5 eggs**
- **2 tablespoons sugar**
- **¾ teaspoon salt★**
- **3 cups all-purpose flour, divided★**
- **1 egg**
- **2 teaspoons water**

In large mixing bowl, soften yeast in warm water. Add butter, 5 eggs, sugar, salt, and 2 cups of the flour. Beat at medium speed until smooth, about 4 minutes. Add remaining flour and beat until smooth, about 1 minute. Cover and let rise in warm place until double in size, 1½ to 2 hours. Using spoon or rubber spatula, beat dough down. Cover and refrigerate overnight. Beat dough down again. Turn out onto lightly floured surface.

Large Loaf

With lightly floured hands, roll three-quarters of the dough into a large ball. Place in lightly greased 5-cup brioche pan. With lightly floured fingers, make a deep indentation (about 2 inches in diameter and 2 inches deep) straight down in center of dough in pan. Roll remaining one-quarter of dough into a small ball and place in indentation. Cover and let rise until dough almost reaches top of pan, 1½ to 2 hours. Beat 1 egg with 2 teaspoons water. Gently brush top of loaf with egg mixture. Bake in preheated 375°F. oven until firm and lightly browned, 35 to 45 minutes. Cool on wire rack 10 minutes. Gently loosen at sides with narrow spatula and remove from pan.

Individual Rolls

Divide dough in half. Cover and refrigerate one-half. (Dough becomes soft and sticky when warm.) Cut ¼ of the remaining dough into 12 equal pieces. With lightly floured hands, roll each piece into a small ball. Set aside. Cut remaining ¾ dough into 12 equal pieces. Roll each piece into a large ball. Place each large ball in lightly greased 2½-inch muffin cup or individual brioche pan. With lightly floured finger, make a deep indentation (about ½ inch in diameter and ½ inch deep) straight down in center of dough in each cup. Place one of the reserved small balls in each indentation. Repeat with remaining refrigerated dough. Cover and let rise until large balls almost reach tops of muffin cups, 30 to 60 minutes. Beat 1 egg with 2 teaspoons water. Gently brush tops of rolls with egg mixture. Bake in preheated 375°F. oven until firm and lightly browned, 15 to 17 minutes. Remove from pans. Cool on wire rack or serve immediately.

★You may substitute 1 package (13¾ ounces) hot roll mix for yeast, salt, and flour.

Early American Croissants; Earth Grains Bread (page 14); Honey Wheat Batter Bread (page 25). Carnation Company

Easy American Croissants

Makes 16 croissants
- **2½ cups all-purpose flour**
- **1 package quick-rise yeast**
- **2 tablespoons sugar**
- **1 teaspoon salt**
- **½ cup undiluted Carnation® Evaporated Milk**
- **¼ cup water**
- **2 eggs**
- **½ cup cold butter**
- **1 tablespoon water**

Combine 1 cup flour, yeast, sugar, and salt. Combine evaporated milk and ¼ cup water; heat to 120°F. Combine flour mixture, evaporated milk mixture and 1 egg in small mixer bowl; beat 3 minutes. Cut cold butter into remaining flour until butter particles are the size of large peas. Combine flour-butter mixture and yeast mixture until all flour is moistened. Refrigerate 2 hours. Knead dough on floured surface 10 to 15 times, or until smooth. Divide in 2. Roll each part into a 14-inch circle. Cut each circle into 8 wedges. Roll each wedge, starting with wide end. Place on ungreased cookie sheets, point side down. Curve into crescent shape. Cover; let rise in warm place until double, about 30 minutes. Combine remaining egg and 1 tablespoon water; brush over croissants. Bake in moderate oven (350°F.) 15 minutes.

Tearoom Refrigerator Rolls

Makes about 48 rolls

- 1 cup diced raw potatoes
- ½ cup vegetable shortening
- ⅓ cup sugar
- 1 tablespoon salt
- 1 package (¼ ounce) active dry yeast
- 5 to 6 cups Martha White All-Purpose Flour, divided
- 2 eggs, lightly beaten
  Vegetable oil
- 2 tablespoons butter or margarine, melted

Grease large bowl; set aside. Cook potatoes in unsalted water; reserve 1½ cups potato water. Heat reserved potato water in saucepan until very warm (120° to 130°F.). Combine potato water, potatoes, and shortening in blender container; blend well; set aside. Combine sugar, salt, yeast, and 2 cups flour in separate bowl. Stir in potato mixture. Add eggs; blend well. Stir in enough remaining flour to make a fairly stiff dough. Turn out onto floured board or pastry cloth. Knead 8 to 10 minutes, or until smooth and elastic. Place dough in prepared bowl. Turn once to grease top. Cover and let rise in warm place, free from draft, 2 hours, or until double in bulk. Punch dough down. Grease 2 large baking sheets; set aside. Shape dough into rolls as desired. Place on prepared baking sheets. Brush tops of rolls lightly with oil. Cover and let rise in warm place, free from draft, 45 minutes, or until double in bulk. Preheat oven to 400°F. Bake 15 to 20 minutes. Transfer to wire racks to cool. Brush tops with butter.

Note: This dough keeps well. If you want to bake only a portion, cover and refrigerate remaining dough until ready to use, up to 4 days. Remove dough from refrigerator when ready to use. Punch down. Shape into rolls as desired. Place on prepared baking sheets. Cover and let rise in warm place, free from draft, 2 hours, or until double in bulk. Bake as directed above.

Hot Muffin Rolls

Makes 24 rolls

- 1¼ cups milk
- ½ cup vegetable shortening
- 3¼ cup Martha White All-Purpose Flour, divided
- ¼ cup sugar
- 1 package (¼ ounce) active dry yeast
- 2 eggs, lightly beaten
- 2 tablespoons butter or margarine, melted

Heat milk and shortening in a saucepan until very warm (120° to 130°F.). Combine 2 cups flour, sugar, and yeast in bowl. Stir in heated mixture. Add eggs and enough remaining flour to make a stiff batter. Beat until smooth. Cover and let rise in warm place, free from draft, 1 hour, or until double in bulk. Grease 24 muffin cups. Stir down batter. Fill prepared muffin cups two-thirds full. Brush tops with butter. Cover and let rise in warm place, free from draft, 30 minutes. Preheat oven to 375°F. Bake 25 minutes, or until golden brown. Serve hot.

Apricot Muffins

Makes 12 to 14 muffins

- 2 cups all-purpose flour
- 3 teaspoons baking powder
- ½ tablespoon sugar
- ½ teaspoon salt
- 1 egg
- 1 cup milk
- 4 tablespoons melted butter or other shortening
- ½ cup Simon Fisher Apricot Butter

Sift flour, baking powder, sugar, and salt together. Combine egg, milk, and shortening and add all at once to dry ingredients, stirring quickly until lumpy in appearance. Fill greased muffin pans one-third full. Place 1 teaspoon apricot butter in each. Then fill muffin pans two-thirds full and bake in hot oven (425°F.) for about 25 minutes.

Pineapple-Bran Muffins

Makes 1 dozen muffins

- 1 cup shredded all-bran cereal
- ½ cup milk
- 1 cup (8¾-ounce can) crushed pineapple, undrained
- ¼ cup raisins
- ¼ cup shortening
- 1 egg
- ½ cup firmly packed C & H Dark Brown Sugar
- 1 cup all-purpose flour
- 2 teaspoons baking powder
- ½ teaspoon salt
- ¼ teaspoon baking soda

Preheat oven to 400°F. Combine cereal, milk, pineapple, and raisins. Stir in shortening and egg; mix thoroughly. Combine remaining ingredients and add to cereal mixture. Mix until ingredients are moistened. Spoon batter evenly into 12 paper-lined muffin cups. Bake 25 to 30 minutes.

Quick-and-Easy Muffins

Muffins are quick breads (although there are a few yeast-raised kinds) baked as small, round, single servings in pans especially designed for the purpose, now known as muffin tins but once called, more attractively, gem pans. Next to the corn ones, blueberry muffins—thickly studded with berries that purple-stain the batter surrounding them—are the best known. But there are many others: whole wheat, bran (usually with raisins), banana, walnut (or pecan or whatever nuts are available—they all make good muffins better), orange, cinnamon-apple, and a dozen more.

Accommodatingly, muffins will accept almost any inclusions you happen to have—cooked rice, cooked pumpkin or yam, corn kernels stripped off the cob, berries of most kinds and all sorts of mashed or cut-up fruit, grated cheddar or Swiss cheese, spices, herbs, whatever. Surprise muffins are created by filling muffin tins about one-quarter full, adding a cube of cheese or a dab of jam or jelly or a sprinkling of streusel mixture, then covering with more batter.

The "muffin method of mixing," as home economics classes refer to it, is simple. Dry ingredients are combined. Liquid ingredients, eggs and shortening such as oil or melted butter, are separately combined, the wet dumped into the dry, and the mixture stirred just enough to moisten the dry ingredients. This produces a lumpy, rough-looking batter, into which the inclusions—if any—are gently folded. The whole point is to keep mixing to a minimum.

Fruit Muffins

Makes 12 to 15 muffins

    1 cup buttermilk
    ¾ cup uncooked kasha
    ¼ cup shortening
    3 tablespoons sugar
    2 tablespoons molasses
    1 egg
    1½ cups all-purpose flour
    2 teaspoons baking powder
    ½ teaspoon baking soda
    ½ teaspoon salt
    ¼ teaspoon ground ginger
    ¼ teaspoon ground cinnamon
    ⅛ teaspoon ground cloves
    ¼ cup raisins or candied mixed fruit

Pour buttermilk over kasha and let set while measuring and mixing other ingredients. Cream shortening, sugar, molasses, and egg until fluffy. Sift dry ingredients together. Add dry ingredients to creamed mixture alternately with the kasha-buttermilk, stirring only until dry ingredients are moistened. Stir in raisins or mixed fruit. Fill well-oiled muffin pans half full of batter. Bake at 425°F. for 20 minutes, or until done.

Always-Ready Bran Muffins

Makes 2 dozen muffins

    3 cups wheat bran morsel cereal, divided
    ½ cup shortening
    1 cup sugar
    2 eggs
    2 cups buttermilk
    2½ cups all-purpose flour
    2½ teaspoons baking soda
    ½ teaspoon salt
    1 cup Sun-Maid® Seedless Golden Raisins

Grease twenty-four 2½-inch muffin cups. Pour 1 cup boiling water over 1 cup of the bran; let stand for 20 minutes. Preheat the oven to 400°F. In a large mixing bowl, cream the shortening and sugar until light and fluffy. Add the eggs and buttermilk and beat well. Beat in the remaining 2 cups of dry bran. Combine the flour, baking soda, and salt and add to the buttermilk mixture. Fold in the bran-water mixture and the raisins. Spoon into the prepared muffin cups, filling two-thirds full. Bake for 18 to 20 minutes.

Rye Muffins

Makes 1 dozen muffins

    1 cup Elam's Stone Ground 100% Whole Rye
        Flour
    1 cup Elam's Stone Ground 100% Whole Wheat
        Flour or Elam's Unbleached White Flour
        with Wheat Germ
    ¼ cup turbinado★
    3 teaspoons baking powder
    ¾ teaspoon salt
    1 cup milk
    2 eggs, beaten
    ¼ cup butter, melted

Combine and mix first 5 ingredients in bowl. Mix milk, eggs, and melted butter. Add liquids to dry ingredients and stir just until dry ingredients are moistened. Fill greased 2½x1¼-inch muffin cups three-quarters full. Bake in hot oven (425°F) until done and lightly browned, about 20 minutes.

★Turbinado, a partially refined cane sugar, may be omitted for sugar-free diets.

Cranberry Whole Wheat Muffins. Ocean Spray Cranberries

Sunflower-Nut Muffins (page 75). Courtesy of Bisquick®

Muffins. Courtesy of Bisquick®

(page 75)

Q. *How warm is warm?*
A. "Dissolve yeast in warm water," the recipe instructs you. How warm? Because temperature in this case is critical, if you're going to do a lot of baking invest in a yeast thermometer. But you can, if you pay careful attention to what you're doing, test the warmth on the inside of your wrist. Active dry yeast should be dissolved in liquid of 105° to 115°F., which will feel comfortably, pleasantly warm, but not hot, on your wrist. Compressed yeast should be dissolved in liquid of 95°F. This is virtually blood temperature, so the liquid should feel neither warm nor cool on the inside of your wrist.

Cranberry Whole Wheat Muffins

Makes 12 medium or 30 small muffins
  1½ **cups Ocean Spray Fresh or Frozen Cranberries,**
       coarsely chopped
  ¼ **cup sugar, divided**
  1 **egg**
  1 **cup milk**
  ¼ **cup vegetable oil**
  1 **cup sifted all-purpose flour**
  1 **cup whole wheat flour**
  2 **teaspoons baking powder**
  1 **teaspoon salt**

Preheat oven to 400°F. In small bowl, combine cranberries and ¼ cup sugar; set aside. In large bowl beat egg lightly with a fork; stir in milk and oil until well blended. Stir in all-purpose flour, whole wheat flour, sugar, baking powder, and salt just until moistened. Blend in cranberries. Spoon evenly into paper-lined medium-size muffin pans. Bake in oven for 25 minutes, or until wooden toothpick inserted inside comes out clean.

Muffins

Makes 12 muffins
  1 **egg**
  2 **cups Bisquick baking mix**
  ¼ **cup sugar**
  ⅔ **cup milk**
  2 **tablespoons vegetable oil or margarine or**
       butter, melted

Heat oven to 400°F. Grease bottoms only of 12 medium muffin cups, 2½x1¼ inches, or line with paper baking cups. Beat eggs lightly; stir in remaining ingredients just until moistened. Divide batter evenly among cups. Bake until golden brown, 15 to 18 minutes; cool, wrap securely, label and freeze up to 1 week. To serve, place frozen muffins on ungreased cookie sheet. Heat in 400°F. oven until warm, 6 to 8 minutes.

Granola-Bran Muffins

Makes 1 dozen muffins
  ¼ **cup firmly packed C & H Golden Brown Sugar**
  1 **cup granola**
  ¾ **cup unprocessed bran**
  ¾ **cup whole wheat flour**
  1 **teaspoon** *each* **baking soda and ground cinna-**
       mon
  ½ **teaspoon salt**
  1 **egg**
  ¾ **cup buttermilk**
  ¼ **cup vegetable oil**

Preheat oven to 400°F. Grease 12 muffin cups. Combine all ingredients in bowl. Mix just until dry ingredients are moistened. Spoon into muffin cups. Bake 15 minutes, or until toothpick inserted in center comes out clean.

Cranberry-Bacon Muffins

Makes about 16 medium muffins

1½ cups Ocean Spray Fresh or Frozen Cranberries,
     coarsely chopped
¼ cup sugar
2 cups plus 2 teaspoons sifted all-purpose flour
1 tablespoon baking powder
2 tablespoons sugar
½ teaspoon salt
1 egg, beaten
1 cup milk
2 tablespoons vegetable oil
2 tablespoons bacon drippings
¼ cup cooked minced crisp bacon

Preheat oven to 425°F. In small bowl, combine cranberries and ¼ cup sugar; set aside. In large bowl sift together dry ingredients. Add beaten egg, milk, vegetable oil, and bacon drippings just until dry ingredients are moistened. Add bacon bits and cranberries just until mixed. Spoon evenly into paper-lined medium-size muffin pans. Bake in oven for 25 minutes, or until a wooden toothpick comes out clean.

Cranberry Oatmeal Muffins

Makes 12 medium or 30 small muffins

1½ cups Ocean Spray Fresh or Frozen Cranberries,
     coarsely chopped
¼ cup sugar
1 cup rolled oats
1 cup buttermilk
⅓ cup vegetable shortening
½ cup firmly packed light brown sugar
1 egg
1 cup sifted all-purpose flour
1 teaspoon baking powder
½ teaspoon baking soda
1 teaspoon salt

In small bowl, combine cranberries and ¼ cup sugar; set aside. In another bowl, combine oats and buttermilk; let stand 1 hour. In a large mixing bowl, combine shortening, brown sugar, and egg until well blended. In a medium mixing bowl, sift together flour, baking powder, baking soda, and salt; stir into shortening mixture alternately with oat-buttermilk mixture until just moistened. Blend in cranberries. Preheat oven to 400°F. Spoon evenly into paper-lined medium-size muffin pans. Bake in oven for 25 minutes, or until wooden toothpick inserted comes out clean.

Another Day, Another Way

Today's bakeries, and even supermarkets, offer breads and rolls in wide variety. But if you always use store-bought breads, you'll never know the joys of home baking, never experience the flavor and texture, like no other, of home-baked breads. If you aren't the world's greatest cook and hold back from home baking through fear of failure, start with a halfway step: try some of the mixes, refrigerated doughs, and frozen doughs your supermarket has to offer. **Bread Mixes—** There are many of these; boxed, they are shelved near the cake mixes. You'll find hot roll mix, a variety of sweet/tea breads with nuts and fruits, several kinds of mixes to make muffins, mixes for corn and other quick breads, and yeast mixes to make chubby little loaves of white or whole wheat or rye "hearth" bread. **Frozen Dough—**Find this near the ready-to-eat breads in the grocer's freezer. From this dough you can make white or whole wheat loaves, as well as a number of baked goodies such as cinnamon rolls. (Give yourself time; the dough must thaw, then rise, before it can be baked.) Frozen roll dough is available, too, already shaped into plump tea buns, neat cloverleafs, Parker house or pocketbook rolls. **Refrigerated Dough—** Because it needs refrigeration, this is usually shelved close to the dairy or deli departments. Here, again, there is considerable variety to choose among: whole French-type loaves, flaky crescents, several kinds of biscuits, Parker house rolls, bread sticks, cinnamon rolls, Danish-type rolls, and more.

Apricot-Bran Muffins

Makes 8 muffins

1 egg
⅓ cup milk
1 tablespoon brown sugar
½ teaspoon ground cinnamon
1 package (7 ounces) Martha White Bran Muffin
   Mix
⅓ cup chopped dried apricots

Preheat oven to 425°F. Grease 8 muffin cups; set aside. Beat egg in bowl with fork. Add milk, brown sugar, and cinnamon; stir until sugar is dissolved. Add muffin mix and apricots; stir just until blended; batter will be lumpy. Fill prepared muffin cups two-thirds full. Bake 15 to 18 minutes, or until golden brown. Serve warm.

Raisin-Oatmeal Muffins

Makes 1 dozen muffins
  1 cup whole wheat flour
  ¾ cup rolled oats
  ½ cup Sun-Maid® Seedless Raisins
  ¼ cup firmly packed light brown sugar
  1 tablespoon baking powder
  ½ teaspoon baking soda
  ¾ teaspoon salt
  ¼ teaspoon ground nutmeg
  1 egg, lightly beaten
  1 cup milk
  ¼ cup vegetable oil

Preheat oven to 400°F. Grease twelve 2½-inch muffin cups well, or line with paper baking cups. Mix the flour, oats, raisins, sugar, baking powder, baking soda, salt, and nutmeg in a large bowl. In a separate bowl, blend the egg, milk, and oil. Add to flour mixture all at once, stirring just until the dry ingredients are moistened. Spoon into the prepared muffin cups, filling each about half full. Bake for 20 to 25 minutes, or until muffins are well browned.

Pecan Buttermilk Muffins

Makes 2 dozen muffins
  2 cups sifted cake flour
  1 teaspoon baking powder
  ½ teaspoon salt
  2 tablespoons sugar
  ½ teaspoon baking soda
  1 cup buttermilk
  3 tablespoons butter, melted
  1 egg, beaten
  ½ cup chopped pecans

Sift together dry ingredients. Combine buttermilk, butter, and egg. Add milk mixture all at once to dry ingredients. Add pecans and mix only enough to combine; do not beat. (Mixture will be slightly lumpy.) Fill well-oiled muffin pans two-thirds full. Bake in preheated 400°F. oven 20 to 25 minutes, or until muffins are puffed and lightly browned.
Helpful to know: Reheat leftover muffins, loosely wrapped in aluminum foil, in a preheated 450°F. oven for 5 minutes.

Muffin Magic
  If you are making muffins of any kind and you do not have enough batter or dough to fill all of the cups, place 1 to 2 tablespoons water in the empty cups. This will keep them from burning or warping and prolong the life of the pan.

Date-Filled Bran Muffins

Makes 1 dozen muffins
  1 cup all-bran cereal
  1 cup milk
  1 egg
  ¼ cup soft butter or margarine
  1 cup all-purpose flour
  2½ teaspoons baking powder
  ½ teaspoon salt
  ¼ cup sugar
  ½ can (6 ounces) Solo Date Filling

Preheat oven to 400°F. Generously butter twelve 2½-inch muffin-pan cups. Combine all-bran and milk. Let stand until most of the moisture is absorbed. Add egg and butter and beat well. Sift together flour, baking powder, and salt. Stir in sugar. Add to bran mixture and stir just until dry ingredients are moistened. (Batter will be lumpy.) Divide mixture among prepared muffin pan cups. Place a heaping teaspoonful of date filling in center of each muffin. Bake about 20 to 25 minutes, or until muffin springs back when lightly pressed with finger. Cool slightly on wire rack. Turn out of pan to cool completely.

All-Bran Muffins

Makes 1 dozen muffins
  1 cup sifted all-purpose flour
  2½ teaspoons baking powder
  1 teaspoon salt
  3 tablespoons soft shortening
  ¼ cup molasses
  1 egg
  1 cup all-bran cereal
  ½ cup milk

Heat oven to 400°F. Grease twelve 2½-inch muffin-pan cups. Sift flour, baking powder, and salt into medium-size bowl. Put shortening, molasses, egg, all-bran, and milk into blender container. Cover; blend at high speed until well mixed. Pour over dry ingredients; stir just until moistened. Fill muffin cups two-thirds full. Bake 15 minutes, or until done.

Six-Way Muffins with Blueberries. Hamilton Beach Scovill, Inc.

Applesauce Muffins

Makes 1 dozen muffins
  2 cups sifted Martha White Self-Rising Flour
  ⅓ cup sugar
  ¼ teaspoon ground nutmeg
  ¼ teaspoon ground cinnamon
  1 egg
  1 cup applesauce
  ½ cup milk
  3 tablespoons vegetable shortening, melted, or
      vegetable oil

Preheat oven to 425°F. Grease 12 muffin cups; set aside. Sift flour, sugar, and spices into bowl; set aside. Break egg into separate bowl; beat lightly with fork. Add applesauce, milk, and shortening. Add flour mixture; stir just until blended. Fill muffin cups about three-quarters full. Bake 20 minutes, or until golden brown.

Six-Way Muffins

Makes 1 dozen muffins
  2 cups sifted all-purpose flour
  2½ teaspoons baking powder
  ½ teaspoon salt
  2 tablespoons sugar
  1 cup milk
  1 egg
  ½ cup soft shortening

Heat oven to 400°F. Grease twelve 2½-inch muffin-pan cups. Sift flour, baking powder, salt, and sugar into medium-size bowl. Put remaining ingredients into blender container in order listed. Cover; blend at low speed until well mixed. Pour over dry ingredients; stir just until moistened. Fill muffin cups two-thirds full. Bake 20 to 25 minutes, or until done.

Date-Nut Muffins
Add ¾ cup pitted dates and ¼ cup walnuts to ingredients in blender container. Cover; blend at low speed until dates and nuts are finely chopped. Proceed as for Six-Way Muffins.

Raisin Muffins
Add 1 cup seedless raisins to ingredients in blender container. Cover; blend at low speed until raisins are finely chopped. Proceed as for Six-Way Muffins.

Carrot Muffins
Add 1 carrot, pared and cut up, to ingredients in blender container. Cover; blend at low speed until carrot is finely chopped. Proceed as for Six-Way Muffins.

Cranberry Muffins
Add 1 cup whole cranberries and ¼ cup sugar to ingredients in blender container. Cover; blend at low speed until cranberries are chopped. Proceed as for Six-Way Muffins.

Blueberry Muffins
Prepare batter in Six-Way Muffin recipe. Fold in 1 cup washed fresh blueberries. Bake as for Six-Way Muffins.

Strawberry Yogurt Muffins

Makes 8 muffins
  ½ cup (4 ounces) strawberry yogurt
  1 package (7 ounces) Martha White Strawberry
      Muffin Mix
  ¼ cup water

Preheat oven to 425°F. Grease 8 muffin cups; set aside. Stir yogurt to blend fruit. Combine muffin mix, yogurt, and water in bowl; stir just to moisten. Fill prepared muffin cups two-thirds full. Bake 15 minutes, or until golden brown.

Strawberry Yogurt Muffins; Apricot-Bran Muffins; Praline Muffins (page 75). Martha White Foods

Sour Cream-Date Muffins

Makes 1 dozen muffins
    ¾ cup C & H Granulated Sugar
    1¾ cups all-purpose flour
    1 tablespoon baking powder
    ½ teaspoon salt
    ½ cup snipped dates
    ½ pint (1 cup) sour cream
    1 egg
    ½ cup butter, melted and cooled
    ½ teaspoon ground cinnamon

Preheat oven to 400°F. Grease 12 muffin cups. Combine ¼ cup sugar, the flour, baking powder, and salt in bowl. Stir in dates. Combine sour cream, egg, and 2 tablespoons of the butter. Stir into dry ingredients, mixing just until moistened. Spoon into muffin cups. Bake 20 minutes, or until toothpick inserted in center comes out clean. Combine ½ cup sugar and the cinnamon in bowl. Dip tops of hot muffins in remaining melted butter, then cinnamon-sugar. Serve warm.

Cheese Muffins

Makes 1 dozen
    2 cups sifted all-purpose flour
    4 teaspoons baking powder
    1 tablespoon sugar
    ½ teaspoon salt
    1 egg
    1 cup milk
    3 tablespoons butter or margarine, softened
    ½ pound sharp cheddar cheese, cubed

Preheat oven to 350°F. Grease muffin pans well. Sift flour, baking powder, sugar, and salt into large bowl of Sunbeam Mixmaster Mixer. Put egg, milk, and butter into blender, cover, and process at Mix until smooth. Remove feeder cap, add cheddar, and process at Chop only until cheddar is finely chopped. Pour into dry ingredients. Set dial at lowest. Mix only until flour is moistened. Fill prepared tins two-thirds full. Bake 15 to 25 minutes.

Ginger-Date Bran Muffins

Makes 8 muffins
    1 egg
    ⅓ cup milk
    1 tablespoon sugar
    ⅓ cup chopped dates
    1 tablespoon slivered crystallized ginger
    1 package (7 ounces) Martha White Bran Muffin
      Mix

Preheat oven to 425°F. Grease 8 muffin cups; set aside. Beat egg in bowl with fork. Add milk and sugar; stir until sugar is dissolved. Add dates, ginger, and muffin mix; stir just until blended. Fill prepared muffin cups two-thirds full. Bake 15 to 18 minutes, or until golden brown. Serve warm.

Banana Muffin Surprise

Makes 12 to 14 muffins
    ½ cup uncooked oats, quick or regular
    ½ cup milk
    1 cup unsifted all-purpose flour
    ¼ cup sugar
    2½ teaspoons baking powder
    ½ teaspoon baking soda
    ½ teaspoon salt
    ½ teaspoon ground cinnamon
    ¼ teaspoon ground nutmeg
    ¼ cup butter or margarine, melted
    1 egg
    1 cup mashed ripe bananas (3 medium)
    ½ cup sunflower seeds

In medium bowl, combine oats and milk; set aside until milk is absorbed. In medium bowl, mix flour, sugar, baking powder, baking soda, salt, cinnamon, and nutmeg. Add butter, egg, and bananas to oat mixture; add to dry ingredients and stir just until moistened. Stir in sunflower seeds. Fill greased 2½-inch muffin cups two-thirds full. Bake in 425°F. oven 15 minutes, or until cake tester inserted in center comes out clean.

Pecan-Filled Muffins

Makes 10 muffins
    1 egg, lightly beaten
    ½ teaspoon vanilla extract
    1 tablespoon butter or margarine, melted
    ⅓ cup firmly packed brown sugar
    ½ can (6¼ ounces) Solo Pecan Filling
    1 can (8 ounces) refrigerated biscuits

Preheat oven to 375°F. Combine egg, vanilla, butter, and brown sugar and blend well. Stir in pecan filling and mix well. Separate biscuit dough into 10 biscuits and press each out slightly with the hands. Press each biscuit into a 2½-inch muffin-pan cup. Press as far up the sides as possible, making the dough as thin as possible. Fill with 1 tablespoon of the pecan mixture. Bake about 15 minutes, or until lightly browned. Remove from pans and serve warm.

English Bran Muffins

Makes 1 dozen muffins
  1 cup wheat bran cereal
  ⅔ cup milk
  1 egg
  ¼ cup vegetable oil
  1 cup sifted Martha White Self-Rising Flour★
  ¼ cup sugar

Preheat oven to 400°F. Grease 12 muffin cups; set aside. Combine cereal and milk in bowl; let stand until liquid is absorbed. Add egg and oil; mix well with fork. Sift flour and sugar into egg mixture; stir just until blended. Fill muffin cups two-thirds full. Bake 25 minutes, or until golden brown.
★If using Martha White All-Purpose Flour, add 2½ teaspoons baking powder and ½ teaspoon salt.

Easy Cheesy Muffins

Makes 1 dozen muffins
  1 cup sifted Martha White Self-Rising Flour
  1 cup Martha White Self-Rising Corn Meal
  ¼ cup sugar
  ⅔ cup grated sharp cheddar cheese
  1 egg
  1 cup milk
  2 tablespoons vegetable shortening, melted, or vegetable oil

Preheat oven to 325°F. Grease 12 muffin cups; set aside. Combine dry ingredients and cheese in bowl. Break egg into separate bowl; beat lightly with fork. Stir in milk and shortening. Add to flour-cheese mixture; blend thoroughly. Fill muffin cups about two-thirds full. Bake 20 minutes, or until golden brown.

Put It Away for Another Day

Breads and rolls, coffee cakes and quick breads, sweet rolls and Danish rolls—all may be freezer stored for later use, at 0°F. or lower. It pays, then, to make up a recipe that supplies more loaves or rolls than the family can eat at once. Freezer storage is also a good idea because homemade breads, having no preservatives, go stale quite rapidly. Wrap the baked goods securely, airtight, in heavy-duty foil or freezer paper. (If a frosting or glaze is called for, postpone that until after the bread is later thawed for use.) Date the packages, and freezer-store for up to 3 months. Three months is also the optimum freezer storage time for unbaked doughs, as well as for store-bought baked goods.

Crescents o' Corn Meal

Makes 32 rolls
  2 packages (¼ ounce each) active dry yeast
  ½ cup warm water (110° to 115°F.)
  1 cup scalded milk
  ½ cup butter or margarine
  ½ cup sugar
  2 teaspoons salt
  4½ to 5 cups all-purpose flour
  1¼ cups Quaker or Aunt Jemima Enriched Corn Meal
  2 eggs
  Butter or margarine, softened
  Melted butter
  2 tablespoons grated Parmesan cheese

Dissolve yeast in warm water. In large bowl, pour milk over ½ cup butter, sugar, and salt; cool to lukewarm. Stir in dissolved yeast, 1 cup flour, 1 cup cornmeal, and eggs. Add enough remaining flour to make soft dough. Knead on lightly floured surface for 6 to 8 minutes, or until smooth and elastic. Grease 2 large cookie sheets; sprinkle each with about 1 tablespoon cornmeal. Divide dough in half; roll out each half to form 12-inch circle. Spread each circle with about 2 tablespoons softened butter; cut each into 16 wedges. Roll up each wedge, beginning with wider end, shaping to form crescents. Place crescents point side down on prepared cookie sheets. Brush crescents lightly with melted butter. Combine remaining 2 tablespoons cornmeal and cheese; sprinkle over crescents.★ Cover with towel; let rise in warm place about 1 hour and 15 minutes, or until double in size. Heat oven to 400°F. Bake for 15 to 20 minutes, or until golden brown.
★At this point, dough can be covered with plastic wrap and refrigerated up to 24 hours. When ready to let rise, remove from refrigerator; remove plastic wrap. Cover; let rise in warm place about 2½ hours or until nearly double in size. Bake as recipe directs.

Oatmeal Muffins

Makes 12 muffins
  3 cups Elam's Scotch Style Oatmeal
  3 teaspoons sugar
  3 teaspoons baking powder
  ¾ teaspoon salt
  1½ cups milk
  1 egg, beaten
  3 tablespoons cooking oil or melted shortening

Combine first 4 ingredients in bowl; mix. Combine milk, egg, and oil; beat lightly. Add liquids to dry ingredients; stir just until dry ingredients are moistened. Fill greased 2½x1½-inch muffin cups about seven-eighths full using an equal amount of batter in each cup. Bake in hot oven (425°F.) until done and lightly browned, 20 to 25 minutes.

Sunflower-Nut Muffins

Makes 12 muffins
   2 cups Bisquick baking mix
   ¼ cup grated Parmesan cheese
   ¼ cup roasted salted sunflower nuts
   ½ cup mayonnaise or salad dressing
   ¼ cup milk
   2 tablespoons sugar
   2 tablespoons snipped chives or sliced green
      onion tops
   2 eggs
   2 tablespoons roasted salted sunflower nuts

Heat oven to 400°F. Grease bottoms only of 12 medium muffin cups, 2½x1¼ inches, or line with paper baking cups. Mix all ingredients except 2 tablespoons sunflower nuts; beat vigorously 30 seconds. Fill muffin cups about ⅔ full; sprinkle each with ½ teaspoon sunflower nuts. Bake until golden brown, 15 to 18 minutes. Wrap and freeze up to 2 months. To serve, place frozen muffins on ungreased cookie sheet. Heat in 400°F. oven until warm, 6 to 8 minutes.

Raisin English Muffins

Makes about 1 dozen muffins
   3 to 4 cups all-purpose flour
   2 packages (¼ ounce each) active dry yeast
   2 tablespoons sugar
   1 teaspoon salt
   1 cup milk
   ¼ cup water
   2 tablespoons oil
   1 cup raisins
      Cornmeal (about ⅓ cup)

Combine 1½ cups flour with yeast, sugar, and salt in large mixer bowl. In small saucepan, heat milk, water, and oil until warm (120° to 130°F.). Pour into dry ingredients and mix until smooth. Stir in enough remaining flour to make a soft dough. Turn out onto floured board and knead in raisins. Continue to knead an additional 2 to 3 minutes until dough is smooth and satiny. Cover; let rest 30 to 40 minutes. Meanwhile, sprinkle several tablespoons cornmeal onto waxed paper; set aside. On floured board, roll out dough to about ½-inch thickness. Cut into muffins with a 3- to 4-inch round cutter (a 6- or 7-ounce tuna can with ends removed works well). Transfer muffins onto waxed paper. Sprinkle remaining cornmeal on tops of muffins. Cover; let rest 30 to 40 minutes, or until slightly raised. Bake muffins on a lightly greased skillet or griddle over low heat until golden brown, 8 to 10 minutes on each side.★ Cool on wire racks.

★An electric skillet also works well. Cook muffins at the 275°F. setting.

Praline Muffins

Makes 1 dozen muffins
   6 tablespoons butter or margarine, melted
   ½ cup firmly packed brown sugar
   6 teaspoons water
  36 pecan halves
   1 cup (8 ounces) sour cream
   ¼ cup milk
  1½ cups Martha White BixMix

Preheat oven to 425°F. Spoon 1½ teaspoons butter, 2 teaspoons brown sugar, and ½ teaspoon water into each of 12 ungreased muffin cups. Arrange 3 pecan halves on top of brown sugar mixture in each cup. Combine sour cream, milk, and baking mix in bowl; stir until well blended. Spoon dough evenly into muffin cups. Bake 12 to 15 minutes, or until golden brown. Immediately invert pan onto serving plate. Let stand until syrup drizzles over sides of muffins.

Basic Muffins

Makes 12 muffins
   1 egg
   1 cup milk
   3 tablespoons vegetable shortening, melted, or
      vegetable oil
   2 cups sifted Martha White Self-Rising Flour
   2 tablespoons sugar

Preheat oven to 425°F. Grease 12 muffin cups; set aside. Break egg into bowl; beat lightly with fork. Stir in milk and shortening. Add flour and sugar; stir just until blended. Fill muffin cups about two-thirds full. Bake 20 minutes, or until golden brown.

Basic Muffins with Blueberries

Add 1 cup fresh or frozen blueberries to batter. Bake as for Basic Muffins.

Q. *My family likes muffins and quick breads such as orange-raisin or apple-pecan. Mine have good flavor, but the texture is coarse and has a lot of holes. What am I doing wrong?*
A. You're being too good to them, probably—beating them too much. In fact, don't beat them at all. Stir, and then only until the dry ingredients are completely moistened. The batter will look lumpy but the texture of the finished product will be good.

Honey Muffins

Makes 1 dozen muffins
- ¼ **cup margarine**
- ½ **cup honey or sugar**
- 2 **eggs**
- 1 **cup cooked Riceland Rice**
- 1 **cup buttermilk**
- 2 **cups sifted all-purpose flour**
- 1 **tablespoon baking powder**
- 1 **teaspoon salt**
- ½ **teaspoon baking soda**

Beat margarine and honey or sugar until light. Add eggs and rice and continue beating 2 to 3 minutes. Add milk and dry ingredients that have been sifted together. Stir with spoon only until well blended. Fill greased muffin pan two-thirds full. Bake at 400°F. for 20 minutes, or until done. Remove from pan at once.

Pumpkin-Raisin Muffins

Makes 1 dozen muffins
- 1 **package (16.1 ounces) nut bread mix**
- 1½ **cups Libby's Pumpkin Pie Mix**
- ½ **cup raisins**
- 1 **egg, beaten**
- 1 **tablespoon sugar**
- ½ **teaspoon ground cinnamon**

Preheat oven to 375°F. Grease bottom only, or line medium-size muffin pans with liners. Combine nut bread mix, pumpkin pie mix, raisins, and egg; mix until just moistened. Spoon into muffin pans, filling each cup two-thirds full. Sprinkle top of each muffin with combined sugar and cinnamon. Bake 20 to 25 minutes, or until wooden toothpick inserted in center comes out clean. Cool 5 minutes; remove from pans.

Whole Wheat-Bran Muffins

Makes 10 muffins
- ½ **cup whole wheat flour**
- 1½ **cups wheat bran morsel cereal**
- ¼ **cup firmly packed light or dark brown sugar**
- 1 **teaspoon baking powder**
- ½ **teaspoon baking soda**
- ½ **teaspoon salt**
- ½ **cup Sun-Maid® Puffed Seeded Muscat Raisins**
- 1 **egg**
- ⅔ **cup buttermilk**
- 3 **tablespoons vegetable oil**
- **Butter and jam**

Grease ten ½-inch muffin cups well, or line with paper baking cups. Preheat the oven to 400°F. In a large mixing bowl, toss the flour, bran cereal, sugar, baking powder, baking soda, salt, and raisins until very well mixed and raisins are coated. Beat the egg lightly in a small mixing bowl and stir in the buttermilk and oil. Add buttermilk mixture to flour mixture all at once. Stir lightly with a fork until the ingredients are fairly well mixed but the batter is still somewhat lumpy. Spoon the batter into the prepared muffin cups, filling each about two-thirds full. Bake for 18 to 20 minutes, or until muffins are well browned. Remove from pans and serve immediately with butter and jam.

Date-Bran Muffins

Makes 1 dozen muffins
- ¼ **cup soft shortening or butter**
- ¼ **cup Sue Bee Honey**
- 1 **egg**
- ¾ **cup milk**
- 1 **cup whole bran**
- 1 **cup pitted dates, snipped**
- 1 **cup sifted all-purpose flour**
- 2 **teaspoons baking powder**
- ½ **teaspoon salt**

Cream together shortening and honey. Add egg, beat well. Stir in milk, bran, and dates. Sift together flour, baking powder, and salt. Add to batter. Stir just to moisten ingredients. Batter will look lumpy. Spoon into 12 greased 2½-inch muffin-pan cups. Fill two-thirds full. Bake at 400°F. for 20 to 25 minutes, or until done.

English Muffins

A large number of people start the day with a split and toasted English muffin, eaten austerely plain or slathered with jam, jelly, honey, or marmalade. English muffins are leavened with yeast; not kneaded, after their first rising they are rolled out on a board sprinkled with cornmeal, cut in 3- to 4-inch rounds, set to rise again on a cornmeal-covered board, then stove-top-baked on an ungreased griddle. Available almost everywhere, in both restaurants and food markets, English muffins once came in only one kind—plain white—but there are now cornmeal English, sourdough, whole wheat, and raisin-studded bran, among others.

English muffins aren't the only yeast-raised muffins. There are several kinds, baked conventionally in muffin tins in the oven, that are raised with yeast or sourdough. But those leavened with baking powder or soda—the quick-bread muffins of all kinds—are by far the more popular in this country.

Baking Pans for Breads

Both shape and size are important when you choose a pan in which to bake your bread: shape, because the shape of the pan will determine the shape of the finished product, and size, because a too-large or too-small pan can result in a disappointing product. **Loaves** —Pans to bake loaves of bread (and meat loaf, and any other loaf-shape food) are longer than they are wide, and provided with high sides up which the bread can "climb" as it rises. The most common size, used for white or whole wheat loaves, is 9 inches long by 5 inches wide; a slightly smaller size, 8 by 4 inches, is used for sweet fruit and/or nut loaves. **Cottage Loaves**—These and their cousins, squaw bread and sheepherder's bread, are round, slightly flattened in shape, and crusted on the sides as well as the top. These are shaped and baked on baking sheets or any other low-sided pan larger than the finished loaf will be. **Rolls and Biscuits**—The distinction here is that rolls are yeast-raised, while biscuits are leavened with baking powder or soda. Simple shapes of either are baked on baking sheets or smaller pans with low to medium sides. You must know whether the sides of the biscuits or rolls are meant to be soft or crusty. If soft, they should be baked close together, their sides touching; if crusty, spaces between will allow the heat to form a crust on both sides. Some rolls, such as cottage or white mountain, meant to be pulled apart before serving, are baked in 8- or 9-inch square pans. Cloverleaf rolls, each formed of three balls of dough, are baked in muffin tins. **Sweet Rolls**—Again, whether they are meant to be crusty or soft on the sides governs whether they are placed close together, sides touching, or spaced a bit further apart. In either case, use a baking sheet for sweet rolls, which do not rise high—Danish, snails, elephant ears, and such; the same baking sheet does well for sweet rolls that are a bit thicker and "breadier," such as bear claws. Old-fashioned cinnamon rolls are baked close together in a square or oblong pan; the closeness forces them to rise up because they cannot expand sideways, exactly the desired condition for these rolls. Sticky buns are sometimes baked in a square pan, with sides high enough to contain the gooey mixture in which they are placed, and sometimes in individual muffin tins. **Popovers**— Each popover requires individual baking space. Heavy muffin tins will do, but old-fashioned black iron gem pans, dear to Grandma's heart, produce higher, crustier popovers. Or, if you wish, custard cups may be used, as long as they are the proper shape: deeper than they are wide. **Coffee Cakes**—These, if they are circular, are shaped and baked on baking sheets or in round pans, such as large layer-cake pans, or pizza bakers. Coffee cakes with lots of topping, such as crumb cakes or streusel breads, are better off in square pans with higher sides than baking sheets offer to contain those good toppings. **Muffins and Quick Breads**— These bake in a variety of pans. Muffins go into muffin tins, not surprisingly, which come in an assortment of cup sizes from one mouthful to a hearty 3-inch diameter; old-fashioned gem pans, of black iron, are staging a comeback and are fine for muffins, too— some of them produce a number of attractive shapes. Quick breads are generally baked in loaf pans—smaller than those used for yeast breads—but sometimes in ovenproof ring molds. **Casserole and Batter Breads**—These, yeast raised or leavened, need high sides to climb and are baked in casserole or other deep dishes.

Peanut Butter Muffins

Makes 1 dozen muffins

- **1 cup Elam's Unbleached White Flour with Wheat Germ**
- **4 teaspoons baking powder**
- **¾ teaspoon salt**
- **1 cup Elam's Stone Ground 100% Whole Yellow Corn Meal★**
- **⅓ cup turbinado or firmly packed brown sugar**
- **½ cup Elam's Natural Peanut Butter with Defatted Wheat Germ**
- **1 cup milk**
- **1 egg, beaten**
- **¼ cup cooking oil or melted shortening**

Combine and sift first 3 ingredients into bowl. Stir in cornmeal and turbinado or brown sugar. Add peanut butter; cut in with pastry blender or knives until mixture resembles coarse crumbs. Combine and mix milk, egg, and oil or melted shortening. Add liquids to dry ingredients; stir just until dry ingredients are moistened. Fill greased 2½x1¼-inch muffin cups three-quarters full. Bake in hot oven (400°F.) until done and lightly browned, about 20 minutes.

★Elam's Organically Grown Stone Ground 100% Whole Yellow Corn Meal may be substituted, if desired.

Sweetness and Light

Coffee cake is everyone's favorite, streusel-topped or sugared or iced, rich with nuts or fruit or a sweet filling. Make a pair, freeze one for later.

Almond Kringle

Makes 2 coffee cakes

4 cups all-purpose flour
1 teaspoon salt
2 tablespoons sugar
1 cup butter or margarine, softened
¼ cup warm water (105° to 115°F.)
1 package (¼ ounce) active dry yeast
¾ cup milk
2 eggs, well beaten
1 can (12½ ounces) Solo Almond Filling
Browned Butter Icing (recipe follows)

Sift together flour, salt, and sugar. Using a pastry blender or 2 knives, cut butter into mixture. Into a warm bowl, measure water. Sprinkle in yeast; stir until dissolved. Combine milk and eggs. Add to flour mixture along with yeast, mixing just enough to dampen flour. Cover and refrigerate overnight. Divide dough in half. Return half to refrigerator. On a lightly floured board, roll remaining half to an 18x16-inch rectangle. Spread half the almond filling in a lengthwise strip down center of dough. Fold one side over filling and overlap with other side. Pinch ends together. Turn dough over on a baking sheet so lapped side is down. Form into an oval shape. Cover dough and let rise in a warm place, free from draft, until double in bulk, about 1 hour. Repeat with remaining dough. Preheat oven to 375°F. Bake 25 minutes, or until golden brown. While warm, frost with Browned Butter Icing.

Browned Butter Icing

⅓ cup butter or margarine, softened
3 cups sifted confectioners sugar
3 tablespoons light cream
1½ teaspoons vanilla extract

Place butter in saucepan and brown lightly over medium heat. Add sugar and blend. Stir in cream and vanilla until smooth.

Prune Ring (page 93); Coconut Rolls (page 105); Apricot-Rum Baba (page 81). Solo Food Products

Sweet Dough for Coffee Cakes

Makes 2 coffee cakes

½ cup milk
½ cup sugar
¼ teaspoon salt
½ cup butter or margarine
½ cup warm water (105° to 115°F.)
2 packages (¼ ounce each) active dry yeast
2 eggs, well beaten
½ teaspoon almond or vanilla extract
4 to 5 cups all-purpose flour

Scald milk. Stir in sugar, salt, and butter. Cool to lukewarm. Measure warm water into a large warm bowl. Sprinkle in yeast. Stir until dissolved. Stir in lukewarm milk mixture, beaten eggs, desired extract, and half the flour. Beat until smooth. Stir in enough additional flour to make a slightly stiff dough. Turn out onto a lightly floured board. Knead until smooth and elastic, about 8 minutes. Place in a greased bowl, turning to grease top of dough. Cover; let rise in a warm place, free from draft, until double in bulk, about 1 hour. Use this dough in any recipe that you desire, using desired fillings or shapes.

Good idea: If you have an electric oven, a great place to let bread rise is in the oven with the oven light on. The light provides warmth and the oven itself is virtually draft-free.

Granola Coffee Ring

Makes one 10-inch coffee cake
- 1 cup granola
- ¾ cup sour cream
- 1 cup all-purpose flour
- ¾ teaspoon baking soda
- ¾ teaspoon baking powder
- ½ teaspoon salt
- ½ teaspoon mace
- ½ cup butter, softened
- ½ cup sugar
- 3 eggs
- ½ cup firmly packed brown sugar
- 2 tablespoons sour cream
- ½ teaspoon ground cinnamon
- 1 cup (6-ounce package) Nestlé Butterscotch Flavored Morsels

In a large bowl, combine granola and sour cream; let stand 15 minutes to soften cereal. Preheat oven to 350°F. In a small bowl, combine flour, baking soda, baking powder, salt, and mace; set aside. Beat butter, sugar, and eggs into granola-sour cream mixture. Stir in flour mixture; set aside.

In a small bowl, mix brown sugar, nuts, sour cream, and cinnamon. Spread half the granola batter into greased and floured 10-inch tube pan; dot with half the brown sugar mixture and sprinkle with Nestlé Butterscotch Flavored Morsels. Cover with remaining batter; top with remaining filling. Bake 50 minutes. Loosen edges. Cool cake completely; remove from pan.

Coffee Ring

Makes one 8-inch ring or 10 biscuits
- 1 dozen toasted almonds
- 1 dozen maraschino cherries
- 1 package (8 ounces) refrigerated biscuits
- ¼ cup butter or margarine, melted
- ½ cup sugar
- ½ can (6¼ ounces) Solo Almond Filling
- 2 tablespoons light cream or sherry

Preheat oven to 400°F. Grease an 8-inch ring mold. Arrange almonds and cherries in bottom of mold. Cut refrigerated biscuits in half lengthwise. Dip each half in melted butter, then in sugar. Place half the biscuits in bottom of prepared pan. Combine filling and cream or sherry, blending to make a smooth mixture. Spread over top of biscuits. Top with remaining biscuit halves. Bake 20 to 25 minutes, or until lightly browned. Let stand on wire rack about 3 minutes. Invert onto serving plate and remove pan. Serve either warm or cold. The ring can be cut when cold, or the individual biscuits can be pulled off.

Walnut-Apple Ring

Makes one 10-inch ring
- 1 cups unsifted whole wheat flour
- 1½ cups all-purpose flour
- 1 tablespoon baking powder
- 1 teaspoon salt
- ¾ teaspoon baking soda
- ⅔ cup Hollywood Safflower Oil
- 1⅔ cups firmly packed light brown sugar, divided
- 6 egg whites or 4 whole eggs
- ¼ cup milk
- 2¼ teaspoons vanilla extract
- 1½ teaspoons ground cinnamon
- ¼ teaspoon ground allspice
- 4 cups diced tart apples, unpeeled
- 1 cup coarsely chopped walnuts, divided
- Confectioners Glaze (recipe follows) (optional)

Preheat oven to 350°F. Grease and flour a 10-inch tube pan; set aside. In a large bowl, combine whole wheat and all-purpose flours, baking powder, salt, and baking soda; set aside. In a large mixing bowl of an electric mixer, beat safflower oil and 1⅓ cups of the brown sugar until combined. Gradually beat in eggs until blended. Mix in milk and vanilla; beat until sugar is dissolved, about 2 minutes. Gradually mix in reserved flour mixture, blending just until combined. In a medium bowl, combine remaining ⅓ cup brown sugar with cinnamon and allspice; add apples and ½ cup of the walnuts; mix well. Stir into batter. Spoon into prepared pan. Sprinkle the top of batter with remaining ½ cup walnuts. Bake until a cake tester inserted into center comes out clean, about 1 hour and 15 minutes. Let cake cool in pan for about 30 minutes. Loosen edges with a spatula and turn out onto a serving plate. Serve warm. Or, if desired, spoon Confectioners Glaze over cake. Wrap cake and store in refrigerator.

Confectioners Glaze
- 1 tablespoon milk
- ½ cup confectioners sugar
- ½ teaspoon vanilla extract

In a small saucepan, heat milk until hot. In a small bowl, combine confectioners sugar with 1½ teaspoons of the hot milk and vanilla. Gradually stir in more hot milk until mixture is the consistency of a thick white sauce.

> ## "Come for Brunch"
> A weekend or holiday buffet brunch is a splendid way to entertain and—a bonus—is likely to be much less costly than a dinner for the same number of guests. To serve as the focal point of the buffet table, plan on a pair of handsome and delicious homemade coffee cakes. They can be baked the day before or, if you like, any time up to a month in advance and frozen.

Prune Pinwheels

Makes 10 rolls

    3 cups all-purpose flour
    4 teaspoons baking powder
    ½ teaspoon salt
    ½ cup butter or margarine, softened
    1 cup milk
    1 can (12 ounces) Solo Prune Filling or any
        desired nut filling
      Brown sugar (optional)
      Nuts (optional)

Preheat oven to 400°F. Heavily butter a 9-inch layer cake pan. Stir together flour, baking powder, and salt. Using a pastry blender or 2 knives, cut in butter until mixture resembles coarse crumbs. Add milk and stir until well blended. Turn dough out onto a lightly floured board and knead 10 to 12 times, or until a smooth ball is formed. Roll dough into a 10x16-inch rectangle. Spread prune filling over top of dough. Starting at the long side, roll dough up, jelly roll fashion. Moisten edge and press gently together to seal. Cut roll into 10 slices. Place slices cut side down in prepared pan. Bake 35 minutes, or until lightly browned. Serve warm. If desired, for added taste, sprinkle the bottom of the pan with brown sugar and a few nuts before rolls are placed in it.

Apricot-Rum Baba

Makes 6 to 8 servings

    ¾ cup warm water (105° to 115°F.)
    1 package (13¾ ounces) hot roll mix
    ⅓ cup sugar
    6 tablespoons butter or margarine, softened
    2 eggs
    ½ cup Solo Apricot Filling
    ¼ cup rum

Grease a 6½-cup baba pan. Measure water into a large warm bowl. Sprinkle yeast from roll mix over water; stir until dissolved. Add sugar, butter, and eggs and blend well. Stir in roll mix and beat well. Spoon batter into prepared baba pan. Cover and let rise in a warm place, free from draft, until almost double in bulk, 30 to 45 minutes. Preheat oven to 400°F. Bake 30 minutes. (If top of cake begins to brown too much, cover with a piece of aluminum foil.) In a small saucepan, heat apricot filling until warm. Stir in rum. Turn baba out of mold into a shallow pan. Spoon sauce over baba immediately. Combine basting with mixture until baba has absorbed all of the mixture. Cool before serving.

Swedish Tea Ring

Makes 3 coffee cakes

    1½ cups milk
    1¼ cups plus 2 tablespoons butter or margarine,
        divided
    1½ cups sugar, divided
    2 packages (¼ ounce each) active dry yeast
    1½ teaspoons salt
    6½ to 7 cups sifted Martha White All-Purpose
        Flour, divided
    3 eggs
    ½ teaspoon vanilla extract
    1 tablespoon ground cinnamon
    1 cup confectioners sugar
    1½ to 2 tablespoons milk

Grease large bowl; set aside. Heat 1½ cups milk and 1 cup butter in saucepan until very warm (120° to 130°F. Butter need not melt completely). Combine ½ cup sugar, yeast, salt, and 2 cups flour in large mixing bowl. Gradually beat in warm milk mixture at low speed of electric mixer until blended. Beat at medium speed 2 minutes. Add eggs, vanilla, and 2½ cups flour; beat 2 minutes. Use wooden spoon to stir in enough remaining flour to make a soft dough. Turn out onto lightly floured board or pastry cloth. Knead 8 to 10 minutes, or until smooth and elastic. Place dough in prepared bowl. Turn once to grease top. Cover and let rise in warm place, free from draft, 1 hour, or until double in bulk. Punch dough down; divide into thirds. Return two-thirds to bowl; set aside. Grease 3 large baking sheets; set aside. Roll one-third dough into 20x7-inch rectangle on lightly floured board or pastry cloth. Melt 2 tablespoons butter and brush evenly over dough within 1 inch of edges. Combine remaining 1 cup sugar and cinnamon in small dish; blend well. Sprinkle ⅓ cup sugar-cinnamon mixture evenly over dough within 1 inch of edges. Roll up, jelly roll fashion, from long side; pinch edges to seal. Place roll, seam side down, on prepared baking sheet. Shape into a ring; pinch ends to seal. Use scissors to cut dough at 1-inch intervals around ring, cutting two-thirds through roll with each cut. Gently turn each cut piece of dough on its side, slightly overlapping slices. Repeat with remaining two-thirds dough. Cover rings and let rise in warm place, free from draft, 45 minutes, or until double in bulk. Preheat oven to 375°F. Bake 20 to 25 minutes, or until golden brown. Transfer to wire racks. Combine confectioners sugar and 1½ tablespoons milk in small bowl; blend well. Drizzle over rings while warm.

Sour Cream Coffee Cake (page 92). Caloric Corporation

Mama's Indiana Bread. The Reynolds Wrap Kitchen

Mama's Indiana Bread

Makes 2 loaves

    2 packages (¼ ounce each) active dry yeast
    ½ cup warm water (105°F.)
    ½ cup butter or margarine, softened
    ½ cup sugar
    2 teaspoons salt
    ½ cup boiling water
    4 eggs
    6 cups all-purpose flour, divided
    ⅓ cup raisins
    ⅓ cup chopped nuts
      Oil

Dissolve yeast in warm water; set aside. Combine butter, sugar, and salt in large bowl. Stir in boiling water. Beat in eggs with electric mixer. Stir in half of flour with wooden spoon; blend in yeast mixture. Add enough flour to form a soft dough. Toss raisins and nuts with 1 tablespoon flour; spread on well-floured board. Turn out dough onto raisins and nuts; knead until smooth and elastic, 6 to 8 minutes. Place dough in well-oiled bowl; turn dough once. Cover with damp towel and let rise in a warm place until double in size, about 2 hours. Punch down dough. Divide and shape. Place in 2 greased Reynolds Redi-Pan loaf or round cake pans. Cover with damp towel until doubled. Bake in preheated 350°F. oven 40 to 50 minutes, or until golden brown. Remove from pans; cool on wire rack 10 minutes. Brush with melted butter. Serve warm.

Clara's Holiday Orange-Nut Bread

Makes 1 loaf

    2¼ cups all-purpose flour
     ¾ cup sugar
      1 tablespoon grated orange peel
    2¼ teaspoons baking powder
     ½ teaspoon salt
     ¼ teaspoon baking soda
      1 cup Orange Peel Preserves, finely chopped
     ½ cup mixed candied fruit
      2 tablespoons shortening
      1 large egg
     ¾ cup Florida orange juice
      1 cup chopped walnuts

Grease a 9x5x3-inch loaf pan; set aside. In a large bowl, mix flour, sugar, grated orange peel, baking powder, salt, and baking soda. Add Orange Peel Preserves and candied fruit; toss to coat fruit. Add shortening, egg, and orange juice; stir with a wooden spoon until dry ingredients are moistened. Stir in nuts. Spread

Clara's Holiday Orange-Nut Bread. Florida Department of Citrus

batter evenly into prepared pan. Bake in a 350°F. oven 50 to 60 minutes, or until a cake tester inserted in center of bread comes out clean. Remove from oven; cool 5 minutes. Turn out of pan; cool completely on wire rack. Wrap tightly in plastic wrap or foil; let stand 24 hours.

Coconut Coffee Cake

Makes 2 coffee cakes

    1 recipe Sweet Yeast Dough (see index)
    3 cups grated coconut, divided
    ½ cup sugar
    ½ cup butter or margarine
    ¼ cup honey
    2 tablespoons milk
    ¼ teaspoon almond extract
      Confectioners Icing (see index)

Prepare Sweet Yeast Dough. While dough is rising, combine 2½ cups coconut, sugar, butter, honey, and milk in saucepan; bring to a boil, stirring constantly. Remove from heat; let stand until cool. Stir in almond extract. When dough is double in bulk, punch down; let rest 10 minutes. Divide dough in half. Roll out each half into 14 x 8-inch rectangle. Spread half of the coconut filling lengthwise down center 3 inches of 1 rectangle. Beginning 2 inches from 1 end on long side of dough and up to the filling, make 6 slits at 2-inch intervals to outside edge of dough. (This will make 7 strips.) Repeat for other side of dough. Beginning on 1 end, overlap 1 strip from each side over filling. Pull end strips down and under, tucking them in. Repeat with remaining dough rectangle. Cover and let rise in warm place, free from draft, 35 minutes, or until almost double in bulk. Preheat oven to 350°F. Bake 30 to 35 minutes, or until golden brown. Frost with Confectioners Icing while still warm. Sprinkle each coffeecake with 1/4 cup remaining coconut.

Mexican Sweet Bread

Makes about 32 buns

   1 recipe Sweet Yeast Dough (see index)
   2 cups sugar
   2 cups sifted Martha White All-Purpose Flour
   1 cup butter or margarine, melted
   2 eggs, lightly beaten
   1 teaspoon ground cinnamon
     Dash salt

Prepare Sweet Yeast Dough. After dough has risen, punch down; let rest 10 minutes. Grease 2 large baking sheets; set aside. Combine remaining ingredients in bowl; blend well; set aside. Shape pieces of dough into smooth 1¾-inch balls. Flatten balls with palm of hand or rolling pin into 4-inch rounds. Place rounds about 2 inches apart on prepared baking sheets. Place heaping tablespoonful of sugar mixture on center of each round; spread almost to edges. Cover and let rise in warm place, free from draft, 30 minutes, or until double in bulk. Preheat oven to 400°F. Bake 10 minutes, or until lightly browned. Cool 3 to 4 minutes on wire rack before serving.

Carolina Coffee Cake

Makes 1 coffee cake

   ½ cup firmly packed brown sugar
   2 tablespoons Martha White All-Purpose Flour*
   1 teaspoon ground cinnamon
   2 tablespoons butter or margarine
   ¾ cup sugar
   ⅓ cup vegetable shortening
   2 eggs
   1¾ cups sifted Martha White Self-Rising Flour
   ¾ cup milk
   ⅓ cup chopped nuts

Preheat oven to 375°F. Grease 10-inch round baking pan or iron skillet; set aside. Combine brown sugar, all-purpose flour, cinnamon, and butter in small bowl; blend with pastry blender or 2 knives until mixture is consistency of coarse crumbs; set aside. Cream sugar and shortening with electric mixer in mixing bowl until light and fluffy. Add eggs, one at a time, beating well after each addition. Alternately beat in self-rising flour and milk, in thirds. Stir in nuts. Pour into prepared pan. Sprinkle with brown mixture. Bake 30 to 35 minutes, or until wooden toothpick inserted in center comes out clean.

*If using all-purpose flour, sift 2½ teaspoons baking powder and ½ teaspoon salt with flour.

Pecan-Sour Cream Coffee Loaf

Makes 1 loaf

   ½ cup chopped nuts
   3 tablespoons brown sugar
   1 teaspoon ground cinnamon
   ½ cup butter or margarine
   1¼ cups sugar
   3 eggs
   1 cup (8 ounces) sour cream
   1 teaspoon grated lemon peel
   2 cups sifted Martha White Self-Rising Flour

Preheat oven to 350°F. Grease bottom of 9x5x3-inch loaf pan; set aside. Combine nuts, brown sugar, and cinnamon in small bowl; set aside. Cream butter and sugar with electric mixer in mixing bowl until light and fluffy. Add eggs, 1 at a time, beating well after each addition. Stir in sour cream and lemon peel. Gradually add flour, mixing just until blended. Pour half of the batter into prepared pan. Spoon half the nut mixture over batter. Spoon on remaining batter. Sprinkle with remaining nut mixture; press nuts gently into top. Bake 50 to 60 minutes, or until golden brown. Cool in pan 10 minutes. Gently loosen sides of loaf. Turn out onto wire rack to cool completely.

Cinnamon-Raisin Bread

Makes 2 loaves

   1 recipe Sweet Yeast Dough (see index)
   ½ cup raisins
   ¼ cup butter or margarine, melted
   1 cup sugar
   2 tablespoons ground cinnamon
     Confectioners Icing (see index) (optional)

Prepare Sweet Yeast Dough. After dough has risen, punch down; let rest 10 minutes. Grease two 9x5x3-inch loaf pans; set aside. Lightly knead raisins into dough. Divide dough in half. Roll out each half into 9x7-inch rectangle. Brush each rectangle with half of the butter. Combine sugar and cinnamon in small bowl; blend well. Sprinkle each rectangle with half of the sugar-cinnamon mixture. Roll up, jelly roll fashion, from long side. Fold ends under; press edges to seal. Place in prepared pans. Cover and let rise in warm place, free from draft, 45 minutes, or until double in bulk. Preheat oven to 375°F. Bake 30 to 35 minutes, or until loaves sound hollow when lightly tapped. Turn out onto wire racks to cool. Frost with Confectioners Icing, if desired.

Whole Wheat Coffee Cake

Makes 1 coffee cake

     1 **cup boiling water**
     1 **package (8 ounces) dates, chopped**
    ¾ **cup sifted Martha White Self-Rising Flour★**
    ¾ **cup Martha White Whole Wheat Flour**
    ½ **cup firmly packed brown sugar**
    ⅓ **cup sugar**
    ½ **cup butter or margarine, softened**
     2 **eggs, lightly beaten**
    1½ **teaspoons vanilla extract**
       Pecan Glaze (recipe follows)

Combine water and dates in small bowl; let stand until cool. Preheat oven to 375°F. Grease and flour 9-inch square baking pan; set aside. Combine flours and sugars in bowl. Cut in butter with pastry blender or 2 knives until mixture is consistency of coarse crumbs. Add date mixture, eggs, and vanilla; stir just until blended. Pour into prepared pan. Bake 35 to 40 minutes, or until cake shrinks away slightly from sides of pan. Remove from oven. Pour Pecan Glaze over cake in pan. Cool 10 to 15 minutes before cutting into squares.

★If using all-purpose flour, add 1½ teaspoons baking powder and 1 teaspoon salt.

Pecan Glaze

    1½ **cups confectioners sugar**
     3 **tablespoons milk**
     1 **teaspoon vanilla extract**
    ½ **teaspoon almond extract**
    ½ **cup chopped pecans**

Combine all ingredients except pecans in small bowl; stir until smooth. Stir in pecans.

Sunday Brunch Coffee Cake

Makes 16 servings

    ¼ **cup butter or margarine**
     1 **cup sugar**
     2 **eggs**
    1½ **cups plus 2 tablespoons sifted cake flour**
    ¼ **teaspoon salt**
    2¾ **teaspoons baking powder**
    ½ **cup milk**
     1 **tablespoon butter, melted**
     3 **tablespoons sugar**
    ½ **cup chopped walnuts**

Sweetening with Honey

Replace sugar with honey in your own favorite recipes! Substitute honey for the sugar called for, cup for cup. As a rule, reduce the liquid called for by one-fourth cup for every cup of honey used to replace the sugar.

In baked goods, add ½ teaspoon of baking soda to the recipe for every cup of honey substituted and bake at a temperature 25°F. lower than instructions call for. Baked goods made with honey are tender, moist, and have a remarkable "keeping" quality. You can make party desserts well ahead of time, prepare honeyed breads, cookies, and cakes for lunch-box treats or to send off to faraway friends, knowing every bite will stay moist and delicious.

Honey spreads for hot breads, snacks, and hearty sandwiches are quick, easy, and so good! Try honey with drained and mashed frozen strawberries on hot cakes. Or blend cream cheese with honey and a touch of lemon juice as a snack-cracker spread. And don't forget peanut butter and honey for delicious sandwiches!

For a delicious breakfast spread, mix 2 parts whipped margarine with 1 part honey (½ pound to 1 cup). Delicious on toast, French toast, hot cakes, waffles, fried mush—even on grapefruit halves before broiling. Extra good with a sprinkling of ground cinnamon—or lightly frosted with a dab of jelly or preserves!

Honey keeps best in a dry place, because it absorbs moisture. Refrigeration only hastens granulation, so a kitchen shelf is the best place. Granulation is natural for honey and doesn't spoil it. It can be easily reliquified by standing the honey container in hot (not boiling water, or by placing it in a very, very low (200°F. or lower) oven. Honey will remain liquid and unharmed if you prefer to store it in your freezer at a below-zero temperature.

Preheat oven to 350°F. Place butter and 1 cup sugar in large bowl of Sunbeam Mixmaster Mixer. With dial set at medium, cream until fluffy. Add eggs and beat until creamy. Sift dry ingredients together. Add to butter mixture alternately with milk, with dial set at lowest. Pour into a greased 8-inch square pan. Spread melted butter over top. Sprinkle with 3 tablespoons sugar and the walnuts. Bake 45 minutes. Cut in squares and serve hot.

Golden Upside-Down Snack Bread. Cling Peach Advisory Board

Panettone

Makes 1 loaf
- ⅓ cup milk
- 2 packages (¼ ounce each) active dry yeast
- 3¾ to 4¼ cups all-purpose flour, divided
- ½ cup butter or margarine, softened
- ¾ cup sugar
- 4 eggs
- 1 cup Sun-Maid® Zante Currants
- ½ cup finely chopped mixed candied fruit
- ½ cup chopped almonds, divided

Heat the milk until lukewarm (110° to 115°F.) and stir in the yeast until dissolved. Add ¼ cup of the flour and stir until smooth. Cover and let rise in a warm place, free from draft, until bubbly, about 15 minutes. In a large electric mixer bowl, cream the butter and sugar until fluffy. Add the eggs and beat until fluffy. Blend in the yeast mixture and 1 cup of the remaining flour; beat for 2 minutes at medium speed. Add ½ cup of the remaining flour and beat for 5 minutes at high speed, or until the batter is shiny and "sheets" off a spoon. Stir in the currants, candied fruit, ⅓ cup chopped almonds, and about 2 cups of the remaining flour, or enough to make a firm dough. Turn out on a floured surface and knead until smooth and elastic, about 10 minutes. Place in a greased bowl and turn once to grease the surface. Cover and let rise in a warm place, free from draft, until double in bulk, about 1½ to 2 hours. Grease a 10-inch tube pan. Sprinkle with additional sugar and remaining almonds. Punch the dough down and roll it out on a lightly floured surface into a 15x10-inch rectangle. Starting with the long side, roll up the dough jelly roll fashion, pinching the seam to seal. Fit into the prepared pan, seam side down, and pinch the ends to join. Cover and let rise until double in bulk, about 1 hour. Preheat the oven to 350°F. Bake for 45 to 50 minutes, or until the top of the bread is browned and the loaf sounds hollow when tapped with the fingers. (If the bread starts to get too brown during the baking, lightly cover the top with a piece of foil.) Remove from pan and cool on a wire rack.

Blueberry-Nut Coffee Cake

Makes 16 servings
- 2 packages (7 ounces each) Martha White Blueberry Muffin Mix
- 1 cup milk
- ½ cup chopped nuts (optional)
- Crumble Topping (recipe follows)

Preheat oven to 375°F. Grease 9-inch square baking pan; set aside. Pour muffin mix into bowl. Add milk and nuts; stir just until blended. Spread evenly in prepared pan. Sprinkle with Crumble Topping. Use a knife to gently swirl topping into batter; do not mix. Bake 30 to 35 minutes, or until golden brown. Cut into squares and serve warm.

Crumble Topping

- ½ cup firmly packed brown sugar
- 2 tablespoons Martha White All-Purpose Flour
- 1 teaspoon ground cinnamon
- 2 tablespoons butter or margarine

Combine all ingredients in small bowl; mix with pastry blender or 2 knives until crumbly.

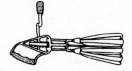

Golden Upside-Down Snack Bread

Makes 6 to 8 servings
- ¼ cup butter
- ½ cup firmly packed brown sugar
- ⅓ cup toasted slivered almonds
- 1 can (29 ounces) cling peach halves
- 2 cups biscuit mix
- 1 cup sour cream
- ¼ cup sugar
- 1 egg
- 2 teaspoons grated lemon peel
- Sour cream (optional)
- Brown sugar (optional)

Grease 9-inch round layer pan with 2 tablespoons butter. Sprinkle bottom with brown sugar and almonds. Drain peaches and arrange on top of mixture. Stir in biscuit mix, sour cream, 2 tablespoons melted butter, sugar, unbeaten egg, and lemon rind just until blended; then beat well, about 30 seconds. Spread mixture evenly over peaches and bake in 400°F. oven 20 to 25 minutes. Cool 5 minutes; turn out onto rack. If desired, spoon dollop of sour cream into each peach cup and sprinkle with brown sugar.

Cinnamon Swirl Bread

Makes 1 loaf

    6 tablespoons C & H Granulated Sugar, divided
    1 package (¼ ounce) active dry yeast
    ½ teaspoon salt
    3 to 3½ cups all-purpose flour
    ½ cup milk
    ¼ cup water
    ¼ cup butter or margarine
    1 egg
    1 tablespoon butter, melted
    ½ teaspoon ground cinnamon

Grease 9x5x3-inch loaf pan. In large bowl, mix ¼ cup sugar, yeast, salt, and 1 cup of the flour. Heat milk, water, and ¼ cup butter until lukewarm (110°F.)—butter will not be melted. Add to flour mixture; beat 1 minute. Add 1 cup additional flour and the egg; beat 2 minutes. With a spoon, stir in 1 to 1½ cups flour until dough holds shape. Turn out onto floured board. Knead 8 minutes, or until dough is smooth and elastic (it should not be firm or sticky). Cover with waxed paper and towel. Let rest 20 minutes. Punch dough down and roll into an 8x15-inch rectangle. Brush with melted butter. Sprinkle with 2 tablespoons sugar and the cinnamon. Starting with narrow end, roll up jelly roll fashion. Seal ends; place seam side down in loaf pan. Cover pan with plastic wrap; refrigerate 2 to 4 hours. Before baking, remove wrap. Pierce any air bubbles with oiled toothpick. Let stand at room temperature 20 minutes while oven preheats to 350°F. Bake 40 to 45 minutes, or until bread sounds hollow when tapped. Turn out onto rack to cool.

Golden Brown Buttermilk Coffee Cake

Makes 12 to 16 servings

    ¾ cup firmly packed C & H Golden Brown Sugar
    ½ cup butter, softened
    3 eggs
    3 cups all-purpose flour
    2 teaspoons baking powder
    1 teaspoon baking soda
    ½ teaspoon salt
    1 cup buttermilk
    1 teaspoon vanilla extract
    Pecan Crumb Filling (recipe follows)

Preheat oven to 350°F. Grease 3-quart fluted tube pan. Cream sugar, butter, and eggs. Combine flour, baking powder, soda, and salt. Add alternately with buttermilk to sugar mixture. Stir in vanilla (batter will be thick). Spoon half the batter into pan, then sprinkle with half the Pecan Crumb Filling. Repeat. Bake 1 hour. Cool 5 minutes, then invert on rack. Serve warm or cool.

Pecan Crumb Filling

    1 cup firmly packed C & H Golden Brown Sugar
    ¼ cup all-purpose flour
    ¼ cup butter
    ⅓ cup minced pecans

Blend sugar and flour. Cut in butter with pastry blender or fingertips until mixture is crumbly. Stir in pecans.

Lemon-Nut Coffee Cake

Makes 1 cake

Topping

    ½ cup walnuts
    1 cup cornflakes
    ¼ cup sugar
    ½ teaspoon ground cinnamon
    ½ cup butter or margarine, melted

Batter

    ½ cup walnuts
    2 cups packaged biscuit mix
    ½ cup milk
    1 egg
    ½ cup firmly packed brown sugar
    3 tablespoons butter or margarine, melted
    ½ lemon rind
    1 tablespoon lemon juice

Have all ingredients at room temperature. Heat oven to 400°F. Grease 8x8x2-inch baking pan. Prepare Topping: Put walnuts into blender container. Cover; blend at medium speed until chopped. Empty into small bowl. Put cornflakes into blender container. Cover; blend at medium speed until crumbled. Add to nuts; stir in sugar, cinnamon, and butter; mix well. Prepare Batter: Put walnuts into blender container. Cover; blend at medium speed until chopped. Empty into medium-size bowl. Add biscuit mix. Put milk, egg, sugar, melted butter, lemon rind, and lemon juice into blender container. Cover; blend at medium speed until rind is chopped. Add to biscuit mix and nuts. Stir just until moistened. Pour into prepared pan. Sprinkle evenly with Topping. Bake 25 minutes, or until done.

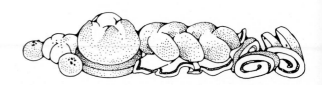

Raisin-Yogurt Coffee Cake

Makes 8 to 10 servings
  1 cup firmly packed C & H Golden Brown Sugar
  ½ cup butter or margarine, softened
  1 teaspoon vanilla extract
  2 eggs
  ½ cup chopped golden raisins
  2 cups all-purpose flour
  1 teaspoon baking powder
  ½ teaspoon salt
  ½ cup plain yogurt
  Walnut Crumb Filling (recipe follows)

Preheat oven to 350°F. Grease a 9-inch square pan. Cream sugar, butter, and vanilla. Add eggs, 1 at a time, beating well after each addition. Stir in raisins. Combine flour, baking powder, and salt. Add to creamed mixture alternately with yogurt, beginning and ending with dry ingredients. Spread half the batter in pan. Sprinkle with half the Walnut Crumb Filling. Repeat. Bake 40 minutes. Serve warm or cool.

Walnut Crumb Filling

  ½ cup firmly packed C & H Golden Brown Sugar
  ¼ cup butter or margarine
  2 tablespoons ground cinnamon
  ¾ cup coarsely chopped walnuts

Blend all ingredients with pastry blender or fingertips until crumbly.

Streusel Swirl Coffee Cake

Makes 10 to 12 servings
  ⅓ cup butter or margarine, softened
  1 cup granulated sugar
  2 eggs
  1 teaspoon vanilla extract
  2½ cups all-purpose flour, divided
  1 tablespoon baking powder
  ½ teaspoon salt
  1 cup milk
  ½ cup Libby's Pumpkin Pie Mix
  ¾ teaspoon ground cinnamon, divided
  ⅔ cup firmly packed brown sugar
  ¼ cup butter or margarine, softened

Preheat oven to 350°F. Cream ⅓ cup butter and granulated sugar until light and fluffy. Blend in eggs and vanilla. Combine 2 cups flour, baking powder, and salt; add alternately with milk, mixing well after each addition. Reserve 1 cup batter. Pour remaining batter into greased and floured 13x9x2-inch baking pan. Combine reserved batter with pumpkin pie mix and ¼ teaspoon cinnamon. Drop pumpkin mixture over

plain batter, swirl with knife for marble effect. Bake 20 minutes. Combine brown sugar, ½ cup flour, and ½ teaspoon cinnamon; cut in ¼ cup butter until mixture resembles coarse crumbs. Sprinkle over cake; continue baking 10 minutes. Serve warm.

Deliciously Dolled-up Delicacies

Dress up muffins, quick breads, or coffee cakes with one of the following delicious-and-easy glazes:

Orange Glaze (particularly good on nut cakes or breads): Blend 1 cup sifted confectioners sugar with 1 tablespoon orange juice. Add more orange juice, a little at a time, until the glaze is thin enough to pour from a spoon. Spoon the mixture over. If you like, decorate the glazed cake or bread with thin slivers of orange peel and/or chopped nuts.

Chocolate Glaze: Break up 1 package (4-ounce) sweet cooking chocolate into a saucepan; add 1 tablespoon butter and 3 tablespoons water. Cook the glaze over moderate heat, stirring until the chocolate is melted. Remove the glase from the heat and beat in 1 cup sifted confectioners sugar, ⅛ teaspoon salt, and 1 teaspoon vanilla extract. Spread the mixture over the cake or bread.

Raspberry Glaze: Thaw and drain 1 package of frozen raspberries and press them through a sieve to purée them and remove the seeds. Stir sufficient purée into 2 cups sifted confectioners sugar to obtain a pouring consistency. Slowly spoon the glaze over the cooled cake or bread, letting it run down the sides.

Mocha Glaze: Over hot water, melt 2 squares (1 ounce each) unsweetened chocolate with 1 teaspoon butter. Stir in 1 cup sifted confectioners sugar. Add 3 tablespoons very strong cold coffee, beating the mixture until smooth. Spoon the glaze over the cake or bread immediately.

Lemon Glaze: Combine ¾ cup sifted confectioners sugar with enough lemon juice so that the mixture will pour slowly off a spoon. Dribble the glaze lightly over the cooled top crust.

Vanilla Glaze: Combine ¾ cup sifted confectioners sugar and ¼ teaspoon vanilla extract with enough milk so that the mixture will pour slowly off a spoon. Dribble the glaze lightly over the cooled top crust.

These glazes may be further ornamented, before they set, with chopped nuts, whole nutmeats, grated chocolate, or colored sugars.

Delicious Peach Coffee Cake

Makes 9 to 12 servings
- ½ cup C & H Granulated Sugar
- 1 egg
- ⅓ cup butter or margarine, melted
- ¾ cup milk
- 2 cups all-purpose flour
- 1 tablespoon baking powder
- ½ teaspoon salt
- Topping (recipe follows)
- 2 fresh peaches, peeled and sliced, or 1 can (16 ounces) sliced peaches, drained

Preheat oven to 400°F. Grease and flour 9-inch square pan. Beat sugar and egg in large bowl until well mixed. Stir in butter and milk. Combine flour, baking powder, and salt; stir into sugar mixture. Spread batter in pan. Sprinkle three-quarters of topping mixture on batter; arrange peach slices over top and sprinkle with remaining topping. Bake 30 minutes.

Topping

- ½ cup firmly packed C & H Golden Brown Sugar
- ¼ cup all-purpose flour
- 1 teaspoon ground cinnamon
- 2 tablespoons butter or margarine, softened

Combine sugar, flour, and cinnamon. Cut butter into sugar mixture until crumbly.

Delicious Peach Coffee Cake. C & H Sugar Co.

Hawaiian Fruitcake

Makes 1 loaf
- ¾ cup C & H Granulated Sugar
- ¾ cup all-purpose flour
- ¾ teaspoon salt
- ¼ teaspoon *each* baking powder and baking soda
- 2 cups (10 ounces) pitted whole dates
- 1 cup (8 ounces) glacéed pineapple pieces
- 1 cup (5 ounces) macadamia nuts (or 2 cups blanched almonds), chopped
- 3 eggs
- ½ teaspoon brandy extract

Preheat oven to 300°F. Grease 9x5x3-inch loaf pan and line bottom with greased paper. In large bowl, mix sugar, flour, salt, baking powder, and soda. Stir in dates, pineapple, and nuts, coating with sugar mixture. Beat eggs until thick and lemon colored. Fold eggs and brandy extract into fruit mixture. Turn into loaf pan. Bake 1½ hours. Cool in pan 10 minutes, then turn out onto rack and peel off paper to finish cooling. Garnish, if desired, with fruit and nuts. To serve, slice thinly. Keeps well, tightly wrapped, up to 2 months.
Note: Firmly packed C & H Golden Brown Sugar may be substituted for the granulated.

Hawaiian Fruitcake. C & H Sugar Co.

Pumpkin-Go-Round Coffee Cake

Makes 2 coffee cakes

Filling

    1 cup Libby's Solid Pack Pumpkin
    ½ cup sugar
    1 package (3¾ ounces) instant butterscotch
        pudding mix
    ½ cup milk
    ½ teaspoon ground cinnamon
    ¼ teaspoon ground ginger
    ⅛ teaspoon ground cloves
    ½ cup chopped nuts

In mixing bowl, combine all Filling ingredients except nuts; beat 2 minutes. Add nuts; refrigerate.

Dough

    4 to 5 cups all-purpose flour, divided
    ½ cup sugar
    1½ teaspoons salt
    2 packages (¼ ounce each) active dry yeast
    ½ cup milk
    ½ cup water
    ¼ cup butter
    2 eggs

In large bowl, mix 1½ cups flour, sugar, salt, and yeast. In saucepan, combine milk, water, and butter; heat until liquids are warm (120° to 130°F). Add to dry ingredients; beat 2 minutes at medium speed, scraping bowl occasionally. Add eggs and ½ cup flour, or enough to make a thick batter; beat at high speed for 2 minutes. Stir in enough additional flour to make a stiff dough. On lightly floured surface, knead dough until smooth and elastic, about 8 to 10 minutes. Place in greased bowl, turning to grease top. Cover; let rise in warm place until double in volume, about 1 hour. Punch dough down; divide in half. Roll half the dough to a 20x7-inch rectangle. Spread with additional melted butter and half the filling. Roll up from wide side. Seal edges; shape into a ring on greased baking sheet with sealed edge down. Seal ends together firmly. Cut slits two-thirds through to center of ring at 1-inch intervals; turn each section on side, working quickly. Repeat with remaining dough and filling. Cover; let rise in warm place, until double in volume, about 1 hour. Preheat oven to 350°F. Bake 15 to 20 minutes. Remove from baking sheets; cool on wire racks. Drizzle Icing over cooled coffee cakes.

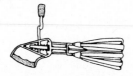

Icing

    2 cups confectioners sugar
    2 tablespoons milk

Combine confectioners sugar and milk; mix well.

Sour Cream Coffee Cake

Makes one 9-inch square cake

    1½ cups sugar
    ½ cup pecans
    1 teaspoon ground cinnamon
    2 cups sifted all-purpose flour
    1 teaspoon baking powder
    ¾ teaspoon baking soda
    ½ teaspoon salt
    ½ cup butter or margarine, softened
    ½ teaspoon vanilla extract
    2 eggs
    1 cup sour cream

Heat oven to 350°F. Grease 9x9x2-inch baking pan. Put ½ cup sugar, pecans, and cinnamon into blender container. Cover; blend at medium speed until nuts are chopped. Empty onto wax paper; set aside. Sift flour, baking powder, baking soda, and salt into medium-size bowl; set aside. Put butter, 1 cup sugar, vanilla, and eggs into blender container. Cover; blend at high speed until well mixed. While blender is running, tip center cap and add half the flour mixture and ½ cup sour cream. If necessary, stop blender during processing and push ingredients toward blades with rubber spatula. Add remaining flour mixture and sour cream. Pour half the batter into prepared pan. Sprinkle evenly with half the sugar-nut mixture. Repeat layers. Bake 40 to 45 minutes, or until done. Cool 15 minutes. Cut into squares and serve warm.

Confectioners Sugar Glaze

Makes ½ cup

    1 cup confectioners sugar
    1 tablespoon milk or light cream
    ¼ teaspoon vanilla extract

In small mixer bowl, mix all ingredients at low speed until of spreading consistency.

German Stollen

Makes 3 stollen
- 1 recipe Sweet Yeast Dough (recipe follows)
- ½ teaspoon grated lemon peel
- ½ cup chopped pecans
- ½ cup raisins
- ½ cup finely chopped mixed candied fruit
  Butter or margarine, softened
  Butter or margarine, melted
  Confectioners Icing (recipe follows)
  Candied fruit and pecans (optional)

Prepare Sweet Yeast Dough, kneading in lemon peel with last addition of flour. Grease 2 large baking sheets; set aside. After dough has risen, punch down. Knead in pecans, raisins, and candied fruits. Divide dough into thirds. Pat one third into 12x8-inch oval. Spread with softened butter. Fold in half lengthwise, bringing one side within ½ inch of opposite side. Press edges together lightly.Place on prepared baking sheet. Brush top with butter. Repeat with remaining two thirds. Cover and let rise in warm place, free from draft, 35 minutes, or until double in bulk. Preheat oven to 375°F. Bake 30 to 35 minutes, or until golden brown and loaves sound hollow when lightly tapped. Cool on baking sheets. Frost while warm with Confectioners Icing. Decorate with additional candied fruit and pecans, if desired.

Sweet Yeast Dough

Makes 1 recipe
- 2 packages (¼ ounce each) active dry yeast
- ½ cup warm water (105° to 115°F.)
- ½ cup sugar
- 2 teaspoons salt
- ½ cup vegetable shortening
- ½ cup hot milk
- 2 eggs, lightly beaten
- 4½ to 5 cups sifted Martha White All-Purpose Flour

Grease large bowl; set aside. Dissolve yeast in water in measuring cup; set aside. Combine sugar, salt, shortening, and milk in bowl. Cool to lukewarm. Add eggs; blend well. Add 2 cups flour; blend well. Stir in yeast mixture. Stir in enough remaining flour to make a soft dough. Turn out onto lightly floured board or pastry cloth. Cover with cloth. Let rest 10 minutes. Knead dough 8 to 10 minutes, or until smooth and elastic. Place in prepared bowl. Turn once to grease top. Cover and let rise in warm place, free from draft, 1½ hours, or until double in bulk. Continue as directed in specific recipes.

Confectioners Icing

Makes 1½ cups icing
- 3 cups sifted confectioners sugar
- ¼ cup hot milk
- ¾ teaspoon vanilla extract

Combine all ingredients in mixing bowl. Beat until smooth.

Prune Ring

Makes 1 coffee cake
- ½ recipe Sweet Dough for Coffee Cakes (see index)
- ½ can (6 ounces) Solo Prune Filling
  Confectioners Sugar Glaze (see index) (optional)

Punch dough down. On a lightly floured board, roll dough into a 10x16-inch rectangle. Spread with prune filling. Roll up from long side, jelly roll fashion, to form a 16-inch roll. Pinch seam to seal. Form into a ring on a greased baking sheet. Using scissors, make cuts from top surface about two-thirds of the way through at 1-inch intervals. Turn one piece toward center, next toward outside of ring; continue in this fashion all the way around ring. Cover; let rise in a warm place, free from draft, until double in bulk, about 1 hour. Preheat oven to 350°F. Bake ring about 25 minutes, or until golden brown. Remove from baking sheet and cool on wire rack. Prune Ring can be drizzled with a thin Confectioners Sugar Glaze before serving, if desired.

Prune Breakfast Wheel

Makes 1 coffee cake
- 2 cups sifted enriched flour
- 3 teaspoons baking powder
- 1 teaspoon salt
- 1 tablespoon sugar
- ¼ cup shortening
- 1 egg
- ¾ cup milk
- ¼ cup Simon Fisher Prune Butter

Sift together flour, baking powder, salt, and sugar. Cut in shortening. Beat egg and add milk. Add to flour mixture. Stir only enough to moisten flour. Spread dough in greased 10-inch cake pan. With fingertips, press top of dough down into inch-wide grooves, making a circular pattern. Make first groove 1 inch from edge of pan and second groove 2½ inches from edge of pan. Fill grooves with prune butter. Bake at 400°F. for about 20 minutes.

Peanut Butter Bread (page 40); Peanut-Date-Filled Coffee Bread (page 96); Double Peanut Gems (page 108). Oklahoma Peanut Commission

Cinnamon Swirl Yeast Bread

Makes 2 loaves

- 1 package (¼ ounce) active dry yeast
- 1½ cups warm water (105° to 115°F.)
- 1¼ cups sugar (about), divided
- 1 cup butter or margarine (about), divided and melted
- 2 eggs
- 1½ teaspoons salt
- 2 teaspoons ground cinnamon, divided
- 1 cup Libby's Solid Pack Pumpkin
- 7 to 7½ cups all-purpose flour
- 1 cup raisins, divided

Dissolve yeast in warm water. Add ⅔ cup sugar, ⅔ cup melted butter, eggs, salt, and 1 teaspoon cinnamon; mix well. Stir in pumpkin and 3 cups flour; beat until smooth. Add enough remaining flour to form soft dough. On floured surface, knead dough until smooth and elastic. Place in greased bowl; brush with melted butter. Cover; let rise in warm place until double in volume, about 1½ hours. Punch down dough; divide in half. On lightly floured surface, roll out each half into an 18x9-inch rectangle. Brush each rectangle with 2 tablespoons melted butter; sprinkle with half of combined ½ cup sugar and 1 teaspoon cinnamon. Sprinkle each with ½ cup raisins. Roll up from narrow end; press ends to seal. Fold ends under loaves; place each, seam side down, in greased 9x5x3-inch loaf pan. Cover; let rise until double in volume, about 1 hour. Preheat oven to 375°F. Brush loaves lightly with additional melted butter. Bake 50 to 55 minutes, or until golden brown and loaves sound hollow when tapped. Remove from pans; cool on wire rack.

Variation

For a sweeter bread, combine 1 cup confectioners sugar and 5 to 6 tablespoons cream or milk to make a glaze consistency. Drizzle over loaves.

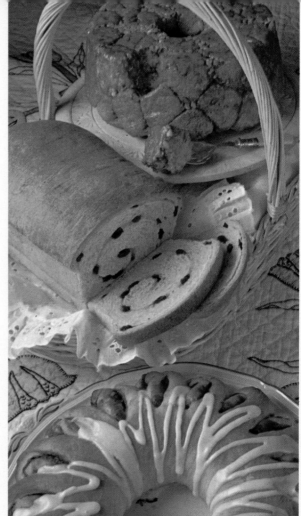

Spiced Bubble Bread (page 25); Cinnamon Swirl Yeast Bread (page 94); Pumpkin Go-Round Coffee Cake (page 92). Libby, McNeill & Libby, Inc., The Great Pumpkin Cookbook, A Harvest of Libby's Favorite Recipes.

Peanut Butter and Jam Swirl Coffee Cake

Makes 1 coffee cake

  1 package (¼ ounce) yeast, dry or compressed
  ¼ cup water (lukewarm for compressed yeast and warm for dry)
  ¾ cup milk
  ⅓ cup brown sugar
  1 teaspoon salt
  2 cups sifted all-purpose flour
  ¼ cup peanut butter
  1 egg
  ⅓ cup raspberry, strawberry, or other red-colored jam

Soften yeast in water. Scald milk. Measure brown sugar and salt into medium-size bowl. Pour milk over sugar, and stir until dissolved. Cool to lukewarm. Add 1 cup flour and peanut butter; beat until smooth. Add softened yeast and egg; beat well. Add more flour to make a thick batter. Beat thoroughly. Cover, let rise in warm place until bubbly and double in size (1 hour). Stir down. Spread in a well-greased 9-inch round pan. With floured fingers, press a spiral-like indentation in top of batter, starting at center and working toward outside of pan. Fill indentation with raspberry jam. Let rise again until double (45 minutes). Bake 350°F. for 30 to 35 minutes. Remove from pan at once if coffee cake is to be served on special plate.

About Baking Powders

All present-day baking powders are a mixture of three essential ingredients: 1) baking soda, the source of the still-necessary carbon dioxide, essential for leavening; 2) some kind of acid, to release the carbon dioxide; and 3) a starch substance, such as flour or cornstarch, to keep the mixture dry and prevent caking. The difference between the various types of baking powder on the market lies in the kind of acid used in each.

Tartrate type: Baking powder containing cream of tartar and tartaric acid. Because this kind releases its gases quickly when it is wetted (combined with a liquid), recipes usually call for more of it than of other kinds. Batters leavened with tartate-type baking powder won't wait. They must be baked as soon as they are mixed or too much carbon dioxide will escape, resulting in a heavy cake, cookie, or quick bread.

Phosphate type: Baking powder containing calcium acid phosphate as its acid ingredient; sometimes contains sodium acid pyrophosphate as well. Somewhat slower acting than the tartrate type, this baking powder releases about two-thirds of its gases at room temperature, the remaining third at oven temperature.

Combination or double-acting type: Two acid ingredients in this baking powder, sodium aluminum sulphate (s.a.s.—this is sometimes called SAS-type baking powder) and calcium acid phosphate. A small portion of the carbon dioxide is released at room temperature, but this type of baking powder releases the major portion of its leavening gases at oven temperature. It produces a more stable batter, one that can wait a few minutes before being baked without any great loss of leavening, or that can be refrigerated for later (same day) baking.

Emergency measures. If you run out of baking powder, you can use a combination of 1 teaspoon baking soda, 1 teaspoon cream of tartar, and ½ teaspoon salt for each cup of flour the recipe calls for. Use only to save the day, however—don't mix and store your own baking powder, because it will not retain its effectiveness for any length of time.

Even commercial baking powders won't remain effective forever. Home cooks who do very little baking should buy baking powder in the smallest available container, store it tightly covered in a cool place, and make certain that the spoons used to measure it with are entirely free from moisture. If you feel the baking powder in your pantry may need replacing, test it before using it. Stir a teaspoon of the baking powder into ¼ cup of hot water—if the mixture bubbles quickly and cheerfully, the leavening is still useful.

Peanut–Date-Filled Coffee Bread

Makes 1 coffee cake
- 1 package (8 ounces) dates, chopped (1½ cups)
- ½ teaspoon grated lemon peel
- 3 tablespoons lemon juice
- ¼ cup water
- 1 cup chopped peanuts
- 1 package (13¾ ounces) hot roll mix
- ¾ cup warm water
- 1 egg
- 2 tablespoons soft butter

Icing
- 1 cup sifted confectioners sugar
- 1 tablespoon peanut butter
- 4½ teaspoons lemon juice
- Milk

Combine dates, lemon peel, lemon juice, and water; bring to a boil. Reduce heat and cook while stirring until dates soften and mixture thickens. Cool and add peanuts. Prepare hot roll mix according to package directions using warm water and egg. Let rise as directed. On a floured surface, roll dough into a 16x9-inch rectangle. Spread with soft butter and date filling. From the long edge, roll up jelly roll fashion. Seal seam and ends. Place on a large greased cookie sheet in a semi-circle. Make cuts two-thirds of the way through the roll at 1-inch intervals; turn each section on its side. Bake in a preheated 350°F. oven for 20 to 25 minutes. Cool. To make icing, combine confectioners sugar, peanut butter, and lemon juice; add enough milk to make of spreading consistency. Spread over coffee cake.

Cinnamon Twists

Makes 12 to 14 twists
- 1 recipe Hot Rize Biscuits (see index)
- 1 cup sugar
- 2 teaspoons ground cinnamon
- ½ cup butter or margarine, melted

Preheat oven to 450°F. Grease large baking sheet; set aside. Prepare biscuit dough. Roll out to ¼-inch thickness on lightly floured board or pastry cloth. Cut into rounds with floured 2-inch doughnut cutter. Combine sugar and cinnamon in small bowl; set aside. Dip each round in butter, then in sugar-cinnamon mixture. Twist ends in opposite directions. Place twists 1 inch apart on prepared baking sheet. Bake 10 to 12 minutes, or until golden brown.

Pineapple-Apricot Squares

Makes 1 coffee cake

3¾ to 4¼ cups all-purpose flour
1 teaspoon sugar
1 package (¼ ounce) active dry yeast
½ cup milk
½ cup water
1 cup butter or margarine
2 eggs
1 can (12 ounces) Solo Pineapple Filling
1 can (12 ounces) Solo Apricot Filling
Confectioners Sugar Glaze (see index)
(optional)

In a large bowl, combine thoroughly 1¼ cups flour, sugar, and dry yeast. Combine milk, water, and butter in a saucepan. Heat over low heat until liquids are very warm (120° to 130°F.). (Butter need not melt entirely.) Gradually add to dry ingredients and beat 2 minutes at medium speed of electric mixer, scraping bowl occasionally. Add eggs and ½ cup flour. Beat at high speed 2 minutes, scraping bowl occasionally. Stir in enough additional flour to make a soft, moist dough. Divide dough in half. Pat out half the dough in the bottom of an ungreased 15x10x1-inch jelly roll pan. Combine pineapple and apricot fillings and spread over dough. Roll out remaining dough on a floured board to a shape the size of the jelly roll pan. Carefully roll dough around rolling pin, transfer to top of pan, and unroll to fit over filling. Seal edges together. Snip surface of dough with scissors to allow steam to escape. Cover and let rise in a warm place, free from draft, until double in bulk, about 1 hour. Preheat oven to 375°F. Bake 35 to 40 minutes, or until lightly browned. Cool cake in pan. If desired, frost with Confectioners Sugar Glaze while still warm. Cut into squares to serve.

Poppy Coffee Ring

Makes one 9-inch ring

2 cups all-purpose flour
½ cup sugar
3 teaspoons baking powder
½ teaspoon salt
½ cup butter or margarine, softened
1 egg
¾ cup milk
½ can (6¼ ounces) Solo Poppy Filling
1 teaspoon lemon juice

Preheat oven to 375°F. Butter a 9-inch ring mold. Sift together flour, sugar, baking powder, and salt. Using a pastry blender or 2 knives, cut in butter. Add egg and milk and stir just until dry ingredients are well moistened. Spoon half the batter into prepared ring

mold. Combine poppy filling and lemon juice and spoon over top of dough in ring. Top with remaining dough. Bake 30 to 35 minutes, or until lightly browned. Let stand about 5 minutes, then turn out of pan onto wire rack. Serve either warm or cold.
Good idea: This is a delicious breakfast bread—however, it is very rich. With a special Solo topping or whipped cream, it would make an excellent dessert.

Coconut Strawberry Circle

Makes 1 coffee cake

1 can (8 ounces) refrigerated biscuits
¼ cup Solo Strawberry or Raspberry Filling
2 tablespoons flaked coconut
Confectioners Sugar Glaze (see index)
(optional)

Preheat oven to 400°F. Butter an 8-inch layer cake pan. Separate biscuit dough into 10 biscuits. Flatten slightly and, using the back of a knife, make a crease down the center of each biscuit. Combine strawberry or raspberry filling and coconut. Place about 1 heaping teaspoon of mixture in center of each biscuit and fold into half circle. Arrange folded biscuits, open side up, crosswise around outer edge of cake pan. Bake 12 to 15 minutes, or until golden brown. Cool slightly in pan before serving. Serve warm with a drizzle of Confectioners Sugar Glaze, if desired.

Solo Swirl Coffee Cake

Makes 1 coffee cake

1½ cups all-purpose flour
½ cup sugar
2 teaspoons baking powder
1 teaspoon salt
½ cup butter or margarine
2 eggs, well beaten
½ cup buttermilk
1 can (12½ ounces) Solo filling, any desired flavor
½ cup all-purpose flour
½ cup sugar
¼ cup butter or margarine
½ teaspoon ground cinnamon
½ teaspoon ground nutmeg

Preheat oven to 375°F. Combine flour, sugar, baking powder, and salt. Using a pastry blender or 2 knives, cut butter into mixture to consistency of cornmeal. Add eggs and buttermilk and stir just until dry ingredients are moistened. Spread batter into greased 9-inch square pan. Spread filling over top and cut through filling and batter with knife, swirling filling for a marble effect. Combine remaining ingredients and sprinkle over top of cake. Bake 30 minutes, or until done.

Gingerbread

Makes one 8-inch loaf

1¼ cups sifted all-purpose flour
¾ teaspoon Calumet Baking Powder
½ teaspoon salt
¼ teaspoon baking soda
½ teaspoon ground cinnamon
½ teaspoon ground ginger
¼ teaspoon ground cloves
½ cup molasses
½ cup water
¼ cup shortening
¼ cup sugar
1 egg
Lemon Sauce (recipe follows)

Sift flour with baking powder, salt, soda, and spices. Combine molasses and water. Cream shortening. Gradually blend in sugar. Add egg and beat well. Add flour mixture alternately with molasses mixture, a small amount at a time, beating after each addition until smooth. Pour batter into greased 8-inch square pan. Bake at 350°F. for 35 minutes, or until cake tester inserted into center comes out clean. Cut in squares. Serve warm or cooled with Lemon Sauce.

Lemon Sauce

Makes about 1⅓ cups sauce

⅔ cup sugar
1 tablespoon cornstarch
⅛ teaspoon salt
1 cup water
1 tablespoon butter or margarine
1 teaspoon grated lemon rind
2 tablespoons lemon juice
2 drops yellow food coloring (optional)

Combine sugar, cornstarch, and salt in saucepan; mix well. Gradually stir in water. Cook and stir over medium heat until mixture comes to a boil. Boil 3 minutes, stirring constantly. Remove from heat and add butter, lemon rind, lemon juice, and coloring. Serve warm or chilled.

Gingerbread with Lemon Sauce. General Foods

Apricot Twist

Makes 1 coffee cake

2½ to 3 cups all-purpose flour, divided
3 tablespoons sugar
1 teaspoon salt
1 teaspoon grated orange peel
1 package (¼ ounce) active dry yeast
¾ cup milk
8 tablespoons butter or margarine, divided
1 egg
½ cup chopped Sun-Maid® Dried Apricots
½ cup Sun-Maid® Puffed Seeded Muscat Raisins
¼ cup firmly packed light or dark brown sugar
Vegetable oil
Glaze (recipe follows)

Mix 1 cup of the flour with the sugar, salt, orange peel, and yeast in a large mixer bowl. Heat the milk with 6 tablespoons of the butter until very warm (120° to 130°F.). Beating at low speed, gradually add the warmed milk and butter to the flour mixture. Increase the speed to medium and beat for 2 minutes. Beat in the egg and ½ cup of the remaining flour, or enough to make a thick batter. Increase the speed to high and beat for 5 minutes. Stir in the remaining 1 cup of the flour, or enough to make a stiff dough. Turn out on a floured surface and knead until the dough is smooth and elastic, about 10 minutes. Cover and let stand for 20 minutes. Meanwhile, grease a large baking sheet. Combine the apricots, raisins, and brown sugar and melt the remaining 2 tablespoons butter. Roll the dough out into a 12-inch square and brush with the melted butter. Spread the apricot-raisin mixture over the dough and roll up jelly roll fashion, pinching the ends to seal. Place seam side down on the prepared sheet. Using scissors, cut from the tip at 1-inch intervals about two-thirds of the way down through the dough. Pull cut pieces out to the right and left on alternate sides, twisting slightly to flatten. Brush with oil. Cover the dough lightly with plastic wrap, sealing the edges to prevent the dough from drying out, and refrigerate from 2 to 4 hours.

To bake, preheat the oven to 375°F. Remove the coffee cake from the refrigerator and carefully take off the plastic wrap. Let stand at room temperature for 10 minutes. Bake for 25 to 30 minutes. Spread with Glaze and serve warm.

Glaze

½ cup confectioners sugar
2 teaspoons orange juice

Stir confectioners sugar and orange juice together until smooth.

Quick Coffee Cake

Makes 8 servings

- ¾ cup chopped walnuts
- ¾ cup firmly packed brown sugar
- ½ teaspoon ground cinnamon
- 1½ cups all-purpose flour
- ½ cup sugar
- 1 teaspoon baking powder
- 1 teaspoon baking soda
- ¾ cup sour cream
- 1 egg, lightly beaten
- ⅓ cup vegetable oil
- ¼ cup milk
- 1 teaspoon vanilla extract

Combine walnuts, brown sugar, and cinnamon; set aside. Combine flour, sugar, baking powder, and baking soda in bowl. Stir sour cream, egg, oil, milk, and vanilla extract in another bowl until smooth. Add to flour mixture all at once and stir until well blended. Pour into greased 8-inch square baking dish. Sprinkle with brown sugar mixture. Preheat oven to 350°F. Bake 30 to 35 minutes until toothpick inserted in center comes out clean. Serve warm.

Poppy Strudel

Makes 2 coffee cake rolls

- 3 to 3½ cups all-purpose flour
- 1½ tablespoons sugar
- ½ teaspoon salt
- 1 package (¼ ounce) active dry yeast
- ½ cup sour cream
- ¼ cup water
- ½ cup butter or margarine
- 2 eggs, at room temperature
- 1 can (12½ ounces) Solo Poppy Filling
  Confectioners Sugar Glaze (see index)
  (optional)

In large bowl of electric mixer, combine 1 cup flour, sugar, salt, and dry yeast. In a saucepan, combine sour cream, water, and butter. Heat over low heat until liquids are very warm (120° to 130°F.). (Butter need not melt entirely.) Gradually add to dry ingredients; beat mixture 2 minutes at medium speed of electric mixer, scraping bowl occasionally. Add eggs and ½ cup flour. Beat at high speed 2 minutes, scraping bowl occasionally. Stir in enough additional flour to make a soft dough. Turn out onto a lightly floured board; knead a few times to form a ball. Cover and let stand 10 minutes. Divide dough in half. Roll each half out into a 14x12-inch rectangle. Spread each with ½ can of filling. Roll each up from one side, jelly roll fashion. Seal edges. Place on greased baking sheet, sealed edges down. Cover and let rise in a warm place, free from draft, until double in bulk, about 1 hour. Preheat oven to 350°F. Bake about 35 minutes, or until lightly browned. Remove from baking sheet and cool on wire rack. When cool, drizzle with Confectioners Sugar Glaze, if desired.

Coconut Toppers

Toasted coconut: Spread the coconut—shredded at home from the whole nut, if you're ambitious, or from a can or bag—on a baking sheet. Place it in a 300°F. oven and bake it, stirring occasionally, for 15 to 25 minutes, until it attains a toasty brown shade.

Colored coconut: Place shredded or flaked coconut in a jar that has a lid and add a few drops of any food coloring you desire. Put the lid on the jar and shake it until the coconut is nicely tinted. Or put the coconut in a plastic bag and add the food coloring. Close the bag and knead and shake it until you get the color you want. Either way, be miserly with the coloring—it's a tint, not a shade, that you're seeking.

Coffee coconut: In a jar or bag, as described above, combine 1½ teaspoons instant coffee powder with an equal amount of water. Add the flaked or shredded coconut and shake the jar or knead the bag until the coconut is colored. Spread the coconut on a baking sheet and bake it in a 300°F. oven for 20 minutes, stirring occasionally, until it is dry. Coffee coconut enhances the appearance and flavor of any mocha icing or glaze, or try it on a lemon cake with a coffee filling and a lemon glaze—it tastes as good as espresso with a twist of lemon peel.

Quick Pecan Ring

Makes 8 to 10 servings

- 2 packages (8 ounces each) refrigerated butter-flake rolls
- ⅔ cup sugar
- ½ teaspoon ground cinnamon
- ½ cup milk
- ¼ cup chopped pecans
- ½ cup confectioners sugar
- 1 tablespoon milk
- ¼ teaspoon vanilla extract
  Chopped pecans

Separate refrigerated dough into 24 rolls. Combine sugar and cinnamon. Dip each roll in the milk and then in cinnamon-sugar mixture, turning to coat all sides. Place half the rolls, slightly overlapping, in bottom of an oiled 6½-cup ring mold. Sprinkle with chopped pecans. Add remaining rolls, forming a second layer of overlapping rolls. Bake in a preheated 375°F. oven for 25 to 30 minutes, or until golden brown. Turn onto serving plate immediately. Combine confectioners sugar and milk and blend well. Stir in vanilla. Drizzle over top and sides of ring. Sprinkle with additional chopped pecans.

Poppy Crown Cake

Makes 1 coffee cake
- 2¾ to 3¼ cups all-purpose flour
- ⅓ cup sugar
- ½ teaspoon salt
- 1 package (¼ ounce) active dry yeast
- ⅓ cup water
- ⅓ cup milk
- 6 tablespoons butter or margarine
- 1 egg, at room temperature
- 1 can (12½ ounces) Solo Poppy Filling
  Confectioners sugar (optional)

In large bowl of electric mixer, combine thoroughly 1 cup flour, sugar, salt, and yeast. Combine water, milk, and butter in a saucepan. Heat over low heat until liquids are very warm (120° to 130°F.). (Butter need not melt entirely.) Gradually add to dry ingredients and beat 2 minutes at medium speed of electric mixer, scraping bowl occasionally. Add egg and ½ cup flour. Beat at high speed 2 minutes, scraping bowl occasionally. Stir in enough additional flour to make a soft dough. Cover and let rise in a warm place, free from draft, until double in bulk, about 50 minutes. Turn dough out onto a lightly floured board. Knead slightly. Roll dough into a rectangle about 9x25 inches. Spread with poppy filling. Roll up from the long side, jelly roll fashion. Form a circle and seal ends together. Place circle in a greased Bundt pan. Cover and let rise in a warm place, free from draft, until double in bulk, about 1 hour. Preheat oven to 350°F. Bake 30 to 35 minutes, or until lightly browned. Let stand in pan about 3 minutes. Turn out onto a wire rack and let cool before serving. Dust with confectioners sugar, if desired.

Oatmeal-Apricot Tea Ring

Makes 1 tea ring
- ¼ cup warm water (105° to 115°F.)
- 1 package (¼ ounce) active dry yeast
- ¾ cup warm milk (105° to 115°F.)
- ¼ cup firmly packed brown sugar
- 1½ teaspoons salt
- 4½ teaspoons butter or margarine
- 3½ to 4 cups all-purpose flour
- ½ cup quick-cooking rolled oats
- ½ can (6 ounces) Solo Apricot Filling
- 1 tablespoon sugar
- ½ teaspoon ground cinnamon
  Confectioners Sugar Glaze (see index)
  (optional)

Measure warm water into a large warm bowl. Sprinkle in yeast and stir until dissolved. Add warm milk, brown sugar, salt, and butter. Add 2 cups flour. Beat with rotary beater until smooth, about 1 minute. Add 1 cup flour and oats. Beat vigorously with a wooden spoon until smooth, about 150 strokes. Add enough additional flour to make a smooth dough. Turn out onto a lightly floured board and knead until smooth and elastic, about 8 to 10 minutes. Cover with plastic wrap, then a towel. Let stand 20 minutes. Roll dough out into a 10x16-inch rectangle. Spread with apricot filling. Sprinkle with sugar and cinnamon. Roll up from long side, jelly roll fashion. Place on a greased baking sheet. Shape into a ring and seal ends. Using a sharp knife or scissors, cut through dough at 1½-inch intervals. Turn each cut piece over and cut to form a circle. Cover; let rise in a warm place, free from draft, until double in bulk, about 1 hour. Preheat oven to 350°F. Bake 25 to 30 minutes, or until golden brown. Remove from baking sheet and cool on wire rack. Drizzle with Confectioners Sugar Glaze, if desired.

Prune Swirls

Makes 2 dozen swirls
- 1½ cups stewed pitted prunes, drained
- ¼ cup syrup from prunes
- 3 tablespoons sugar
- 1 tablespoon lemon juice
  Thin strip lemon rind
- ¼ teaspoon ground cinnamon
- ½ recipe Easy Sweet Rolls dough (see index)

Put prunes, syrup, sugar, lemon juice, rind, and cinnamon into blender container. Cover; blend at medium speed until smooth. Pour into saucepan; cook over low heat, stirring frequently, until mixture is thick enough to mound when dropped from spoon. Chill 30 minutes. Roll dough out on lightly floured surface to rectangle about ½ inch thick. Spread prune filling over dough to within 1 inch of edges. Roll up jelly roll fashion, rolling tightly to seal seam. Cut into 1-inch-thick slices; place, cut sides down, 2 inches apart on lightly greased cookie sheets. Cover with clean towel. Let rise about 1 hour, or until double in bulk. Heat oven to 400°F. Bake swirls 15 to 20 minutes, or until golden brown.

Apricot Swirls

Substitute 1½ cups drained pitted canned apricots and ¼ cup syrup from apricots for prunes and prune syrup. Proceed as for Prune Swirls.

Sticky Buns

Makes 20 buns

   3 to 3½ cups all-purpose flour, divided
   1 package (¼ ounce) active dry yeast
   ⅓ cup sugar
   1 teaspoon salt
   ¾ cup milk
  10 tablespoons butter or margarine, divided
   2 eggs
   ½ cup dark corn syrup or honey
   1½ cups firmly packed light brown sugar, divided
   1½ teaspoons ground cinnamon
   ½ cup chopped nuts
   1 cup Sun-Maid® Seedless Raisins

Combine 1 cup of the flour with the yeast, sugar, and salt in a large electric mixer bowl. Heat the milk with 4 tablespoons of the butter until very warm (120° to 130°F.). Beating at low speed, gradually add the warmed milk and butter to the flour mixture. Increase the speed to medium and beat for 2 minutes. Beat in the eggs and ½ cup of the remaining flour, or enough to make a thick batter. Increase the speed to high and beat for 5 minutes. Stir in about 1½ cups of the remaining flour, or enough to make a firm dough. Turn out on a floured surface and knead until smooth and elastic, about 10 minutes. Place in a greased bowl and turn once to grease the surface. Cover and let rise in a warm place, free from draft, until double in bulk, about 1 hour. Combine the corn syrup and 4 tablespoons of the remaining butter in a small saucepan. Stir over low heat until smooth. Divide between two 9-inch layer pans. Using ½ cup of the brown sugar, sprinkle half of it into each pan. Punch the dough down. Divide in half and roll each half into a 10x15-inch rectangle. Melt the remaining 2 tablespoons of butter and brush over the rolled-out dough. Mix the remaining 1 cup of brown sugar with the cinnamon and nuts. Sprinkle half of the mixture over each rectangle and top with the raisins. Roll up jelly roll fashion from the 10-inch side and cut into 1-inch slices. Arrange in the prepared pans. Cover and let rise until double in bulk. Preheat the oven to 400°F. Bake the buns for 18 to 20 minutes, or until well browned. Invert the buns onto plates and cool slightly before serving.

> **Q:** *How do I thaw frozen breads and coffee cakes?*
> **A.** Thaw frozen bread in its wrapper 2 to 3 hours at room temperature. If bread is wrapped in aluminum foil, it can be thawed quickly by placing it in a 375°F. oven for 20 minutes. Sweet yeast breads should be thawed before frosting and decorating.

Apricot Twist (page 99); Classic Cinnamon-Raisin Bread (page 29); Sticky Buns. Sun-Maid Growers of California

Cinnamon-Raisin Roll-Ups

Makes 12 rolls

   2 cups Bisquick Baking Mix
   ½ cup raisins
   ½ cup sour cream
   3 tablespoons milk
   2 tablespoons margarine or butter, softened
   ¼ cup firmly packed brown sugar
   ¼ cup finely chopped nuts
   ½ teaspoon ground cinnamon
   2 tablespoons margarine or butter, melted
     Sugar
     Margarine (optional)

Heat oven to 400°F. Generously grease 12 muffin cups, 2½x1¼ inches. Mix baking mix, raisins, sour cream, and milk; beat 20 strokes. Smooth into ball on floured cloth-covered board. Knead 10 times. Roll into rectangle, 12x10 inches. Spread with softened margarine. Mix brown sugar, nuts, and cinnamon; sprinkle over dough. Roll up tightly, beginning at 12-inch side. Pinch edge into roll. Cut into 12 slices. Place slices, cut sides down, in cups. Brush melted margarine over tops; sprinkle with sugar. Bake until golden, about 15 minutes. Top with margarine, if desired.

Lemon-Pecan Sticky Rolls (page 104). ReaLemon® Lemon Juice from Concentrate

Sticky Pecan Rolls

Makes 1 dozen rolls
  ½ cup Sue Bee Honey
  6 tablespoons butter or margarine
  ¼ teaspoon ground cinnamon
  ⅓ cup coarsely chopped pecans
  1 package (12) brown-and-serve dinner rolls

Select a baking pan (8- or 9-inch cake or pie pan), providing a "snug" fit for the rolls. Pour honey into pan. Add 4 tablespoons of the butter and the cinnamon. Heat in oven until butter melts. Blend ingredients. Sprinkle with pecans. Arrange rolls, tops up, in honey mixture. Spread roll tops with reserved butter. Bake at 400°F. for 10 to 12 minutes, or until rolls are browned. Cool 5 to 10 minutes before inverting pan over serving plate.
Note: Individual Sticky Rolls may be baked in muffin pans. Spoon honey mixture into bottoms of 12 muffin cups. Place a roll in each cup. Butter tops and bake as directed.

Lemon-Pecan Sticky Rolls

Makes 16 rolls
  ½ cup sugar
  ½ cup firmly packed light brown sugar
  ¼ cup margarine or butter
  ¼ cup ReaLemon® Lemon Juice from Concentrate
  ½ teaspoon ground cinnamon
  ½ cup chopped pecans
  2 packages (8 ounces each) refrigerated crescent rolls

Preheat oven to 375°F. In small saucepan, combine sugars, margarine, ReaLemon, and cinnamon. Bring to a boil; boil 1 minute. Reserving ¼ cup, pour remaining ReaLemon mixture into 9-inch round layer cake pan. Sprinkle with nuts. Separate rolls into 8 rectangles; spread with reserved ReaLemon mixture. Roll up jelly roll fashion, beginning with short side; seal edges. Cut in half. Place rolls, cut side down, in prepared pan. Bake 30 to 35 minutes, or until dark golden brown. Loosen sides. Immediately turn onto serving plate; do not remove pan. Let stand 5 minutes; remove pan. Serve warm.

Stale Bread?
Make nutted cinnamon toast for breakfast. Toast bread slices, butter liberally, then sprinkle with sugar—white or brown or, best of all, maple—and cinnamon. Top with chopped nuts, any kind that comes to hand.

Sour Cream Streusel Coffee Cake

Makes 1 coffee cake
  2 tablespoons butter or margarine, softened
  ½ cup firmly packed light brown sugar
  1 teaspoon ground cinnamon
  1 cup Sun-Maid® Puffed Seeded Muscat Raisins
1½ cups sour cream
  ¼ cup butter or margarine, melted
  3 eggs, beaten
  2 teaspoons grated lemon peel
  1 teaspoon vanilla extract
  3 cups all-purpose flour
  2 cups sugar
  2 teaspoons baking powder
  1 teaspoon salt
  ¾ teaspoon baking soda
  ¼ cup chopped dried apricots
  Confectioners sugar

Mix butter, brown sugar, cinnamon, and raisins together until crumbly. Set aside. Combine the sour cream, butter, eggs, lemon peel, and vanilla. In a separate large bowl, combine the flour, sugar, baking powder, salt, baking soda, and apricots. Gently but thoroughly stir the sour cream mixture into the flour mixture. Preheat the oven to 350°F. Grease a 12-cup Bundt pan. Spoon one-third of the batter into the prepared pan. Sprinkle with half the raisin-cinnamon mixture. Repeat layers, ending with batter. Bake 55 to 60 minutes, or until a toothpick inserted in the center comes out clean. Let stand on a wire rack for 10 minutes before removing from the pan to cool completely on the rack. Sprinkle with confectioners sugar before serving.

Cinnamon Rolls

Makes about 4 dozen rolls
  1 recipe Sweet Yeast Dough (see index)
  ¼ cup butter or margarine, melted
  1 cup sugar
  1 tablespoon ground cinnamon
  2 tablespoons milk
    Confectioners Icing (see index)

Prepare Sweet Yeast Dough. After dough has risen, punch down. Let rest 10 minutes. Grease four 8-inch round baking pans or 48 muffin cups; set aside. Divide dough into 4 portions. Roll out 1 portion into 12x6-inch rectangle. Brush with melted butter. Combine sugar and cinnamon in small bowl. Sprinkle one-fourth of cinnamon-sugar mixture over rectangle. Roll up, jelly roll fashion, from long side; seal edges. Cut into 1-inch slices. Place slices, cut sides down, in prepared pans or muffin cups. Brush tops with milk. Repeat with remaining dough. Cover and let rise in warm place, free from draft, 45 minutes, or until double in bulk. Preheat oven to 350°F. Bake 25 minutes, or until golden brown. Turn out onto wire racks to cool. Frost warm rolls with Confectioners Icing.

Coconut Rolls

Makes 2 dozen rolls
  1 recipe Sweet Dough for Coffee Cakes (see index)
  4 tablespoons butter or margarine, softened
  1 cup flaked coconut
  ¼ cup sugar
  ½ teaspoon mace

Divide sweet dough in half. Roll each half out to an 8x12-inch rectangle. Spread each with 2 tablespoons softened butter. Combine coconut, sugar, and mace and sprinkle mixture over rectangles. Starting at 12-inch side, roll dough, jelly roll fashion. Cut in 1-inch-thick slices. Place slices, cut side down, in buttered muffin pan cups. Cover and let rise in a warm place, free from draft, until double in bulk, 30 to 45 minutes. Preheat oven to 350°F. Bake 20 to 30 minutes, or until done. Remove from pans immediately.

Perfect Prune Gems

Makes 1½ dozen muffins
  2 cups all-purpose flour
  ¼ cup sugar
  2 teaspoons *each* baking powder and grated lemon peel
  ½ teaspoon *each* salt and ground nutmeg
  1 cup milk
  2 eggs, beaten
  ¼ cup butter or margarine, melted
  1½ cups (about 9 ounces) coarsely chopped pitted prunes
  ¼ cup wheat germ
  2 tablespoons sesame seed

In large bowl, combine flour, sugar, baking powder, peel, salt, and nutmeg. Stir in milk, eggs, and butter just to moisten. In another bowl, toss prunes with wheat germ. Fold into flour mixture. Spoon into 18 greased ¾-inch muffin-pan cups. Sprinkle with sesame seed. Bake in 425°F. oven about 15 minutes until lightly browned and springy to the touch. Serve warm.

Nuts for Flavor and Texture

Nuts, plain or toasted or even, in some circumstances, salted, decorate a cake or bread in a way interesting to both eye and palate. Blanched almonds, whole or slivered, plain or toasted, are very good and very pretty. Stud a frosting or glaze all over with almonds for a lovely look. (To blanch almonds at home, place them in boiling water for 1 minute or 2, drain them, and slip off the skins with your fingers.) The lovely yellow-green of pistachios offers handsome contrast to any frosting, light or dark. (Pistachios can be skinned in the same way as almonds.) Brazil nuts are too often overlooked. To make handsome curls, soak the shelled nuts in boiling water for 5 minutes, slice them into thin curls with a sharp knife, and then dry them in a low oven without browning. Pecans and walnuts lose nothing of their flavor and goodness just because they are so commonly used; chop them to sprinkle on top or decorate with plump, nut-brown halves. Whole filberts have a flavor affinity for chocolate. Whole nuts or halves of any kind can be dipped in melted chocolate so that they are only partially covered, then cooled and used for decoration.

Coconut is so versatile it's in a class by itself. Use it plain, or toast it or color it and/or flavor it to make easy-but-beautiful decorations for almost any kind of cake or bread.

Stale Bread?

Make French toast. Cut bread (preferably French bread) in diagonal slices, soak in a mixture of egg and milk 30 minutes, and sauté in butter until golden. Serve with syrup or preserves. Delicious flavors: Add to the milk-egg mixture ½ teaspoon grated orange rind or a few drops of vanilla, coconut, or chocolate extract.

Steamed Boston Brown Bread (page 42); Sour Cream Streusel Coffee Cake (page 104); Mini Hearth Loaves (page 36); Raisin-Oatmeal Muffins (page 69). Sun-Maid Growers of California

Derby Day Rolls

Makes 36 rolls

  2 cups water
  1 cup vegetable shortening
6½ to 7 cups sifted Martha White All-Purpose
     Flour, divided
1½ cups sugar, divided
  1 teaspoon salt
  1 package (¼ ounce) active dry yeast
  2 eggs, at room temperature
  4 teaspoons ground cinnamon
  ¼ cup butter or margarine, melted
     Rum Icing (recipe follows)

Grease large bowl; set aside. Heat water and shortening in saucepan until very warm (120° to 130°F.). Combine 3 cups flour, 1 cup sugar, salt, and yeast in mixing bowl. Add heated mixture and eggs; beat with electric mixer until smooth. Add 2 cups flour; blend well. Stir in enough remaining flour to make a soft dough. Turn out onto lightly floured board or pastry cloth. Cover and let rest 10 minutes. Knead 8 to 10 minutes, or until smooth and elastic. Shape into ball. Place in prepared bowl. Turn once to grease top. Cover and let rise in warm place, free from draft, 1½ hours, or until double in bulk. Combine remaining ½ cup sugar and cinnamon in small dish; set aside. Grease 36 muffin cups; set aside. Punch dough down; divide in half. Roll out each half on lightly floured board or pastry cloth into 15x10-inch rectangle. Brush each with half of the butter. Sprinkle each with half of the sugar-cinnamon mixture. Roll up, jelly roll fashion, from long side. Cut into ¾-inch-thick slices. Place slices, cut sides down, in prepared muffin cups. Cover and let rise in warm place, free from draft, 30 minutes, or until double in bulk. Preheat oven to 400°F. Bake 20 minutes. Transfer to wire racks to cool. Drizzle tops with Rum Icing.

Rum Icing

1½ cups confectioners sugar
  ¼ cup milk
  1 teaspoon rum extract

Combine all ingredients in small mixing bowl; beat with electric mixer until smooth.

Note: If you do not have 36 muffin cups, you can bake 12 rolls, cut sides down, in greased 8-inch round baking pan. Sides of rolls will be soft.

Peanut Crescent Rolls

Makes 6 to 8 servings
- ½ cup chopped salted peanuts
- ¼ cup sugar
- 2 tablespoons all-purpose flour
- 2 tablespoons butter, melted
- 1 tablespoon grated orange peel
- 1 package refrigerated crescent dinner rolls
  Peanut Butter Frosting (recipe follows)
- ¼ cup chopped salted peanuts

To make rolls, combine peanuts, sugar, flour, butter, and orange peel in a bowl; set aside. Press seams of crescent rolls together and roll to form a 14x7-inch rectangle. Sprinkle rectangle with reserved peanut mixture. Roll rectangle from long side as if to form a jelly roll. Place roll in a semicircle on a lightly buttered baking sheet; make cuts 1 inch apart about two-thirds way through. Bake at 375°F. for 20 to 25 minutes. Remove from oven and cool slightly. Frost peanut crescent rolls with frosting and sprinkle with chopped peanuts.

Peanut Butter Frosting
- ¼ cup peanut butter
- 2 tablespoons honey
- 2 tablespoons milk
- ¼ cup confectioners sugar

Combine peanut butter, honey, milk and confectioners sugar in mixer bowl; mix until well blended.

Easy Pumpkin Swirl Rolls

Makes 10 to 12 servings
- 1 cup Libby's Pumpkin Pie Mix
- ½ cup chopped dried apricots
- 2 packages (8 ounces each) refrigerated crescent dinner rolls
  Sugar

Preheat oven to 350°F. In saucepan, combine pumpkin pie mix and apricots. Cook over low heat about 10 minutes, or until thick. Cool. Separate crescent roll dough into 4 rectangles. On a surface lightly sprinkled with sugar, roll out each rectangle to 7x4 inches. Press to seal perforations. Divide pumpkin mixture evenly among rectangles. Spread mixture almost to edges. Roll dough from wide end. Place on cookie sheet; cover and refrigerate. When dough is firm enough to slice, about 10 minutes, cut into 1-inch slices. Arrange in two 9-inch buttered cake pans. Sprinkle lightly with additional sugar. Bake 25 minutes, or until golden brown.

Jewel Scones

Makes 1 dozen scones
- 1¾ cups all-purpose flour
- 3 tablespoons sugar, divided
- 1 tablespoon baking powder
- 1 teaspoon grated lemon peel
- ½ teaspoon salt
- ⅓ cup butter or margarine
- 2 eggs
- ½ cup light cream
- 1 egg white, lightly beaten
- 1 can (12 ounces) Solo filling, any desired fruit flavor

Preheat oven to 425°F. Combine flour, 2 tablespoons sugar, baking powder, grated lemon peel, and salt. Using a pastry blender or 2 knives, cut in butter or margarine until mixture has consistency of coarse crumbs. Beat eggs and cream together. Add to dry ingredients and stir until mixture is moistened. Turn out onto a lightly floured board and knead gently, about 15 strokes. Using a lightly floured rolling pin, roll dough into a circle about ¼ inch thick and 8 inches in diameter. Cut circle into quarters, then cut each quarter into 3 wedges. Place wedges, 1 inch apart, on a large ungreased baking sheet. With the thumb make a 1-inch indentation in center of broad section of scone. Brush remaining portion of tops with egg white, then sprinkle with 1 tablespoon sugar. Fill each indentation with a scant 2 teaspoons of desired filling. Bake 12 minutes, or until light golden brown. Serve warm with butter, if desired.

Good idea: There is no need to transfer unused portions of Solo fillings into glass containers, as the cans are lacquered. Unused portions can be refrigerated for several weeks, if covered.

Quick Caramel Buns

Makes 10 buns
- ½ cup firmly packed light brown sugar
- ⅓ cup butter, melted
- 1 tablespoon light corn syrup
- ½ cup coarsely chopped walnuts
- 1 package (9½ ounces) refrigerated flaky biscuits

In a small mixing bowl, blend sugar, butter, syrup, and walnuts. Spoon a heaping tablespoon of the mixture into each of ten 3-inch muffin-pan cups. Open biscuits according to package directions. Place 1 biscuit in each cup on top of mixture. Bake in a preheated 375°F. oven for 12 to 14 minutes, or until tops are golden brown. Remove from oven and immediately invert muffin pan onto a large piece of aluminum foil. Let pan remain over buns for 1 minute. Gently remove pan.

Peanut-Honey Buns

Makes 2 dozen buns
    ½ cup milk
    ¼ cup butter
    ¼ cup sugar
    ½ teaspoon salt
    2 packages (¼ ounce each) or cakes yeast, active
        dry or compressed
    1 egg
    3¼ cups (about) all-purpose flour
    1 cup chopped salted peanuts, divided
    ⅓ cup firmly packed dark brown sugar
    ⅔ cup honey
    4 tablespoons melted butter, divided
    ½ cup firmly packed dark brown sugar

Scald milk. Stir in butter, sugar, and salt. Cool to lukewarm. Measure ½ cup warm (105° to 115°F.) water into a large warm bowl. Sprinkle or crumble in yeast; stir until dissolved. Add lukewarm milk mixture, egg, and 2 cups of the flour. Beat until smooth. Stir in enough additional flour to make a soft dough. Turn out on a lightly floured board. Knead about 10 minutes until smooth and elastic. Place in an oiled bowl, turning once to oil top of dough. Cover and let rise in a warm place, free from draft, until double in bulk, about 40 minutes. Combine ½ cup of the chopped peanuts, ⅓ cup dark brown sugar, honey, and 3 tablespoons melted butter. Mix until blended. Divide this mixture evenly among 24 oiled muffin cups, 2¾x1½ inches. When dough is double in bulk, punch down. Turn out onto a lightly floured board and divide in half. Roll out half into a rectangle 12x9 inches. Brush lightly with remaining melted butter. Combine remaining ½ cup peanuts with ½ cup brown sugar. Sprinkle rectangle with half of this mixture. Roll tightly from 12-inch side, jelly roll fashion. Seal edges firmly. Cut into 1-inch slices. Place, cut side up, into 12 of the prepared muffin cups. Repeat with remaining half of dough and peanut-brown sugar mixture. Cover pans. Let rise in a warm place, free from draft, for about 40 minutes, or until double in bulk. Bake in a preheated 375°F. oven for 15 to 20 minutes. Turn out of pans immediately onto wire racks. When cool, serve as desired, or put buns on a baking sheet, place in freezer and freeze until firm. Remove from freezer, and package in moisture- and vaporproof material. Seal, label, and freeze.

To serve, remove buns from freezer and remove wrappings. Let stand at room temperature until thawed, or place on a baking sheet and heat in a preheated 300°F. oven for about 10 minutes.

Calas

Makes 2 dozen cakes
    1½ cups cooked Riceland Rice, very soft
    1 package yeast, active dry or compressed
    ½ cup warm water
    3 eggs, beaten
    1¼ cups sifted all-purpose flour
    ¼ cup sugar
    ½ teaspoon salt
    ¼ teaspoon ground nutmeg
        Chef-way Oil for frying
        Confectioners sugar, or sugar-cinnamon
        mixture

Mash rice and cool to lukewarm. Soften yeast in warm water and stir into lukewarm rice; mix well. Cover and let rise overnight. In the morning, add eggs, flour, sugar, salt, and nutmeg. Beat only until smooth. Let stand in a warm place for 30 minutes. Drop by tablespoonfuls into deep hot Chef-way (360°F.) and fry until golden, about 3 minutes. Serve sprinkled with confectioners sugar or sugar mixed with cinnamon.

Rice tip: Make muffins, pancakes, and waffles more nutritious by adding cooked rice to the batter.

Double Peanut Gems

Makes 12 muffins
    ¼ cup butter, cut into 12 pieces
    ⅓ cup brown sugar
    ¼ cup salted peanuts
    1 cup all-purpose flour
    2 teaspoons baking powder
    ½ teaspoon salt
    ½ cup finely chopped peanuts
    1 cup bran flakes
    1 cup milk
    ¼ cup shortening
    ¼ cup brown sugar
    1 egg

Grease twelve (2¾-inch) muffin cups. Put 1 piece of butter in each; divide the brown sugar among the cups. Put in oven for a few minutes to melt. Put 5 or 6 peanuts in each cup and set pan aside. Combine flour, baking powder, salt, and chopped peanuts. Put bran flakes in a small bowl and cover with milk. Cream shortening and brown sugar together; add egg and blend well. Stir in softened bran flakes. Add dry ingredients and stir just until they are moistened. Spoon batter into muffin cups, over peanuts. Bake in a preheated 400°F. oven for 20 to 25 minutes. Loosen edges of muffins and turn out of pan. Serve while warm.

Rugelach

Makes 24 rolls

    1 cup butter or margarine, softened
    1 package (8 ounces) cream cheese, at room
       temperature
    2 cups all-purpose flour
    ⅛ teaspoon salt
    ⅔ cup Sun-Maid® Zante Currants or Sun-Maid®
       Puffed Seeded Muscat Raisins, chopped
    ½ cup chopped walnuts
    ½ teaspoon ground cinnamon
    2 tablespoons sugar

Combine the butter and cream cheese. Add flour and salt and knead by hand or beat until well mixed and smooth. Divide dough in half. Wrap each half and refrigerate until dough is well chilled, several hours or overnight. Combine currants, walnuts, cinnamon, and sugar. On lightly floured board, roll each dough half into a 12x8-inch rectangle. Sprinkle each rectangle with half of the currant mixture, to within about ¼ inch of the edges. Preheat oven to 350°F. Starting with the 12-inch side, roll dough into a long tube. Moisten the edge with water and pinch seam lightly to hold in place. Cut into 1-inch-thick slices and place on lightly greased baking sheet. Bake for 18 to 20 minutes, or until pastry is very lightly browned. Remove from pan and cool slightly on wire rack.

Danish Doughnuts

Makes about 2 dozen doughnuts

    2 cups buttermilk
    2 eggs, separated
    2 cups all-purpose flour
    ½ teaspoon salt
    1 teaspoon sugar
    1 teaspoon baking soda
       Sugar
    1 can (12 ounces) Solo Prune Filling or other fruit
       filling

Beat buttermilk and egg yolks together. Sift together flour, salt, 1 teaspoon sugar, and baking soda. Stir into buttermilk mixture. Beat egg whites until stiff but not dry. Fold into buttermilk batter. Heat the aebleskiver pan. Brush with butter or margarine, using enough to leave a small amount in bottom of each cup. Fill each hole in pan two-thirds full of batter and cook slowly, until bottom is lightly browned. Using a long skewer, turn the balls and lightly brown the uncooked side. Serve immediately with sugar and a dab of fruit filling.
Good idea: Aebleskiver pans are made of cast iron and have hemispherical depressions. They can be pur-

chased in department stores, specialty shops, and in most Scandinavian stores. For a delicious variation on this recipe, drop a teaspoonful of Solo Prune or Poppy Filling into the batter of each doughnut before cooking.

Chocolate-Coconut Doughnuts

Makes 16 doughnuts

    4 cups all-purpose flour
    4 teaspoons baking powder
    ¾ teaspoon salt
    ¼ teaspoon baking soda
    2 eggs
  1¼ cups sugar
    2 envelopes (2 ounces) Nestlé Choco-bake
       Unsweetened Baking Chocolate Flavor
    ¼ cup vegetable oil
    1 teaspoon coconut extract
    ¾ cup buttermilk
       Vegetable oil
       Chocolate Frosting (recipe folows)
       Toasted coconut (optional)

In a small bowl, combine flour, baking powder, salt, and baking soda; set aside. In a large bowl, combine eggs and sugar; beat until thick and lemon colored, about 5 minutes. Stir in Choco-bake Unsweetened Baking Chocolate Flavor, oil, and coconut extract. Add flour mixture alternately with buttermilk. Beat just until flour is combined. Divide dough in half; wrap each half separately with waxed paper. Chill in refrigerator about 2 hours. On a lightly floured board or pastry cloth, roll out half the dough to ½-inch thickness. Cut with a 3-inch doughnut cutter. Repeat with remaining chilled dough. In a deep fryer or electric skillet set at 375°F., fry doughnuts in hot oil until browned (about 1½ minutes on each side). Drain on paper towels; cool. Spread tops of doughnuts with Chocolate Frosting. Garnish with toasted coconut, if desired.

Chocolate Frosting

Makes ½ cup frosting

    1 envelope (1 ounce) Nestlé Choco-bake Unsweet-
       ened Baking Chocolate Flavor
    1 cup sifted confectioners sugar
    2 tablespoons butter, melted
    2 tablespoons boiling water
    ¼ teaspoon vanilla extract

In a small bowl, combine Nestlé Choco-bake Unsweetened Baking Chocolate Flavor, confectioners sugar, butter, boiling water, and vanilla extract; beat until smooth.

The Real, Down-Home Kind

Crispness is the feature of these crackers, biscuits, breadsticks, flatbreads, and the like, plus unparalleled homemade flavor the store-bought kind can't match.

Best-Ever Biscuits

Makes about 2 dozen biscuits
- 1¾ cups sifted all-purpose flour
- 1 teaspoon salt
- 2 teaspoons baking powder
- 6 tablespoons cold butter
- ⅔ cup milk

Sift together dry ingredients into a bowl. With 2 knives or a pastry blender, cut in butter until the mixture is the consistency of coarse cornmeal. Add milk all at once and stir briefly until dough leaves the side of the bowl. Turn dough out on a floured board and knead gently and quickly about 20 seconds. Pat out dough to about ½-inch thickness. Cut with a biscuit cutter dipped into a very little flour and place on a lightly oiled baking sheet. Brush tops of biscuits with milk and bake in a preheated 450°F. oven for 12 to 15 minutes.

Sausage Show-Offs

Makes 12 biscuits
- 1 recipe Hot Rize Biscuits (see index)
- 1 pound pork sausage meat

Preheat oven to 350°F. Prepare biscuit dough. Roll out dough on lightly floured board or pastry cloth into ¼-inch thick rectangle. Spread sausage over dough almost to edge. Roll up, jelly roll fashion. Cut into ½-inch thick rounds. Place rounds on ungreased baking sheet. Bake 30 minutes, or until golden brown. Serve immediately.

Hot Rize Biscuits (page 112); Thimble Biscuits (page 112); Sausage Show-Offs. Martha White Foods

Riz Biscuits

Makes 18 biscuits
- 2¾ cups sifted Martha White Self-Rising Flour
- 3 tablespoons sugar
- ¼ teaspoon baking soda
- 1 package (¼ ounce) active dry yeast
- ⅓ cup vegetable shortening
- 1 cup warm buttermilk (105° to 115°F.)
- 2 tablespoons butter or margarine, melted

Grease 2 baking sheets; set aside. Combine flour, sugar, baking soda, and yeast in bowl. Cut in shortening with pastry blender or 2 knives until mixture is consistency of coarse crumbs. Quickly stir in buttermilk until just moistened. Turn out onto lightly floured board or pastry cloth. Knead just until smooth. Roll out to ¼-inch thickness. Cut into rounds with floured 2-inch biscuit cutter. Brush tops of rounds with butter. Stack 1 round on top of another to bake a double biscuit. Repeat with remaining rounds. Place on prepared baking sheets. Cover and let rise in warm place, free from draft, 1 hour, or until double in bulk. Preheat oven to 375°F. Bake 12 to 15 minutes, or until golden brown.

Sour Cream Biscuits

Makes 1 dozen biscuits
- 2 cups sifted all-purpose flour
- 1 tablespoon baking powder
- ¼ teaspoon baking soda
- 1 teaspoon salt
- 1 cup sour cream
- ¼ cup milk

Sift together flour, baking powder, baking soda, and salt. Blend in sour cream. Stir in milk to make a soft dough. Knead gently on a lightly floured board. Pat out to ½-inch thickness. Cut in rounds with a 2-inch biscuit cutter. Place on lightly oiled baking sheet. Bake in a preheated 450°F. oven for 10 minutes.

Hot Rize Biscuits

Makes 12 to 14 biscuits
  2 **cups sifted Martha White Self-Rising Flour**
  ¼ **cup vegetable shortening**
  ¾ **cup milk**

Preheat oven to 450°F. Lightly grease large baking sheet; set aside. Place flour in bowl; cut in shortening with pastry blender or 2 knives until mixture is consistency of coarse crumbs. Add milk; stir with fork just until dough leaves sides of bowl. Turn out onto lightly floured board or pastry cloth. Knead just until smooth. Roll out dough to ½-inch thickness. Cut into rounds with floured 2-inch biscuit cutter. Place on prepared baking sheet. Bake 10 to 12 minutes, or until golden brown.

Thimble Biscuits

Makes 12 to 14 biscuits
  1 **recipe Hot Rize Biscuits (see above)**
  2 **to 3 tablespoons jelly or jam**

Preheat oven to 450°F. Lightly grease large baking sheet; set aside. Prepare biscuit dough. Roll out dough on lightly floured board or pastry cloth to ¼-inch thickness. Cut into rounds with floured 2-inch biscuit cutter. Place half of biscuits on prepared baking sheet. Use a thimble, or other small cutter, to cut a hole in center of each remaining biscuit. Place a biscuit with center removed on top of each whole biscuit. Fill each hole with about ½ teaspoon jelly. Bake 10 to 12 minutes, or until golden brown.

Biscuit Mix

Makes 48 to 56 biscuits
  8 **cups Martha White Self-Rising Flour**
  1 **cup vegetable shortening**

Sift flour into large bowl. Cut in shortening with pastry blender or 2 knives until mixture is consistency of coarse crumbs. Store in airtight container at room temperature. Mix keeps at least 4 months. To use, stir in milk to make a soft dough. (Use ⅓ cup milk for each 1 cup mix.) Preheat oven to 450°F. Roll out dough on lightly floured board or pastry cloth to ½-inch thickness. Cut into rounds with floured 2-inch biscuit cutter. Place biscuits on lightly greased baking sheet. Bake 10 to 12 minutes, or until golden brown.

BixMix Rize Biscuits

Makes 12 biscuits
  1⅓ **teaspoons active dry yeast**
  ⅓ **cup warm water (110° to 115°F.)**
  1 **tablespoon sugar**
  1 **package (5½ ounces) Martha White BixMix**
  2 **tablespoons butter, melted**

Dissolve yeast in warm water in small bowl; set aside. Grease large baking sheet; set aside. Combine baking mix and sugar in bowl. Stir in yeast mixture. Turn out onto lightly floured board or pastry cloth. Knead 10 times, or until smooth. Roll out to ¼-inch thickness. Cut into rounds with floured 2-inch biscuit cutter. Brush tops of rounds with butter. Stack 1 round on top of another to make a double biscuit. Repeat with remaining rounds. Place on prepared baking sheet. Cover and let rise in warm place, free from draft, 40 minutes, or until double in bulk. Preheat oven to 375°F. Bake 12 to 15 minutes, or until golden brown.

Baking Powder Biscuits

Makes 1½ dozen biscuits
  2 **cups sifted all-purpose flour**
  1 **teaspoon salt**
  3 **teaspoons baking powder**
  ⅓ **cup soft shortening or butter**
  ¾ **cup (about) milk**
  Butter

Preheat oven to 450°F. Sift flour, salt, and baking powder into large Sunbeam Mixmaster Mixer bowl. Add shortening; beat at lowest speed about 1½ minutes, or until consistency of coarse meal. Pour in milk, adding just enough to form a soft dough. Beat about 30 seconds, only long enough to mix. Turn out onto lightly floured surface. Knead gently, folding over a few times to even texture. Pat or roll ½ to ¾ inch thick. Cut with floured cutter or cut into squares with a knife. Place on ungreased baking sheet—far apart for crusty sides or close together for soft sides. Bake 12 to 15 minutes, or until brown. Serve piping hot with plenty of butter.

About Baking Biscuits
If you place biscuits on sheet with sides touching, they will be soft; if you place each separately, they will be crusty—have them the way you like them best.

Cheese and Bacon Biscuits

Makes 12 to 14 biscuits
- 2 cups sifted Martha White Self-Rising Flour
- ¼ cup vegetable shortening
- 1 cup (4 ounces) grated sharp cheddar cheese
- ¼ cup (4 strips) crumbled crisp-cooked bacon
- ¾ cup milk

Preheat oven to 450°F. Lightly grease baking sheet; set aside. Place flour in bowl. Cut in shortening with pastry blender or 2 knives until mixture is consistency of coarse crumbs. Stir in cheese and bacon. Add milk; stir with fork just until dough leaves sides of bowl. Turn out onto lightly floured surface or pastry cloth. Knead until smooth. Roll out to ½-inch thickness. Cut into rounds with floured 2-inch biscuit cutter. Place on prepared baking sheet. Bake 10 to 12 minutes, or until golden brown.

Italian Garlic Biscuits

Makes about 10 biscuits
- 2 cups sifted all-purpose flour
- 1 tablespoon sugar
- 2½ teaspoons baking powder
- ½ cup Wish-Bone® Italian Dressing
- ½ cup milk

Into bowl, sift flour, sugar, and baking powder. Stir in Wish-Bone Italian Dressing and milk until all ingredients are moistened. Preheat oven to 425°F. On floured board, knead dough lightly about 5 or 6 times. Roll dough 1 inch thick and cut with a floured 2-inch biscuit cutter. Place 1 inch apart on ungreased baking sheet and bake 12 to 15 minutes, or until biscuits are golden brown.

Sweet Potato Biscuits

Makes 16 to 20 biscuits
- 1½ cups all-purpose flour
- 4 teaspoons baking powder
- ¾ teaspoon salt
- ½ cup shortening
- ¼ cup milk
- 1¼ cups mashed cooked sweet potatoes
- 5 slices crisp cooked bacon, crumbled

Sift flour, baking powder, and salt together. Cut in shortening until mixture is like coarse meal. Combine milk, sweet potatoes, and bacon; mix well. Blend into flour mixture. Roll or pat out to ½-inch thickness on lightly floured surface. Cut with floured 2½-inch biscuit cutter. Place on baking sheet and bake in hot oven (425°F.) about 15 minutes, or until golden brown.

General Method for Making Biscuits

With a pastry blender or 2 knives, cut in shortening until mixture is the consistency of coarse crumbs. These bits of shortening make biscuits flaky. Make a well in the dry ingredients. Add liquid all at once. Stir with a fork, until the dough leaves the sides of the bowl and forms a ball. Turn the dough out onto a floured board or pastry cloth. Roll the dough around to coat lightly with flour. Knead gently to combine ingredients thoroughly. With a rolling pin, roll evenly to desired thickness, usually about ½ inch. Biscuits will double in weight during baking. Cut close together with floured biscuit cutter so there is less dough to reroll. Use straight downward motion, not a twisting one. Gently press leftover dough together and reroll. The best utensil for baking biscuits is a shiny, lightly greased baking sheet.

Old-Fashioned Buttermilk Biscuits

Makes 12 to 14 biscuits
- 2 cups sifted Martha White Self-Rising Flour
- ¼ teaspoon baking soda
- ¼ cup vegetable shortening
- ⅞ cup buttermilk

Preheat oven to 450°F. Lightly grease baking sheet; set aside. Combine flour and baking soda in bowl. Cut in shortening with pastry blender or 2 knives until mixture is consistency of coarse crumbs. Add buttermilk; stir with fork just until dough leaves sides of bowl. Turn out onto lightly floured board or pastry cloth. Knead gently just until smooth. Roll out to ½-inch thickness. Cut into rounds with floured 2-inch biscuit cutter. Place on prepared baking sheet. Bake 10 to 12 minutes, or until golden brown.

Homemade Melba Toast

Make the melba toast at home—it's an excellent way to use up bread that threatens to go stale. Cut bread of any kind into ⅛-inch slices; if you freeze it, you'll be able to get the thinness you want very easily. Cut shapes from the slices with cookie cutters if you wish, or simply divide the slices in half. Place a rack on a baking sheet, spread out the bread pieces on the rack. Bake in a 250°F. oven until they are dry and the shade of golden brown that suits you. Thin slices of rolls or buns may also be used.

Potato Breadsticks; Country Rye Bread (page 11). Wisconsin Potato Growers Auxiliary

Potato Breadsticks

Makes 20 to 24 sticks

 1 medium potato, washed, cooked, peeled, and
　　mashed; reserve ⅔ cup potato water
 3½ to 4 cups all-purpose flour, divided
 1 package (¼ ounce) active dry yeast
 ¼ cup vegetable oil
 1 teaspoon sugar
 1 teaspoon salt
 1 egg white
　Toasted sesame seed

Grease a baking sheet; set aside. Heat reserved potato water in small saucepan to 120° to 130°F. Combine potato, warm potato water, 1½ cups flour, yeast, oil, sugar, and salt in large bowl. Beat with electric mixer on high 2 minutes. Stir in remaining flour. Divide into 20 to 24 equal parts. Roll each part into a ½- to ¾-inch rope. Place 1 inch apart, on prepared baking sheet. Cover with oiled waxed paper. Let rest 20 minutes. Preheat oven to 350°F. Beat egg white and 1 tablespoon water with fork in small bowl. Brush over breadsticks. Sprinkle with sesame seed. Bake 25 to 30 minutes, or until golden brown. Cool before serving.

Caraway Breadsticks

Makes 24 breadsticks

 1 package (¼ ounce) active dry yeast
 1¼ cups warm water (105° to 115°F.)
 3½ cups sifted Martha White All-Purpose Flour
 3 tablespoons sugar
 3 teaspoons caraway seed, divided
 1½ teaspoons salt
 1 tablespoon butter

Grease large bowl; set aside. Dissolve yeast in water in another bowl. Add flour, sugar, 2 teaspoons caraway seed, salt, and butter; blend well. Turn out onto lightly floured board or pastry cloth. Knead 8 to 10 minutes, or until smooth and elastic. Shape into ball. Place in prepared bowl. Turn once to grease top. Cover and let rise in warm place, free from draft, 1 hour, or until double in bulk. Punch dough down. Grease 2 large baking sheets; set aside. Shape dough into long roll. Cut into 24 pieces. Use palms of hands to roll each piece into 12-inch stick. Place sticks 1 inch apart on prepared baking sheets. Sprinkle lightly with remaining teaspoon caraway seed. Cover and let rise in warm place, free from draft, 1 hour, or until double in bulk. Preheat oven to 400°F. Bake 15 to 20 minutes, or until golden brown. Transfer to wire rack to cool.

Sour Cream Biscuits (page 111). Caloric Corporation

Popovers. Caloric Corporation

Popovers

Makes 6 servings

- **3 tablespoons butter or margarine**
- **1 cup milk**
- **3 eggs**
- **½ teaspoon salt**
- **1 cup all-purpose flour**

Grease six 6-ounce custard cups. Place ½ teaspoon butter in each cup. Place cups on ceramic cooking shelf in preheated oven 5 minutes. Beat milk, eggs, and salt in small mixing bowl. Beat in flour until smooth and thickened. Pour batter into hot custard cups. Preheat oven to 400°F. Bake 45 to 50 minutes until crisp and well browned.

Biscuit Bonanza

Biscuits are soda- or baking powder-leavened quick breads (similar small yeast breads are buns or rolls), generally round but sometimes square, and now and then somewhat lopsided because the cook has taken a short-cut and made drop biscuits rather than cutting out the dough. Baked in a hot oven they puff up high, have crisp sides if they've been placed on the baking sheet with space between them, soft sides if they've baked huddled together. They are—or should be—flaky within. Serve hot, then split and toast the leftovers, if there are any, for another meal.

Easy to make and quick to bake, biscuits have all sorts of uses. At breakfast or brunch (once breakfast wasn't worthy of the name without a pan of biscuits), hustle them to the table, split and butter while they're still steaming, and serve with honey, jam or jelly, or preserves. An old-fashioned dish that deserves greater current popularity is fricasséed chicken and biscuits; the hot biscuits are split and spread on a platter, some of the gravy is dribbled over them, the chicken is placed on top, and extra gravy is brought to the table. Split, buttered, slathered with sweetened strawberries between and on top and drenched with thick cream, biscuits make a most superior shortcake. However and whenever you serve them, you aren't likely to find anyone who says "No, thanks," to fresh, hot biscuits.

Water biscuits and beaten biscuits are 2 of the South's innumerable culinary claims to fame. The former are hard, with a ring of shiny brown mounds around their top edges and a depression in the center just right for a good dab of jam or peanut butter. Beaten biscuits are small, not browned, and bear neat fork-pricks on their tops. They take their name from one of the preparation steps—they are literally beaten, not in a bowl but on a board. Any handy instrument, such as a mallet, can be used. (One recipe suggests the flat side of an ax.) Twenty minutes to an hour is a proper beating time—reflecting long gone days of gracious living, when not only did the lady of the house have a cook but the cook had helpers to spell her in her more arduous tasks. Split and sandwiched with a sliver of sharp, salty Virginia-style ham, beaten biscuits were often a feature of buffets and hunt breakfasts.

If you are not in any way a home baker, help is at hand. In the refrigerated case at the supermarket, you'll find biscuits of various kinds, packed in tubes. All you need to do is put them on a baking sheet and bake them. Bakeries, too, often make biscuits, but they cannot be served hot from the oven as can your homemade ones, or the home-baked ones from the supermarket. Be sure to check the metal top of the tube in which the biscuits are packed. It's dated—don't buy the biscuits if the date has passed.

Freezing Biscuits

Although biscuits are best when baked soon after mixing the dough, the dough can be frozen for later use.

To freeze, prepare biscuit dough according to the recipe. Roll out, cut, and place biscuits on a lightly greased baking sheet. Brush the tops lightly with milk. Place in the freezer. When frozen hard (about 1 hour), remove the baking sheet from the freezer. Place biscuits in a plastic bag; seal the bag and return it to freezer.

When ready to use, remove the bag from the freezer and place the biscuits on a lightly greased baking sheet. Preheat oven to 450°F. Biscuits do not have to thaw before baking. Bake 12 to 15 minutes, or until golden brown.

Homemade Crackers

Makes 70 crackers

1 package (6½ ounces) Martha White Pizza Crust Mix
Coarse salt

Preheat oven to 375°F. Grease 2 large baking sheets; set aside. Prepare pizza dough according to package directions. After dough rests 5 minutes, divide in half. Use rolling pin to roll out each half on lightly floured board or pastry cloth into 14x10-inch rectangle. (Dough must be very thin to make crisp crackers.) Ease rolled dough onto prepared baking sheets. Use sharp knife to score into squares. Sprinkle with coarse salt. Bake 12 to 15 minutes. Watch closely; crackers will brown quickly.

Almond-Wheat Crackers

Makes about 8 dozen crackers

⅔ cup water
⅓ cup vegetable oil
2 tablespoons firmly packed brown sugar
1½ cups *each* whole wheat flour and rolled oats
1 cup ground almonds
½ teaspoon salt

In large bowl, combine water, oil, and sugar. Stir in flour, oats, almonds, and salt. Knead on floured board 5 minutes, adding flour as needed to make a non-sticky dough. Roll out to ⅛-inch thickness. Cut into strips 3x1 inch. Place apart on oiled baking sheets. Bake in 350°F. oven 10 to 15 minutes until lightly browned. Cool on racks. Store in airtight container.

Crisp Whole Wheat Crackers

Makes 48 crackers

  1 cup Elam's Stone Ground 100% Whole Wheat
    Flour
  ½ teaspoon baking powder
  ½ teaspoon baking soda
  ½ teaspoon salt
  ½ cup cold water
  1 tablespoon cooking oil
  1 tablespoon butter, melted (optional)
  2 tablespoons caraway seed (optional)

Combine and mix first 4 ingredients in bowl. Add water and oil; mix well and shape into 2 flat patties of equal size. Cover dough; let stand 10 minutes. Place 1 patty on ungreased baking sheet sprinkled generously with additional Elam's Stone Ground 100% Whole Wheat Flour. Turn patty to coat second side with flour. Roll into 12x8-inch rectangle on baking sheet. Cut into 2-inch squares using a floured pizza wheel or sharp knife. If desired, brush lightly with melted butter. Sprinkle each square with 1 teaspoon caraway seed. Repeat with second dough patty. Bake in moderate 350°F. oven until crisp and done, 15 to 20 minutes.

Peanut Butter-Wheat Crackers

Makes about 40 crackers

  1 cup all-purpose flour
  1 cup whole wheat flour
  ¼ cup wheat germ
  1½ teaspoons caraway seed
  1 teaspoon salt
  ½ teaspoon baking soda
  1 cup Skippy Super Chunk Peanut Butter
  ½ cup (about) water
  2 tablespoons cider vinegar
    Milk
    Coarse salt (optional)

In large bowl, mix together flour, whole wheat flour, wheat germ, caraway seed, salt, and baking soda. With pastry blender or 2 knives, cut in peanut butter until coarse crumbs form. Add water and vinegar; mix until dough holds together.(If mixture is too dry, additional water may be added, 1 tablespoon at a time.) Divide dough in half. On lightly floured surface, roll half of dough out to ⅛-inch thickness. Cut with 3-inch round cookie cutter. Repeat with scraps and remaining half of dough. Place on ungreased cookie sheet. Brush surface with milk. If desired, sprinkle with coarse salt. Bake in 375°F. oven 13 to 15 minutes, or until browned and crisp. Remove from pan and cool on wire racks. Store in airtight container.

Scotch Oat Crackers

Makes 2 to 3 dozen crackers

  1 cup Elam's Scotch Style Oatmeal
  ½ teaspoon salt
  ¼ teaspoon baking soda
  4 to 5 tablespoons cold water
  2 tablespoons melted shortening or drippings

Combine first 3 ingredients in bowl; mix. Add 4 tablespoons water and melted shortening or drippings; stir just until dry ingredients are moistened. Add remaining water if needed to make a pliable dough that can be shaped into a ball. Roll dough as thin as possible (about ⅛ inch) on a board sprinkled with Elam's Scotch Style Oatmeal. Cut into 2-inch diamonds or squares using a floured cookie cutter, or cut into bars using a sharp knife or pizza wheel. Bake on hot, lightly greased griddle (375°F.) until crisp and lightly browned, 4 to 5 minutes, turning once. Cool.

Swedish Flatbread

Makes 12 crackers

  2¼ cups Martha White Whole Wheat Flour, divided
  1 cup buttermilk
  1 teaspoon salt
  1 teaspoon baking soda
  ¼ cup butter or margarine, melted

Preheat oven to 350°F. Grease large baking sheet; set aside. Combine 1½ cups flour, buttermilk, salt, baking soda, and butter in bowl; stir until smooth. Gradually stir in enough remaining flour to make a stiff dough. Turn out onto floured board or pastry cloth. Knead 3 or 4 times. Divide into 12 portions. Roll each portion into 8-inch circle. Ease dough circles around rolling pin. Lift onto prepared baking sheet. Prick well with fork. Bake 15 minutes, or until lightly browned. Transfer to wire rack to cool. Store in airtight container.

Spreading the Goodness Around

There is only one way to make homemade breads better, and that's to serve them with luscious homemade jams and jellies, savory spreads and butters.

California Wine Jelly

Makes about 2½ pints jelly
- 3 cups C & H Granulated Sugar
- 2 cups dry or sweet wine, sherry, or port
- 1 packet liquid pectin

Combine sugar and wine in top of double boiler. Place over rapidly boiling water and heat 2 minutes, or until sugar is dissolved, stirring constantly. Remove from heat and stir in liquid pectin at once. Pour into hot sterilized jars. Seal immediately.

Minted Wine Jelly

Use white port in place of sweet wine or sherry. Add 10 to 12 drops mint extract plus green food coloring, if desired, to sugar and wine in double boiler. Or bring 1½ cups crushed mint leaves to boil in pot with the wine and marinate until cool. Strain wine, remeasure, adding more wine if necessary, and follow recipe as for California Wine Jelly.

Spiced Port Jelly

Use port in recipe above. Add ⅛ teaspoon *each* ground cinnamon and ground cloves to sugar and wine in double boiler. Follow recipe as for California Wine Jelly.

Honeyed Port Jelly

Makes four 8-ounce jars
- 2½ cups Sue Bee Honey
- ¾ cup port
- ½ bottle (3 ounces) liquid pectin
- 2 tablespoons lemon juice

Combine honey and port and bring to a boil. Add pectin, stirring constantly. Return to a full rolling boil. Add lemon juice and remove from heat. Pour hot jelly into sterilized jars. Seal.

Mint Jelly

Makes about 3 pints jelly
- 2 cups fresh mint leaves
- 2½ cups apple juice
- 2 tablespoons lemon juice
  Green food coloring (optional)
- 3½ cups C & H Granulated Sugar
- 1 packet liquid pectin

Wash mint leaves and place in large saucepan. Mash. Add apple juice. Bring to boil. Remove from heat, cover pan, and let stand for 10 minutes. Strain. Add lemon juice and a few drops green food coloring. Measure 1¾ cups of this mixture. Combine with sugar in large pan. Bring back to full boil, stirring constantly. Stir in pectin, return to full boil for 1 minute, stirring constantly. Remove from heat. Skim off foam. Pour into hot sterilized jars. Seal immediately.

Cranberry Jelly

Makes about 2 pints jelly
- 4 cups cranberries
- 2 cups water
- 2 cups C & H Granulated Sugar

Cook cranberries and water in saucepan until most of berries have burst. Force through coarse strainer. Return purée to saucepan; add sugar. Cook over low heat until sugar dissolves, swirling pan occasionally. Boil briskly, stirring frequently, to jelly stage (220°F. on candy thermometer) or until syrup drops in a sheet from a metal spoon and is as thick as desired when tested on a cold saucer. Pour into hot sterilized jars. Seal immediately.

Note: For holiday and special occasions, mold in a ring and serve filled with Waldorf salad.

Making Jams, Jellies, and Butters at Home

- Check entire jar for defects.

- Make sure you have the required supply of new lids and bands.

- Lids are not reusable, because the sealing compound with not seal twice.

- Bands are reusable only if in good, unwarped, un-rusted condition.

To Fill Jars

- Prepare checked-over jars by washing in hot soapy water and rinsing them thoroughly.

- Keep jars in hot water until ready to fill.

- Wash and rinse lids and bands.

- Put lids and bands in saucepan of water and bring water to simmering point. Do not boil. Remove from heat, but leave lids and bands in water until needed.

- Fill clean, hot jars with prepared fruit, but fill only as many as will properly fit in the canning kettle at one time.

- Leave ¼ inch air or headspace for butters, conserves, jams, jellies, marmalades, and preserves. Leave ½ inch headspace for jellies when sealing with paraffin.

- Release tiny trapped air bubbles after filling by running a wooden or plastic spatula around the inside of each jar next to the glass. Never use metal spatula or knife to free bubbles. Tiny chips or cracks may result.

- Jar rims and threads must be wiped clean.

- Place a lid on top of each jar with the sealing compound down, next to the glass rim.

- Screw band tight, but do not use force.

Jellies

Jelly is the only preserve which can safely be prepared by the open kettle method. The boiling hot mixture is cooked and poured immediately into hot, sterilized jars and sealed with 2-piece lids or paraffin.

Paraffin should be heated in a double boiler and be used hot, but not smoking. Pour ⅛ inch thick for the best seal. Single, thin layers seal better than thick layers. Prick air bubbles to prevent spoilage.

Boiling Water Bath Method

- Butters, conserves, jams, marmalades, and preserves require boiling water bath processing for 5 to 15 minutes. (Refer to your recipe.) Paraffin cannot be used to seal anything except jelly.

- Boiling water bath canners should be kettles deep enough to allow space for 1 or 2 inches of water above the tops of the jars, plus a little extra space for water to boil in. Kettle should be equipped with a close-fitting cover and a wire or wood rack to keep jars from touching each other on the bottom or sides of the container.

- Put filled canning jars into rack and add hot water to bring water 1 or 2 inches above jar tops.

- Bring water to a rolling boil. Follow recipe for length of boiling time, beginning to time when water has reached a full boil.

- Carefully remove jars after processing, and cool away from drafts.

- *Check manufacturer's directions carefully to make sure each jar is properly sealed before storing!*

Testing for Doneness

Spoon or sheet test. Dip a cool metal spoon in boiling jelly. Raise spoon at least 12 inches above the kettle, out of the steam, and turn spoon so syrup runs off the side. If the syrup forms 2 drops that flow together and fall off the spoon as 1 sheet, the jelly should be done. This test is not for jams, marmalades, or preserves.

Refrigerator test. Pour a small amount of boiling jelly on a cold plate, and put it in the freezing compartment of the refrigerator for a few minutes. If the mixture jells, it should be done. While using this testing method, remove kettle from heat. This test may also be used for butters, jams, marmalades, and preserves.

Plum Jelly

Makes about 2 pints jelly
   4 pounds fully ripe plums (preferably sour cling-
      stone)
   1 cup water
   4 cups C & H Granulated Sugar

Crush plums with potato masher or food processor (do not peel or pit). Add water and bring to boil in large heavy kettle. Boil vigorously 10 minutes, or until plums are tender, crushing occasionally. Ladle into jelly bag or large bowl lined with muslin towel that has been wrung out in cold water. Bring ends together, tie a loop around them, and hang from hook until all juice drains out. Measure 4 cups juice into kettle. Add sugar. Stir constantly until mixture begins to boil. Boil vigorously without stirring until syrup jells (220°F. on candy thermometer) or until syrup drops in a sheet from a metal spoon and is as thick as desired when tested on a cold saucer. Skim off any foam. Pour into hot sterilized jars. Seal immediately.

Pectin Method
To 4 cups juice add 6½ cups C & H Granulated Sugar. Bring to boil, stirring constantly. Immediately stir in 1 packet liquid pectin. Bring to full rolling boil for 1 minute, stirring constantly. Remove from heat. Skim off any foam. Bottle and seal.
Note: If sweet plums are used, substitute ¼ cup strained lemon juice for ½ cup plum juice.

Quince-Apple-Cranberry Jelly

Makes about 4 pints jelly
   10 medium apples
    5 quinces
    4 cups (1 pound) cranberries
    9 cups water
    3 cups C & H Granulated Sugar

Wash fruit. Core and chop apples. Rub fuzz from quinces with cloth; core and chop. In 3 separate covered saucepans, cook quinces, apples, and cranberries with 3 cups water each until soft. (Allow about 30 minutes for quinces, 20 minutes for apples, and 10 minutes for cranberries.) Drain all fruits through several layers of dampened cheesecloth, squeezing and pressing with spoon. Combine juices. Measure 4 cups juice into large saucepan; add 3 cups sugar. Cook over low heat until sugar dissolves, swirling pan occasionally. Boil briskly, stirring frequently, to jelly stage (220°F. on candy thermometer) or until syrup drips in a sheet from a metal spoon and is as thick as desired when tested on a cold saucer. Pour into hot sterilized jars. Seal immediately. Repeat with equivalent amount of sugar for remaining juice.

Grape Jelly

Makes about 2½ cups
   1 envelope Knox® Unflavored Gelatine
   ¼ cup sugar
   2½ cups unsweetened grape juice

In a medium saucepan, mix Knox Unflavored Gelatine with sugar. Blend in grape juice. Stir over low heat until gelatine is completely dissolved, about 3 minutes. Ladle into jars. Cover and cool slightly before refrigerating.
Note: Use the conventional purple grape juice for this, or vary by using the newer red or white grape juices.

Apricot-Pineapple-Almond Marmalade

Makes about ½ pints marmalade
    6 cups fresh ripe apricots
    6 cups C & H Granulated Sugar
    1 cup canned crushed pineapple, drained
    ¼ teaspoon salt
    1 large lemon or ½ orange
   12 blanched almonds

Wash, halve and pit apricots. Combine sugar, apricots, pineapple, and salt in large saucepan. Cut lemon in half lengthwise, trim off ends, then slice thin, discarding seeds. Add lemon slices to saucepan. Heat to boiling, stirring constantly, until syrup jells (220°F. on candy thermometer) or is as thick as desired when tested on a cold saucer. Stir in almonds. Skim off any foam. Ladle into hot sterilized jars to ⅛ inch from the top. Seal immediately.

Three-Citrus Marmalade

Makes 3½ pints marmalade
   2 large oranges
   1 lime
   1 lemon
   6 cups water
   5 cups C & H Granulated Sugar

Wash fruit. Cut in half lengthwise, then cut into very thin crosswise slices. Remove all seeds. Place fruit in large bowl. Add water and soak overnight. Place water and fruit in large saucepan. Bring to boil and cook until fruit is tender. Add sugar and stir until it dissolves. Boil briskly, stirring frequently, 15 to 30 minutes, until syrup jells (220°F. on candy thermometer) or is as thick as desired when tested on a cold saucer. Skim off any foam. Ladle into hot sterilized jars to ⅛ inch from the top. Seal immediately.

*Lemon Tea Bread (page 53); Orange Butter Spread (page 126); Almond
Butter Spread (page 126); Honey Cream Spread (page 126); Orange
Cream Spread (page 126).* Martha White Foods

Peach Jam

Makes about 3 cups

    5 cups sliced peeled peaches (about 2½ pounds)
    ⅓ cup sugar
    1 tablespoon lemon juice
    1 envelope Knox® Unflavored Gelatine
    ¼ cup cold water

In medium saucepan, combine peaches, sugar, and lemon juice. Heat 5 minutes, crushing peaches slightly. Bring to a boil; boil rapidly, stirring constantly, 1 minute.

In small bowl, sprinkle Knox Unflavored Gelatine over water. Let stand 1 minute. Add to peach mixture and heat, stirring until gelatine is dissolved, about 3 minutes. Let jam stand 5 minutes, skimming off foam with a spoon. Ladle into jars. Cover and cool slightly before refrigerating.

Strawberry Jam

Makes about 2 cups

    4 cups sliced strawberries (about 2 pints)
    ⅓ cup sugar
    2 tablespoons lemon juice
    1 envelope Knox® Unflavored Gelatine
    ½ cup cold water

In medium saucepan, combine strawberries, sugar, and lemon juice. Heat 5 minutes, crushing berries slightly. Bring to a boil; boil rapidly, stirring constantly, 3 minutes.

In small bowl, sprinkle Knox Unflavored Gelatine over cold water. Let stand 1 minute. Add to strawberry mixture and heat, stirring until gelatine is completely dissolved, about 3 minutes. Let jam stand 5 minutes, skimming off foam with a spoon. Ladle into jars. Cover and cool slightly before refrigerating.

Grape Jelly (page 121); Peach Jam; Strawberry Jam. Knox Gelatine, Inc.

Blueberry-Strawberry Jam

Makes six to seven ½-pint jars

    3 pints (about) strawberries
    2 pints (about) blueberries
    3 cups sugar
    1½ cups Karo Light Corn Syrup
    ⅓ cup lemon juice

Rinse and stem strawberries; fully crush berries 1 layer at a time to let juice flow freely. Measure 3 cups. Rinse blueberries; fully crush berries 1 layer at a time to let juice flow freely. Measure 3 cups. In 6-quart stainless steel or enamel saucepan, stir together strawberries, blueberries, sugar, corn syrup, and lemon juice. Stirring constantly, bring to hard boil over high heat. Reduce heat; stirring frequently, boil rapidly 40 to 50 minutes, or until mixture thickens or sheets from spoon. To test thickness, pour small amount of boiling mixture on small cold plate. Place in freezer for a few minutes. If mixture gels it is done. Remove from heat; skim surface. Immediately ladle into clean hot ½-pint jars, leaving ¼-inch headspace. With nonmetallic utensil, remove air bubbles. Wipe top edge with damp towel. Seal according to jar manufacturer's directions. Process in boiling water bath 5 minutes. Cool jars on wire rack or folded towel.

Apricot-Pineapple Jam

Makes eight 8-ounce jars
- 1¼ cups dried apricots
- 1 can (20 ounces) crushed pineapple
- 6 cups sugar
- ½ cup lemon juice
- ½ bottle (6 ounces) liquid fruit pectin
- ⅓ cup slivered maraschino cherries, well drained

Combine the apricots with 2 cups water and let stand 4 hours or overnight. Strain the liquid into a large saucepan. Finely chop the apricots. Add the apricots to the saucepan along with the pineapple, sugar, and lemon juice and bring to a full rolling boil over high heat, stirring constantly. Boil for 1 minute, stirring constantly; remove from heat and stir in pectin and cherries. Skim off foam. Stir and skim for 5 minutes. Ladle into hot sterilized jars. Seal at once.

No-Cook Nectarine Jam

Makes eight ½-pint containers
- 2¼ pounds ripe fresh nectarines or peaches
- 5½ cups sugar
- 1 cup Karo Light Corn Syrup
- 1 teaspoon ascorbic acid crystals (optional)
- 2 pouches (3 ounces each) liquid fruit pectin
- ⅓ cup lemon juice

Pit, peel, and fully crush fruit. Measure exactly 2¾ cups. In large bowl, stir together fruit, sugar, corn syrup, and ascorbic acid crystals until well blended. Let stand 10 minutes. Mix pectin and lemon juice. Stir into fruit mixture. Continue stirring vigorously 3 minutes (a few sugar crystals will remain). Ladle into clean ½-pint freezer containers, leaving ½ inch head-space. Cover with tight lids. Let stand at room temperature until set. (It may take up to 24 hours.) Jam to be eaten within a week or two may be stored in refrigerator. Store remaining containers in freezer and transfer to refrigerator as needed.

Cherry Preserves

Makes about 1½ pints preserves
- 2 cups C & H Granulated Sugar
- ½ cup water
- Pinch salt
- 2 cups pitted sour cherries

In large saucepan, combine 1 cup sugar, water, and salt. Cook over low heat until sugar dissolves, swirling pan occasionally. Boil until syrup reaches 236°F. on candy thermometer (soft ball stage). Add 1 cup cherries; boil 10 minutes. Add remaining sugar and cherries and boil 10 minutes longer. Cool in pan, stirring occasionally to plump cherries. Ladle into hot sterilized jars to ⅛ inch from the top. Seal immediately.

Brandied Peach Preserves

Makes about 4 pints preserves
- 5 cups C & H Granulated Sugar
- 1 cup cold water
- 10 large firm-ripe peaches
- 6 whole cloves
- ½ cup good-quality brandy
- ¾ cup chopped walnuts or pecans

In large heavy saucepan, combine 1½ cups of the sugar and the water. Cook over low heat until sugar dissolves, swirling pan occasionally. Scald, peel, pit, and quarter peaches. Add to sugar and simmer gently about 25 minutes, until transparent. With slotted spoon, remove peaches from syrup. Add remaining sugar and the cloves. Cook over low heat until sugar dissolves, then boil until reduced to a thick syrup. Stir in brandy. Sieve syrup over peaches; add nuts. Ladle peaches into hot sterilized jars. Cover with hot syrup to ⅛ inch from top. Seal immediately.

Grape Orange Conserve

Makes about 5½ pints conserve
- 4 pounds Concord or other slipskin grapes
- 8 cups C & H Granulated Sugar
- 3 medium oranges
- 2 lemons
- 1 to 2 cups coarsely chopped walnuts

Wash grapes; squeeze pulp from skins (save skins). Cook pulp until seeds loosen, then press through wire strainer. Add skins and sugar to pulp. Squeeze juice from oranges and lemons; add to grapes. Carefully remove citrus rinds, taking as little of the white pith as possible; cut into fine strips. Cover rinds with cold water and heat to boiling. Drain and add to grapes. Simmer, stirring frequently, about 40 minutes, until thick. Add nuts. Ladle into hot sterilized jars. Seal immediately.

Parsley Butter

Makes about ½ cup butter

¼ **cup parsley sprigs**
½ **cup butter or margarine, softened**
1 **tablespoon light cream or milk**
¼ **teaspoon salt**

Start blender at medium speed. While blender is running, tip center cap and gradually add parsley, blending until chopped. Add remaining ingredients to blender container in order listed. Cover; blend at low speed until thoroughly mixed. If necessary, stop blender during processing and push ingredients toward blades with rubber spatula.
Serving suggestions: Use on broiled steak, cooked vegetables, corn on the cob, Italian bread.

Herb Butter

Substitute 2 tablespoons of a fresh cut-up herb, such as chives, tarragon, or dill, or a combination of fresh herbs, or 1 teaspoon dried herbs, for parsley. Proceed as for Parsley Butter.

Garlic Butter

Add 1 large clove garlic, halved, to blender container with parsley sprigs. Proceed as for Parsley Butter.

Nutted Pineapple-Cream Cheese Spread

Makes 1¼ cups spread

1 **package (8 ounces) cream cheese, cubed and softened**
2 **slices canned pineapple, drained and cut up, or**
  ⅓ **cup canned crushed pineapple, drained**
1 **tablespoon liquid from pineapple**
¼ **cup walnuts**

Put all ingredients into blender container in order listed. Cover; blend at medium speed until pineapple and nuts are chopped and mixture is thoroughly combined. If necessary, stop blender during processing and push ingredients toward blades with rubber spatula.

Fruit Cream Spread

Makes about ½ cup spread

1 **package (3 ounces) cream cheese, at room temperature**
2 **tablespoons jelly, jam, preserves, or drained crushed pineapple**

Combine all ingredients in small bowl; blend thoroughly.

All About Butters

Any one of these savory or sweet butters will dress up any bread you bring to your brunch table. Cream ¼ pound (1 stick) softened butter thoroughly with any suggested addition.

Savory Butters

½ cup grated cheddar and a pinch of dry mustard
4 tablespoons horseradish
2 tablespoons chopped chutney
½ tablespoon curry powder
¼ cup finely snipped parsley, mint, or basil leaves and a few drops of lemon juice
2 tablespoons snipped chives
1 teaspoon chopped fresh tarragon and a few drops of onion juice
2 tablespoons caraway seed
2 tablespoons sesame seed
1 tablespoon anchovy paste or 6 mashed anchovy fillets
1 teaspoon Worcestershire sauce
2 tablespoons well-drained India relish
2 teaspoons lime or lemon juice plus 1 teaspoon grated peel

Sweet Butters

3 tablespoons honey
2 tablespoons maple sugar
⅓ cup ground walnuts, pecans, cashews, black walnuts, or filberts
1 teaspoon vanilla extract plus 1 tablespoon confectioners sugar
1 teaspoon ground cinnamon plus 1 tablespoon confectioners sugar
½ teaspoon ground nutmeg plus 2 teaspoons firmly packed light brown sugar
6 ripe strawberries, mashed, plus 1 tablespoon confectioners sugar and a few drops lemon juice
20 ripe raspberries plus 1 tablespoon confectioners sugar and a few drops lemon juice

Maple Butter

Makes 16 servings

¾ **cup butter, softened**
¼ **cup firmly packed light brown sugar**
½ **teaspoon maple flavoring**

Beat ingredients together until well blended. Refrigerate until ready to serve.

Cinnamon-Honey Butter

Makes 1⅓ cups butter
   6 **tablespoons butter**
   ¼ **teaspoon ground cinnamon**
     Freshly grated nutmeg
   1 **cup honey**

Melt butter in a small saucepan. Blend in cinnamon and a dash of nutmeg. Add honey and heat just to the boiling point. Serve warm.

Peanut Butter

Makes about 1 cup peanut butter
   1½ **cups salted peanuts**
     1 **to 2 tablespoons vegetable oil**

Start blender at high speed. While blender is running, tip center cap and gradually add nuts, blending until finely chopped. Add 1 tablespoon oil. Cover; blend at high speed until smooth, adding more oil if needed. If necessary, stop blender during processing and push ingredients toward blades with rubber spatula.
Note: If using dry-roasted peanuts, increase oil as needed.
Nut Butter
Substitute salted cashews or mixed salted nuts for peanuts. Proceed as for Peanut Butter.

Honey Cream Spread

Makes about ½ cup spread
   1 **package (3 ounces) cream cheese, at room temperature**
   1 **tablespoon honey**
   1 **teaspoon lemon juice**

Combine all ingredients in small bowl; blend thoroughly.

Secrets to Making Spreads, Butters, and Sandwiches

A thin layer of butter spread on bread slices to be used for sandwiches will prevent sogginess. Soften the butter first so that it will spread more easily and go farther, and then spread the slices right to the edges.

Use an ice cream scoop to measure out salad spreads and other mixed fillings.

When toasting bread for sandwiches, avoid stacking the slices to prevent sogginess.

When blending spreads and fillings, stop blender when necessary during processing and push the ingredients toward the blades with a rubber spatula.

Almond Butter Spread

Makes about ½ cup spread
   ½ **cup butter or margarine, softened**
   1 **tablespoon finely chopped almonds**
   ½ **teaspoon almond extract**

Combine all ingredients in small bowl; blend thoroughly.

Orange Butter Spread

Makes about ½ cup spread
   ½ **cup butter or margarine, softened**
   1 **tablespoon orange juice**
   1 **tablespoon grated orange peel**

Combine all ingredients in small bowl; blend thoroughly.

Orange Cream Spread

Makes about ½ cup spread
   1 **package (3 ounces) cream cheese, at room temperature**
   1 **tablespoon orange juice**
   1 **teaspoon grated orange peel**

Combine all ingredients in small bowl; blend thoroughly.

Ginger Cream Spread

Makes about ½ cup spread
   1 **package (3 ounces) cream cheese, at room temperature**
   2 **tablespoons finely chopped crystallized ginger**
   2 **tablespoons finely chopped almonds**
   1 **teaspoon milk**

Combine all ingredients in small bowl; blend thoroughly.

Devon Cream

Makes about ½ cup cream
   1 **package (8 ounces) cream cheese, at room temperature**
   ⅓ **cup sour cream**
   1 **tablespoon sugar**

Combine all ingredients in small bowl; blend thoroughly.

Index